SOURCES IN WESTERN CIVILIZATION

The Nineteenth Century, 1815–1914

THE

Sources in Western Civilization

GENERAL EDITOR, *Herbert H. Rowen*

RUTGERS UNIVERSITY

I. THE ANCIENT NEAR EAST, *Jonas C. Greenfield*

II. ANCIENT GREECE, *Truesdell S. Brown*

III. ROME, *William G. Sinnigen*

IV. THE EARLY MIDDLE AGES, *Robert Brentano*

V. THE HIGH MIDDLE AGES, *Bryce D. Lyon*

VI. RENAISSANCE AND REFORMATION, *Donald Weinstein*

VII. THE SEVENTEENTH CENTURY, *Andrew Lossky*

VIII. THE EIGHTEENTH CENTURY, *George Rudé*

IX. THE NINETEENTH CENTURY, *John C. Cairns*

X. THE TWENTIETH CENTURY, *Arthur P. Mendel*

NINETEENTH CENTURY

1815·1914

EDITED BY

John C. Cairns

UNIVERSITY OF TORONTO

THE FREE PRESS, NEW YORK

Collier-Macmillan Limited, London

A DIVISION OF THE MACMILLAN COMPANY
Printed in the United States of America

Collier-Macmillan Canada, Ltd., Toronto, Ontario

Library of Congress Catalog Card Number: 65–11890

Third Printing June 1966

CONTENTS

"THE world on the verge of its catastrophe was very brilliant. Nations and Empires crowned with princes and potentates rose majestically on every side, lapped in the accumulated treasure of the long peace. . . . The old world in its sunset was fair to see."

—Winston Churchill

"YOU are astonished that I am so sad, I, one of the Olympians living in perpetual bliss and immortal joy? Indeed, we possessed everything: glory, heavenly beauty, eternal youth, everlasting pleasure, and yet we were not happy. . . . We were not good, and hence we had to perish."

—Jakob Burckhardt

INTRODUCTION

1. 1815: PROLOGUE TO PEACE

Twenty years had passed since the shouts of "Down with the tyrant!" brought an end on the scaffold to the apocalyptic vision of an immanent Republic of Virtue. It was ten since old Pope Pius VII journeyed to Paris to anoint but not to crown the meteoric self-made Prince over the ruins of whose imperial domain the gentlemen at Vienna presided that autumn of 1814. Robespierre weighed like a half-remembered nightmare from a time of improbable hopes and appalling fears; Bonaparte was merely lordling of 140 square miles of Mediterranean rock, lodged by the will of Europe in the Mulini Palace above Portoferraio, master now of no more than this tiny pinnacle of a sunken mountain range. From Austerlitz to Elba the distance was immeasurable; nothing remained but the determination of the Emperor of Austria's guests to banish the possibility of a reappearance of France in arms, masking her national designs with the language of the Abbé Sieyès or the *Social Contract.*

Nearly a quarter of a century of war was over, save along the Niagara frontier and on Lake Champlain in North America, or off the American coast, where the troops of President Madison and George III still disputed maritime interests and the uncertain lands of the American West. Of Lundy's Lane or the ruins of the White House, however, neither Prince Metternich, Lord Castlereagh, Alexander I, Prince Hardenberg, nor the Prince de Talleyrand nor any in that glittering bureaucratic host in Vienna took much thought. In any event, English and American signatures at Ghent in December ended the indecisive encounter of the War of 1812, inaugurating what was to be an unbroken peace between the imperial power and the former colonies.

In Europe, however, though the politics of conservatism was

unanimously accepted, only the skillful alignment of Bourbon France with London and Vienna secured peace among the victorious allies, by limiting Prussian appetite for Saxony and Russian designs on the corpse of what once had been Poland. From this new abyss the rulers of aristocratic Europe sanely drew back, in order instead to settle boundaries, to replace deposed sovereigns in the name of legitimacy, and, in the summer of 1815, to confront again the restless ruler of Elba. For Louis XVIII's flight from Paris to Brussels, March 19, was an indication less of Bourbon unpopularity than of the strength of the revolutionary myth. And, though the Imperial eagle's flight to the towers of Notre Dame ended suddenly after Waterloo, the exiling of Napoleon to the South Atlantic did not banish the specter of that social upheaval which Metternich's Europe feared — feared even more than its own quarrelsome ambitions — and the prisoner on Saint Helena so spuriously claimed to represent. Thus the Second Treaty of Paris was more harsh, the victors' renewal of the Quadruple Alliance more pointed, the Declaration of the Holy Alliance — to preserve "Justice, Christian Charity and Peace" — more obviously motivated by fear.

2. THE SHIFTING SANDS OF CONSERVATIVE POLITICS

The Habsburg monarchy dominated the Germanic Confederation for half a century after the Congress of Vienna; Tsar Alexander foreswore his early liberal enthusiasms; the Iron Duke set his face against lower-class agitation. All the same the wind of revolution had passed through the Western world: the upper middle classes were in the saddle in England and France, if not in Austria, Prussia or Russia. Louis XVIII recognized the change and died King of France; Charles X refused to accept it and died in exile. Nicholas I, determined to avoid the errors of his unhappy brother, merely postponed reform and bequeathed a crumbling empire to his heir. In England the improbable Lord Eldon gave way to Earl Grey; in America Andrew Jackson replaced the revolutionary aristocracy of the eastern seaboard, and in the Canadas rebellion brought colonial reform. But parliamentary reform at Westminster, the shift of social forces in the United States, and the rule of wealth in Louis Philippe's France did not shake the Austrian Chancellor's determination to defy the oncoming liberal tide. Though the Congress System fell apart, Metternich's conviction never faltered ("My mind has never known error"), even when his intelligence told him long before 1848 that the game was up. His warning to the Tsar in 1821 [1]* represented the deepest thought of the age of declining conservatism, of which he perhaps was the finest flower. That same year, five thousand miles away on the sea-girt rock, the captive Emperor of the French breathed his last. He left a liberal legend to France and history which triumphed in the person of his own nephew almost at the same time as Metternich was driving away from rioting Vienna, a defeated champion of the cosmopolitan world that had been already mortally stricken at the hands of Massachusetts farmers, Whig gentry and Orleanist entrepreneurs. Only the lingering agonies of that world were to be seen in the petty despotisms of divided Germany and the troubled peninsula of Italy.

Nonetheless the revolutions of 1848–49 failed—not so much because the lower orders were so weak as because the bourgeoisie had long since come into their own. They were prepared, as the June massacres in Paris and the miserable end of the Frankfurt Parliament in Stuttgart demonstrated, to ally themselves with conservative reaction rather than admit the social revolution from below—the selfsame force which they had hoped to destroy half a century earlier when Babeuf was dragged to the guillotine. 1848 ended in Chartist defeat in the streets of London, Sardinian-Piedmontese defeat at the hands of General Radetzky near Custozza, Czech defeat in bombarded Prague, Hungarian defeat by Nicholas's troops at Világos. But if General Cavaignac restored order in Paris and General Windischgrätz in Vienna, no army restored Metternich. The reaction which triumphed in Central Europe was parochial. It prevailed farther to the east, was a political liability in Spain and France, but was henceforth impossible in England. "I was not understood," Metternich said. "I became a phantasm, an imaginary being, a thing without substance." With him departed the last semblance of a united front against liberalism. The time when he had boasted, "I have become a moral power in Germany, and perhaps even in Europe," seemed unimaginably long ago.

3. INTIMATIONS OF AN EGALITARIAN SOCIETY

Thomas Jefferson's triumph fifty years before might now have been seen as the first act of a continuing drama in the West. Certainly it would have been difficult to hear any echo of the 1801

* *Bracketed numbers refer to the selection numbers in the text.*

inaugural around the courts of Europe for half a century. There was no recognition of the "sacred principle" that "though the will of the majority is in all cases to prevail, that will to be rightful must be reasonable; that the minority possess their equal rights which equal law must protect." After all, Jackson's contemporaries were the Prince de Polignac, Frederick William III and Ferdinand of Naples. The fall of Wellington and Charles X was still to be followed by armed rebellion in Monmouthshire and republican insurrections in Paris. At Frankfurt the Diet of the Germanic Confederation railed against "the authors, publishers, printers and disseminators of the writings of the literary school known as Young Germany," and in the Chamber of Deputies Guizot succinctly proclaimed the post-revolutionary philosophy of the possessing classes.

But, although wealthy liberals in the West announced the end of the Revolution, the progress of what both new and old conservatives regarded as an egalitarian malady continued. Count Benckendorff and his notorious Third Section of the Imperial Chancery could answer for peace and order in the Russian Empire; but where coal, steam and the iron rails of the Industrial Revolution crept across western Europe, the military suppression of the silk workers' revolt in Lyons by Marshal Soult merely illustrated the intellectual paralysis of the manufacturing and financial oligarchies backed by agrarian allies. Their very enterprises were doomed to increase the urban revolt. All this Alexis de Tocqueville saw early in Louis Philippe's reign; his observations in America only reinforced his analysis of what was in store for Europe. *Democracy in America* reflected his honesty of inquiry as well as his "religious dread" of what was to come: the hope of preparing the upper classes to educate their future masters and the shudder he experienced on observing the House of Representatives in action [2]. In June, 1848, of course, when Cavaignac "delivered the nation from the tyranny of the Paris workmen and restored it to possession of itself," Tocqueville defined the limits of his liberalism. But though he was fearful of the unwashed lower orders in rebellion, Tocqueville's reaction was against violence rather than against social mobility. Far from resenting America, he presented it as admirable: "The Americans have fought the individualism to which equality gives rise with liberty, and they have won." All the trick was to demonstrate this to the bourgeoisie who, "when called upon to assume the government, took it up as a trade," and to show them the lateness of the hour. It seemed to him on the eve of his death that his warning had failed: revolution had begotten reaction and the far shore was perceived still more dimly than before.

Doubtless this conclusion followed in 1859 from the evidence of events in the Hohenzollern and Habsburg monarchies and more especially in the imperial dictatorship of Napoleon III. Yet within the decade the Liberal Empire was a-building in France, and might have survived to complete its political and social transformation, had it not set a collision course with Bismarck's Prussia. Such opportunist appropriation of Liberal Policy as Disraeli's Reform Bill of 1867 brought Tocqueville's vision of the democratic future a little closer, too, even though neither the North German Confederation, the distraught Spain of Isabella II, the newly united Kingdom of Italy nor the reorganized Austro-Hungarian monarchy, let alone Alexander II's faltering reforms in Saint Petersburg, offered much evidence that the lessons of America were deemed relevant in Europe.

4. THE SOCIAL CONSEQUENCES OF INDUSTRIAL PROGRESS

An aristocrat born in 1805, son of a Restoration prefect, might not be expected to display an overly developed social conscience. In fact, Tocqueville's attention was focused principally upon the preservation of liberty and values. Given the brief railroad boom in France, the substantial increases in coal and iron production before 1848, the emergence of a factory system, his view now may even seem narrow. But the French middle classes who reigned in collaboration with the aristocracy were almost prisoners of the social system which they had prevailed over. Thus, despite industrial unrest and occasional governmental inquiry into its character and causes, it was as natural for Tocqueville to concern himself with political liberty as for Richard Cobden or John Bright to assail the landed oligarchy and the tariff structure on behalf of free trade and the betterment of "the intelligent middle and industrious classes." Yet it was Tocqueville who was "of the opinion on the whole that the manufacturing aristocracy which is growing up is one of the harshest which ever existed in the world." Disraeli's observation that free trade was not a principle but an expedient underlined the fact that the middle class preferred cheaper cereals for the workers to industrial legislation. Elementary laws lay disregarded; critics charged that the Factory Act of 1819 "actually encourages vice. It establishes idleness by act of Parliament." Not until the Whig triumph of 1832 did the shocking evidence of industrial inhumanity stun the upper classes. Thereafter legislation made it less easy to employ children under nine in textile factories, or those under eighteen more than sixty-nine hours a week.

Lord Althorp's Factory Act of 1833 no more than began the assault upon commercial traffic in human misery, as Lord Ashley was to show [3]. By 1842, when young Victoria was on the throne ("I incline to think," Palmerston noted, "that she will turn out to be a remarkable person, and gifted with a great deal of strength of character"), the Commons were ready to prohibit the employment of women and boys under thirteen to drag colliery carts behind them on hands and knees through the pits. Nevertheless, the doubts about this state intervention offered a nice commentary on the values of this prosperous Western civilization which now committed its conscience to mill and mine inspectors. It was simpler to abolish slavery overseas than to obtain a ten-hour day for women at home, though both were achieved. If Oliver Twist moved the English reading classes to tears, neither Victor Hugo nor Eugène Sue wrung compassion from the Orleanist masters of what Adolphe Thiers called "the vile multitude." It was not, of course, that Victoria's subjects were more sensitive than Louis Philippe's; moreover, they had distractions aplenty, with rebellion in North America, war in the East and a crisis with France. But somehow the sentiments of Casimir Perier seemed more direct than those, say, of Sir James Graham, who lingered on after cholera carried off that orderly French banker and prime minister in 1832. "The workers," ran one of Casimir Perier's dicta, "must realize that their only salvation lies in patient resignation to their lot." As social doctrine, this pronouncement had the virtue of clarity; but not even the unsuccessful revolution of 1848 could demonstrate its truth. Alphonse de Lamartine and Cavaignac could read this lesson in the presidential election figures that December; Louis Napoleon lived to carry away into exile twenty-two years later much the same conclusion. "We do not want to be dependents," the workingmen's Manifesto of The Sixty had informed him. "We want to be equals. We reject alms. We demand justice. We do not hate men. We want to change things." Like Bismarck's Reich, though more slowly, the Third French Republic was to act on this implacable verdict.

5. THE SPECTER OF SOCIALISM

Social criticism had not waited on the appearance of George Stephenson's steam-driven train, thundering at twenty-six miles an hour down the line to Darlington with a wagonload of musicians fanfaring amidst the thirty-four carriages of stupefied guests, shareholders and officials. Long before this signal event of 1825 — a year when Francis I reluctantly admitted parliamentary procedure for Hungary and John Quincy Adams became the first American President with a properly recorded popular vote — the socialist challenge to the bourgeoisie was flung down. Robert Owen's utopian experiment in Indiana, New Harmony, showed that though radical extremism might be driven underground, reformers prepared to stop short of revolution could still flourish in the West. Nothing so much illuminated the abyss separating the reactions of Romanov and Bourbon as the contrast between the collapse of the December Revolt on a bleak winter day in Saint Petersburg, with the police pushing the corpses through the ice-holes of the Neva, and the calm abdication of Charles X at Rambouillet five years later. Charles was not so wise — he relied, after all, on Polignac, who in turn relied on apparitions of the Virgin — and assassins would still feel compelled to fling bombs at Louis Philippe and Louis Napoleon. The point, however, was that for Colonel Paul Pestel and the Russian opposition, with their vague and relatively conservative ideas ("impertinent, destructive dreams," said the Tsar), no avenue but violence appeared open. Less than a year before Nicholas hanged Pestel, that "hell-born fiend," Henri Saint-Simon died quietly in his bed, predicting the socialist triumph of an industrial society: "At this moment all I can say is that you are entering upon an epoch when united efforts must yield the greatest success. The pear is ripe. You must pluck it. . . ."

Babeuf's strain was not dead, as that professional revolutionist Louis-Auguste Blanqui proved with a lifetime of insurrectionary misadventures. But even Blanqui ("the uncontested chief, who has filled us with revolutionary faith, the resolution to struggle, the scorn of suffering," said Peter Tkachev) died a free man; Michael Bakunin repeatedly acted out the century's revolutionary myth with no positive results and no permanent harm to himself, leaving behind only the undying hostility of Karl Marx and, to anarchism, a legend of furious activity. Others were less fortunate without being more successful. But what the nineteenth-century West seemed to show was that justice and the good society were to be secured less by barricades than by the pen and the ballot-box. Despair and confusion in the Paris Commune of 1871 might hide this conclusion from old Louis-Charles Delescluze, seeking out death that evening in the setting sun, in frock coat, top hat, red sash, with cane in hand, atop the barricade at the Chateau d'Eau; but the authors of the *Communist Manifesto* knew it long before they died. Their triumph was to combine an electrifying analysis of history, pointing to the inevitable collapse of bourgeois society, with a hazy vision of a communist world to come, all with "scientific" proofs more inflexible than judgment from "many-ridged Olympus." Saint-Simon had only harangued the Restoration notables: "You are the successors of Caesar. . . . What are you doing for the poor?" Charles Fourier had only lectured the business community for condemning every individual to "intentional war against the mass." Pierre-Joseph Proudhon had only proclaimed that the bourgeoisie knew that its role was finished and invited it to "give up its soul peacefully."

The utopians were not inconsequential on that account: Saint-Simon's industrial enthusiasm survived the authoritarian overtones of his disciples and their curious search for a Female Messiah; Fourier's fantasy of a harmonious world of self-supporting communities of 1,620 persons expired less because of his failure to plan menus and garbage disposal ahead of time than because funds ran out at Condé-sur-Vesgre, fire ravaged Brook Farm and because, in a more general way, human nature was not up to his expectations. Proudhon's mutualist influence lived on in the organized labor movement. All the same, no social critique rivaled the Marxian [4]. Marx did not lecture or invite; he proclaimed the inevitable demise of a whole world. Much in his forecast would be contradicted by the progress of middle-class society, more than Wilhelm Liebknecht cared to admit; revisionism crept in; the old texts were strained. But the success of Marx and Engels lay in the internecine wars fought in their name, in the hope and fear they aroused long after their century was no more. Beyond the strife of schism and social gospel, Marx, if not "the man of science," "the greatest living thinker," as Engels said in the cemetery at Highgate, was the most commanding critic the contemporary world knew.

6. LIBERAL NATIONALISM ON TRIAL

But the mid-century was rich in critics. In the international arena of 1848 the future "martyrs of the rue des Capucines" jostled the astronomer François Arago and the poet Lamartine ("The more I see of representatives of the people, the more I like my dogs"), and the moderates who had joined rioting students in Vienna in March watched while they were cut down in October. "The reaction has already begun among the bourgeoisie," Rudolf Virchow wrote from Frankfurt. "They are already talking once again of the rabble, and are already considering how to distribute the political rights unequally among the various members of the nations." Criticism of the old order, feudal or bourgeois, was shattered by class interest, stifled by the conflict of historic claims and destroyed by race consciousness. Within months, Gustav von Struve's confident declaration to the Baden government—"A tremendous revolution has flashed across Europe. The old system is waning and falling into ruins."—had been belied by such iron wills as that of General von Wrangel, who marched on Berlin despite rebel threats to his wife, muttering, "I wonder if they have hanged her? I hardly believe so!" From Sicily to Poland the critics of the old order raised the storm, manned their barricades, debated, divided, fought and died or went home or to prison or to exile with disenchantment in their hearts. Carrying their class and national idols before them, they went down, mostly to defeat. "But what," wrote Berthold Auerbach, "is courage alone without talent? It can fight and it can inflame, but it can give no character to human society." The contradictory wealth of their criticism and their ambition was their undoing.

Of those who fled across the map that year, from revolution or reaction, some like Frederick William IV returned stronger than before, some such as Pius IX went back sadder if not wiser, and some like Giuseppe Mazzini, abandoning the revolutionary government of the Eternal City ("I feel . . . rage rising within me at this triumph, all throughout the world, of brutal force over right and justice"), wandered off to last years of futile striving in a cause to be achieved by other men and other means. Principal standard-bearer of a still uncertain nationalism and archfoe of Habsburg dominion, Mazzini was the ill-fated messianic leader of a "predestined" people. Marx might consider Mazzini's provocative policy toward Austria "fundamentally wrong," but although this other guest of England was a prophet like Marx, unlike Marx he had no dialectical certainty of triumph, only the passionate will to revolt and to witness the Italian victory in his own time. Pursued by the bailiff, dependent on his friends and neighbors, Marx sat calmly in the British Museum documenting his apocalyptic insights; expelled from his homeland by his own people, Mazzini fretted in his London room, or launched himself and his followers on still more disastrous adventures [5]. After Cavour, Napoleon III and Bismarck, combining and quarreling, had brought about Italian unity, Mazzini still dreamed of Republican Italy, spurning Parliament and amnesty on the last bitter visit incognito to Italy and, finally, Pisa, where the pale, sad "Mr. Brown" died.

Such a man, oblivious to class conflicts, whose message was to love Humanity, the word of God and the Italian nation, could scarcely escape Marx's condemnation as a merely meddlesome visionary without understanding of the world as it actually was. To the Sage of Soho, he was "Master Mazzini," "an ox," "a demagogue of the old school." Yet even Cavour and the hard-headed Piedmontese who made Italy were touched by the exile's burning faith; Georges Sorel judged that he had done more by his mythmaking than all of them. And a boy who passed the slender old prophet in the streets of Pisa might have lived to see the Republic established in Italy after all.

7. CONTACTS OF CIVILIZATIONS

"Mission" and "destiny" were words that came easily to nineteenth-century lips. They were proud expressions of a restless civilization seeking not only new political forms for itself but fresh contacts in the wider world. Sometimes it was the restlessness of mere cramp, as with Latter Day Saints moving on past the Mississippi to the shores of Great Salt Lake; sometimes it was land hunger leading to armed aggression, as with General Winfield Scott storming the beaches near Vera Cruz and then Mexico City itself. Saint-Simonians such as Michel Chevalier and Barthélemy Enfantin dreamed of joining France to Egypt by rail or piercing the isthmus of Suez. By the time the Empress Eugénie sailed into the Canal on a cloudless November day in 1869 and the strains of *Aïda* were heard in Cairo on Christmas Eve 1871 (despite the Khedive Ismail's importuning, Verdi did not compose for a canal opening), the Mogul

Empire had been replaced at Delhi by the British Raj, the Dutch and Portuguese had spread down the Malayan archipelago to Timor, Count Muraviev had extended Alexander II's domain to Vladivostok and President Johnson's America was established in the Aleutians. Phileas Fogg and Captain Nemo symbolized not merely the unlimited scientific and technological expectancy of a supremely confident generation ("For the last twenty years," Marshal Lyautey was to say, "the advance of the peoples is merely living the novels of Jules Verne") but the familiarity with which the reading public of Manchester, Lille or Chicago contemplated the globe. The *Illustrated London News* had a circulation of five million. Robinson Crusoe's adventures might be read in many languages and even be heard to the music of Jacques Offenbach. By 1885 the English were laughing easily, if too complacently, at *The Mikado.*

For despite all its problems, or perhaps even partly as a consequence of them, the West was increasingly interested in the outside world—interested and aggressive. In the course of a dispute over wheat supply the Dey Hussein of Algiers was so unwise as to strike the French Consul with his fly whisk; the partly punitive expedition of Admiral Duperré and General Bourmont which followed in the summer of 1830 laid the foundation for a great French empire in North Africa. The Emperor Tao Kuang's attempt to discipline corrupt officials and to confiscate the opium stocks of foreign merchants at Canton was paid for with the surrender of Hong Kong and the opening of five ports to the commerce and residence of Western "barbarians." Contacts, where resisted, became brutal encounters. None was more difficult and fateful than that between the commerce-hungry West and the Tokugawa Empire. Only the Dutch were spared the ban upon foreign vessels touching at Japanese ports, but when King William II of Holland proposed that the Shogun abandon the policy of isolation, he was advised: "Henceforth pray cease correspondence." Eight years after that injunction, Commodore Perry's ships arriving off Uraga spelt "finis" to the policy it expressed. The Baltimore *Sun* had castigated the 1853 expedition as "humbug" and "a matter of ridicule abroad and at home," but Perry extracted a first treaty the next year [6]. By the winter of 1868, after repeated negotiations and some conflict with the representatives of many Western states, an Imperial rescript announced that "intercourse with foreign countries shall in future be carried on in accordance with the public laws of the whole world." Almost overnight the feudal order fell away in the era of Mutsuhito, the Emperor Meiji. The consequences of the ensuing extraordinary contact between East and West were eventually to rock Asia, Europe and America. It would be almost a century before the convivial Japanese sentiment expressed that evening of March 31, 1854—"Nippon and America, all the same heart"—came true. As usual, Mr. Dooley observed more accurately: "Whin we rapped on the dure, we didn't go in, they come out."

8. ROMANTICISM AND REALISM

Curious, energetic and aggressive, the nineteenth century expressed itself articulately in every artistic medium. The Enlightenment had a reputation for its classical spirit; the early nineteenth century was wafted in on a wave of Romanticism. It was not surprising, however paradoxical, that one of the official supporters of the Romantic revival should have been Emperor of France. Doubtless the virtues of Chateaubriand's *Génie du Christianisme* were in Napoleon's eyes political, but the impact of its spirit widened out in letters and art long after the Concordat had passed into the records of the Vatican. The classical revival did not wither away. It lingered on along the banks of the Potomac, in the Carolinas and in the place-names of upstate New York towns and villages. It rested securely on Mont Sainte-Geneviève, lived on in Jacques-Louis David's canvases and in Bertel Thorvaldsen's tomb for Pius VII in Saint Peter's. It remained in the structure of Beethoven's quartets. But that was the point: Bach, Handel and Mozart were gone, and in the music of Beethoven, though hardly in the paintings of Ingres, the fusing of classical structure and Romantic mood proclaimed the new age. A generation disenchanted after nearly a quarter century of war in the name of abstract principles was, not surprisingly, receptive to renewed reading of young Werther's sorrows, to the death of John Keats at twenty-six and to Trelawny's burning the body of Shelley on the shore of the Gulf of Spezia near Viareggio. What mattered was not that Jane Austen's provincial clergymen and quiet satire no longer held the reading public but rather that the novel of sensibility could not hold the troubled social conscience of Victor Hugo or Charles Dickens, let alone the tempestuous spirit impelling Lord Byron to a legendary death at Missolonghi.

Romanticism could mean the cult of medievalism in the restoration of Vézelay and Carcassonne. It stood beside the Thames and threw its spires upward over Cologne. It was present in the profound sense of historical continuity expressed earlier by Edmund Burke and erected by Hegel into a philosophy of history. "Do not applaud me, gentlemen," Fustel de Coulanges told his students in Paris. "It is not I who speak to you, but History that speaks through me." Yet, if Romanticism proved tenacious, coursing through the century, say, in Schumann, Wagner, Brahms and Mahler, the attitude to life called Realism drove artists no less passionately. Delacroix's lush color and motion competed with the dynamic accuracy of Daumier's hard-eyed commentaries on business civilization. Where Millet portrayed peasant toil without sentimentality, Balzac stripped the prosperous subjects of the July Monarchy of all disguise. In Gustave Flaubert's provincial druggist, Monsieur Homais, the bourgeois character was pilloried scrupulously and mercilessly. A consuming and uncompromising vocation, Flaubert's Realism reflected the deadly seriousness with which, like Captain Ahab in his relentless pursuit of the white whale, artists, scientists and revolutionaries applied themselves to their tasks [7]. But in Melville the dedication to Realism was infused with symbolism and emotional extravagance: ". . . then all collapsed, and the great shroud of the sea rolled on as it rolled five thousand years ago." *Moby-Dick* expressed much of the Romanticism of that towering century, while Flaubert's superb catalogue of Emma Bovary's bleak journey through life focused the cruelest light on the confident class which had almost inherited the West, if not the world.

9. RELIGION AND THE CHALLENGE OF HUMANISM

The defenders of the old order had defined this bourgeois confidence as the basic ill of their time; Burke had called it "the spirit of innovation," and Metternich termed it "presumption." After Pius VII's early liberalism ("The form of democratic government adopted for us is not at all repugnant to the Gospel. . . ."), the Papacy swung away. Gregory XVI launched his *Mirari Vos* against the liberal Catholic movement of Abbé Lamennais. "We can only describe as proud, or rather as foolish," this Encyclical of 1832 declared, "men who weigh the mysteries of faith, 'which passeth all understanding,' in the scales of human reason, and trust to the reasoning powers of the human mind alone, powers which are, in the present state of our human nature, weak and infirm. . . ." Confronted by the revolutionary violences of 1820–21, 1830–31 and 1848–49, the Papacy set itself against liberalism and materialism. As nationalism gathered strength and the possibility of healing the Catholic-Protestant schism seemed more remote than ever, Rome drew its Church about itself more closely. In an instinctive reaction to the assaults of the Italian state, science and free-thinking, it proclaimed war on "the chief errors and false doctrines of our most unhappy age" in the *Syllabus* of 1864. It was moving toward the promulgation of Papal Infallibility at the Oecumenical Council held in 1869–70 on the eve of the fall of Rome and the total eclipse of temporal power.

Not least of the errors and false doctrine catalogued in the *Syllabus* were secular humanism and faith in science. "Science is truly a religion," Ernest Renan had written in 1848. "Science alone can resolve for man the eternal problems for which his very being urgently demands a solution." With Wilhelm Dilthey, philosophers were to proclaim that only history can tell what man is; with Fustel de Coulanges, historians insisted that true history was pure science. Inevitably the Christian matrix of the Western society came under scrutiny. In Germany, David Strauss pronounced Christ to be a myth, a reflection of the folk soul at work in history. Religion, Ludwig Feuerbach maintained, was an illusion by which man, in creating God, might worship himself: "Christianity is an *idée fixe* which stands in flagrant contrast to our fire and life insurances, our railways and steamships, our galleries of painting and sculpture, our military and commercial schools." Somewhere between the extreme claims of materialism and traditional belief, the humanist conception of Renan's *Life of Christ* found its place in 1863 [8]. "Suddenly overnight," remarked Émile Zola, "[Renan's] face rose above France, with the terrifying profile of Anti-Christ. It was a sacrilege shaking Jesus on his cross." The struggle between religious traditionalism and historical and sociological enquiry could not but shock respectable conservatives. The growth of the new inquisitive spirit was beyond the power of any man or institution to halt. At the level on which the struggle between tradition and science was joined it constituted, at its least, a disquieting fault in the structure of Western culture.

10. SCIENCE AND THE NATURE OF MAN

Where philosophers of science and "scientific" historians had not hesitated to analyze the nature of God, scientists themselves did not fear to investigate the nature of man. *A priori* dogmatisms and the "self-evident facts" of the human past collided with "positivist science" resting upon the rigid collection, classification and examination of observable data. Whether Jesus of Nazareth was divine or merely human, in either case it became difficult to believe any longer with Archbishop Ussher that the earth had been created at 6 P.M. on the evening of October 22, 4004 B.C. (Old Style). Yet Sir Charles Lyell's geological researches made it clear that the static views of Auguste Comte's positivist science were now as unacceptable as the Enlightenment's faith that through Right Reason man and nature might be reconciled. Like the *philosophes,* Comte concluded that since truth existed in society as in nature, science must discover it and formulate society's natural laws ("generalize our scientific conceptions and . . . systematize the art of life"). The challenge to this High Priest of Humanity was old: the notion of organic evolution had long existed. Buffon and Lamarck had espoused evolutionary ideas; now the English naturalists Alfred Wallace and Charles Darwin carried them further. After Darwin's famous books of 1859 and 1871, it was hardly possible to view the science of society as being other than a perpetual quest [9].

Thomas Henry Huxley said that "old ladies of both sexes" considered Darwin thoroughly dangerous; Darwin insisted that he saw "no good reason why [*The Origin of Species*] should shock the religious feelings of any one." If it was true that "the higher animals" had evolved "from the war of nature, from famine and death," still he thought there was "grandeur" in the fact that "whilst this planet has gone cycling on according to the fixed law of gravity, from so simple a beginning endless forms, most beautiful and most wonderful, have been and are being evolved." But in the context of the age, all this was shocking. "The question is this," Disraeli said, "—Is man an ape or an angel? My lord, I am on the side of the angels." Moreover, the uses of a popularized and distorted Darwinism in racial, social and political struggles were often far removed from anything to which Wallace or Darwin might have subscribed. "Your boldness," Darwin wrote even to Ernst Haeckel, "sometimes makes me tremble." Whatever Darwin was to learning, he became the unwilling justifier of an intensified conflict within the West and between East and West, bolstering with "science" the imperialist views of the Deity by which, as Senator Albert Jeremiah Beveridge put it, God had created the English-speaking and Teutonic peoples to be "the master organizers of the world to establish system where chaos reigns" and to "administer government among savage and senile peoples."

II. CULTURAL CONFLICT AND CIVIL WAR

When *The Origin of Species* appeared, *Uncle Tom's Cabin* was six years old, and the United States was already gripped by the acrimonious debate on slavery. John Brown's abolitionist passion had slaughtered innocent Southerners at Pottawatomie Creek, a Southern Senator had caned a Northern colleague into insensibility, and Hinton Helper's *Impending Crisis* heralded an implacable struggle. War, of course, was hardly unknown in the century. The Holy Alliance had embraced neither England nor France—the latent contest between Prussia and Austria cut across it, while a futile war between Nicholas I, on the one hand, and Victoria, Napoleon III and Victor Emmanuel, on the other, destroyed it. If the war in the Crimea demonstrated anything, however, it was that though there were more serious rivalries in Europe, it was possible for English public opinion and the French dictatorship to compel a bloody and inconclusive war so that 800,000 men died in a godforsaken peninsula without anyone but Alexander II being the wiser. Tennyson's hero in *Maud* said "hail once more to the banner of battle unroll'd"; thankful that "the peace, that I deem'd no peace, is over and done," he embraced somewhat fancifully "the purpose of God, and the doom assign'd." Hugo ridiculed his Emperor's last hesitations (*"Soldats! L'empire c'est la peur!"*). But 1854 suggested only that great states could blunder into impossible campaigns on behalf of causes neither scrutinized nor understood.

Whether or not the opening of the American West inevitably dictated a contest to decide the preservation or the destruction of the South's "Peculiar Institution," doctrinaires such as William Yancey of Alabama and William Lloyd Garrison of Massachusetts saw no way out. "I have need to be all on fire," the "Great Abolitionist" insisted, "for I have mountains of ice about me to melt." The Negro slave question was an economic problem; but it was first and foremost a state of mind. It was a race question masquerading as a contest of nationalisms and cultures. Carefully contained by delicate political balance until the spoils from the Mexican War brought on the smouldering debates from which the Union would emerge disrupted, the slavery question had hung fire since 1819. It was not the anti-slavery sentiments of the successful Republican candidate for the Presidency in 1860 which brought South Carolina's declaration of dissolution; rather it was the growing Southern conviction that North and South were fundamentally incompatible. "Then let dissolution come now," the Charleston *Mercury* had declared; "the better for the South that it should be today; *she* cannot afford to wait." Lincoln's election merely precipitated the establishment at Montgomery of a second nation. President Buchanan had only refused recognition of John Calhoun's doctrine of nullification; his successor, faced with an act of armed rebellion in Charleston Harbor, raised an army and made war [10].

The Civil War was protracted and savage, fought with hatred. To preserve his nation, Jefferson Davis had only to survive the assault; to preserve the United States, Lincoln had to conquer the Confederacy. Both camps grew rife with dissension, both inflicted and sustained indelible memories, both flagged. "A large majority on both sides are tired of war; want peace," Alexander Stephens wrote in 1863. ". . . But as we do not want peace without independence, so they do not want peace without union." Europe, divided, watched and kept out. When the surrender came at Appomattox Court House, four years and perhaps a million deaths had been required to restore the Union and liberate the Negro race in America. "The war is over," General Grant said; "the rebels are our countrymen again." But the race conflict and sectionalism survived. Lincoln collapsed, mortally wounded, less than a week after Lee surrendered. Ahead stretched all the injustice and struggle of reconstructing the nation, for politics here was to be so often the continuation of war by other means, and "the byegone South" was not so easily buried.

12. WAR SHIFTS THE EUROPEAN BALANCE

War indeed appeared to be the fate of the West in the two decades following the upheaval of 1848–49. Evidently nationalist strivings, confused and unsuccessful, had unleashed aggressions which could be contained only after the map had been remade and the center of power shifted away from older capitals. A chain of wars ensued. If the Crimean War was not the "monster catastrophe" Lord Clarendon predicted, it revealed the military incapacity of Russia, France and Great Britain. By underlining Austria's hesitations, it encouraged Piedmont's Italian ambitions and convinced the Prussian delegate to the Frankfurt Diet, Otto von Bismarck, that it was possible and desirable to cut Prussia free from "the worm-eaten and old-fashioned man of war," and to squeeze the Habsburgs out of Germany. The Italian war of 1859, plotted and provoked by Cavour and Napoleon III, made united Italy possible. The inconclusiveness of that war rendered the defeat of Austria in the next one the more certain by ensuring the continued hostility of Italians. The armistice of Villafranca committed Napoleon morally to a benevolent neutrality in the German struggle Bismarck was to provoke; it assured the French Emperor of the indifference or contempt of Italy for failing to wrest Venetia away from Austria. Prussia profited from Habsburg weakness, Italian Irredentism and French embarrassment. Moreover, the situation of the Second Empire was worsened by Grant's victory; the abandonment of the Mexican adventure under American pressure rendered Imperial policy the more reckless in Europe. "The Emperor's mind," Palmerston had quipped, "seems as full of schemes as a warren is full of rabbits. . . ." Everything turned to disaster. To conquer Germany, Bismarck had to seem ready only to protect her. Having negotiated Villafranca, Napoleon permitted Sadowa and provoked Sedan.

The war of 1870 did not come because a Hohenzollern prince posed his candidacy for the Spanish throne, for the candidacy was withdrawn ("The affair is finished," said Emile Ollivier). It came rather because, as the candidacy revealed, a transfer of power in Europe was in process. The Imperial party saw no way but by victory in the field to retrieve the humiliation of abandoning Maximilian to execution and Franz Josef to defeat. "Well, disgrace yourselves, if you choose," Eugénie flung at those hesitating in the Council. "But don't disgrace the Emperor!" Ollivier made the best of it: "Since we cannot prevent it, our duty is to render it popular." But the war's popularity expired within weeks; the debacle consolidated Prussia's hegemony in the establishment of the Second Reich at Versailles, January 18, 1871, and the French Empire was swept away in the torrent. "While I more and more feel the deep culpability of France," Gladstone wrote as the siege of Paris by General von Moltke's armies approached an end in December 1870 [11], "I have an apprehension that this violent laceration and transfer is to lead us from bad to worse and to be the beginning of a new series of European complications." In fact, the disputatious team of Bismarck and Moltke, by masterly diplomacy and a nearly masterly direction of armies in the new age of railways, telegraphs and breechloading rifles, had imposed upon Europe a political settlement the consequences of which could be measured only in the twentieth century.

13. THE IMPERIAL URGE

Internally stabilized after 1871, Europe extended its power throughout the world. Colonial enthusiasm had flagged in the 'forties and 'fifties. In Great Britain and France the free-traders condemned colonies as unprofitable ("millstones around our necks"). "The scum of England," it was said, "is poured into the colonies." The July Monarchy had been drawn into the subjugation of Algeria only because of the struggle for prestige with England. Chateaubriand might say scornfully, "After Napoleon nothing!" but Louis Napoleon observed from his prison in 1841 that the Algerian war was purposeless: "These faraway possessions, burdensome in peacetime, disastrous in wartime, are a source of weakness." Nevertheless colonialism never died; even the cost-accounting middle classes were as attached to it as the aristocracy, and the workers (as Cobden observed) were no more intelligent. No matter what the prisoner at Ham had said, Napoleon III acquiesced in General Faidherbe's empire-building in Senegal, if he did not encourage it. Nor did he resist the pressure of admirals and Bordeaux shipping interests for the conquest of Cochin-China, whether it was to protect Catholic missionaries or to penetrate the Chinese market and gain a naval base. The Summer Palace burning at Peking occasioned dark reflections in a British pro-consul ("I thought bitterly," Lord Elgin noted, "of those who for the most selfish objects are trampling underfoot this ancient civilization"); the British electorate opted for Palmerston's aggressive policy. As late as 1881, Bismarck swore that "as long as I am Chancellor we shall not carry on any colonial policy." Within four years colonialist propaganda led to his proclamation of German protection over Southwest Africa, the Cameroon coast, East Africa and Zanzibar.

Europe might be at rest. "We belong," said the German Chancellor, "to what old Prince Metternich called the satiated States." But the nations were in fierce competition. Europe's population was growing at a rate second only to that of America, to which it sent its people; Asia and Africa fell off by comparison, remaining little better than stationary. Added to this demographic push was the new wave of industrialization, with a race for markets and raw materials. Recession at home and a growing tariff system spelled intense competition and seemed to dictate the necessity for seizing faraway lands. "Colonial policy," Jules Ferry said, "is the offspring of industrial policy." But the new colonialism was occasioned by more than economic interests: Ferry spoke also of "*mission civilisatrice,*" Rudyard Kipling of "the White Man's burden" and the White Fathers of "humanitarianism." The antislavery movement in Africa began with Dr. Livingstone and led to the International Association for the Exploration and Civilization of Africa in 1876, but its dedication to "science, humanity and progress" resulted in the pursuit of ivory and rubber and the practice of appalling atrocities on Congo natives. Inevitably the missionary work of Cardinal Lavigerie advanced the North African policies of the Third Republic. The racist doctrines of Gobineau or Houston Stewart Chamberlain, the exhortations of cultured lecturers at Oxford and Berlin and the necessities of the growing popular press offering vicarious romance and exotic adventure—all fed the imperial impulse, and sent up again the age-old cry, "We must have lands, new lands!" The quest was for power and the symbols of power [12]. Imperialism was more than aggression by special interests using national power for their own ends; it was a state of mind. If it was not universal, it prevailed.

14. CUBA: IMPERIALISM IN "A BLOODSMITTEN LAND"

The spectacular imperial gains of the late Victorian age were high tide. Europe's authority was destined to wane, though this was hidden from explorer-adventurers such as Carl Peters and Henry Stanley, from pro-consuls like Alfred Milner and Eugène Jonnart and from Leopold II and Victoria. In the name of Christianity, economic necessity, progress and altruism, the European wave had swept over almost the whole of the Dark Continent in little more than a generation, engulfed India and washed to the frontiers of China in exigence and destruction. Even Gladstone had welcomed Germany to participation in "the great purposes of Providence for the advantage of mankind." Egypt was penetrated and subdued, Tunisia brought under protection, Morocco and Libya were ripe for acquisition, Persia existed at the pleasure of rival empires. With Indochina the process of infiltration was almost complete; Formosa and Korea had been severed from China; the Empress Tzu Hsi, unconstructive and defiant, confronted a barrage of demands for foreign concessions and leases from the Yangtze Valley to Manchuria which implied the elimination of an independent China. The result was United States intervention, rebellion against the demands of the Foreign Devils, defeat and punishment, but not dismemberment. The tide receded. By the time the old Empress died in 1908, a new rival to the Europeans, Japan, had staged a dramatic stroke, defeating the ill-starred forces of Nicholas II at Port Arthur, Mukden and Tsushima. A mere fifty years after Perry's "black ships" dropped anchor in Yedo Bay, less than a decade after General Bartieri's troops were cut to pieces by Ethiopians at Adowa, the Russian disaster of 1904–05 was another harbinger of the passing of the European age.

By the Treaty of Portsmouth Japan demonstrated that it was not only Europeans who could feel within themselves a sense of manifest destiny; fifty-seven years earlier the Treaty of Guadalupe Hidalgo had shown that Americans felt it. "Whether they will or no," Captain Mahan declared, "Americans must now begin to look outward." Having defeated Mexico and survived the Civil War, moving toward such industrial preeminence as Europe could hardly imagine, the United States contemplated imperialist action in the spring of 1898. Napoleon III had been successfully threatened a generation earlier, President Cleveland had taken a tough line with Lord Salisbury over the Venezuelan boundary dispute and Theodore Roosevelt had noted: "Personally, I rather hope that the fight will come soon. The clamor of the peace faction has convinced me that this country needs a war." But now it was more than practitioners of the strenuous life who reacted to events in Cuba: the sugar interests were hard hit, and the mysterious explosion and sinking of the U.S.S. *Maine* caused the eagle to scream. The wrong done by Spanish Regent Christina Maria's government in the second round of that Cuban rebellion stemming from the last days of Queen Isabella's reign struck a sentimental chord in the American people; all the same the worst excesses of "Weyler the Brute" were ended and the virtual capitulation of Madrid to Washington's demands had been achieved when McKinley sent his war message to Congress. "The taste of Empire is in the mouth of the people," commented the Washington *Post,* "even as the taste of blood in the jungle." Years before, Cleveland had warned against "an epidemic of insanity"; McKinley had promised "no jingo nonsense." All was swept aside [13]. Mr. Dooley might smile wryly at T.R.'s Gran' Picnic and Moonlight Excursion to Cubia, but the stunning blow delivered by Admiral Dewey at Manila Bay was as decisive as Admiral Togo's was to be seven years later at Tsushima. It might not be glorious, as William Graham Sumner noted, to knock "to pieces a poor, decrepit, bankrupt old State like Spain," but the victory marked America's coming of age as a power. For Europe the loss of Cuba and the cession of Puerto Rico, Guam and the Philippines signified the emergence of a powerful competitor which, like the Empire of the Rising Sun, would one day dispute the hegemony of the world.

15. JUSTICE IN THE INDUSTRIAL SOCIETY

One of the curiosities of imperialism was the manner in which all classes identified themselves with what James Mill called "a vast system of outdoor relief for the upper classes." The *Communist Manifesto* pronounced the worker without a homeland; yet even the sullen workmen of the Quartier Saint-Antoine, cheering the Emperor on his way to Italy ("We'll behave while you're gone! We'll guard the Empress!"), had given this the lie. Before the Stuttgart Congress of the Second International, Eduard Bernstein spoke approvingly of imperialism: "I estimate that a certain tutelage of the civilized peoples over the uncivilized is a necessity." Unemployed mill workers of Normandy and Lancashire might express sympathy with the plantation slave; the collision of the European and native races in Africa and Asia occasioned other sentiments. In a sense it was true that the workingman had, as Cecil Rhodes had adjured him, woken up to the fact that "The 'three acres and a cow' idea has been found to be humbug. . . ." Nevertheless it had not escaped the nationalistic workingman that all was not well in a society where, if the predicted increasing misery of the proletariat was not a fact, the gap between rich and poor had widened during the century.

The liberal "night-watchman State" was passing but by the turn of the century only the German Empire had instituted legislation directed toward a comprehensive social policy. Elsewhere such gains as could be registered had come through trade union activity and the increasing strength of socialist parties. It was not that the notion of strikes and violence had vanished; indeed it lived on in international syndicalism, achieving its classic statement in Sorel's *Reflections on Violence.* Yet there was this: with the progress of literacy, education, humanitarianism and even political democracy, the idea of mounting the barricades was moribund; it could almost be said that this idea culminated in the catastrophe of the Commune and expired among the exiles of New Caledonia. Blanqui died peacefully, Bakunin somewhat wearily ("Everything will pass, and the world will perish, but the Ninth Symphony will remain"). The future lay less with the bomb-throwers and assassins than with social democracy, although the murders of President Sadi Carnot, King Umberto and President McKinley suggest that anarchism still had a certain vogue. Yet it was true that the Russian Empire constituted the one great exception to the Western pattern of emerging liberalism.

All the same, the social struggle was uphill. Quarreling socialists united with difficulty; the hostility of conservatives, church and state was manifest. "I am free to employ whomever I wish in my workshops and factories," Eugène Schneider had told a workers' deputation in 1870. "I should prefer to see all my blast furnaces extinguished rather than give in to pressure." Before his death the aged Pio Nono inveighed against "the execrable so-called Communist doctrine" and the "criminal systems" of those who would "desecrate all human and divine rights." After him, perhaps because of German state paternalism and a new social awareness in the churches, Rome's point of view became less harsh and more positive. Hostile as it was to Marxism and trade unionism, Leo XIII's Encyclical of 1891 indicated that the crying problems of urban civilization were recognized in high places [14]. This change did not escape the Second International; the Church, commented Hubert Lagardelle, "now has a social conscience and is a party of concession."

16. JUSTICE FOR THE ONE AND THE MANY, IN THE NEW WORLD AND THE OLD

Socialism focused attention upon the plight of the cities. The transfer of some 100 million Europeans from agriculture to industry after 1870, the eclipse of the craftsman, the emergence of the modern corporation, recurring industrial crises, the concentration of wealth (in Great Britain some 5 percent of the population possessed 85 percent of the national wealth) and the rise of unions—

all this suggested that society's primary problems lay in slums, in medicine and sanitation, in elementary education and in articulating effectively the cause of the poor in the political arena. The cities were vast and the social effort required to deal with their troubles scarcely realized. London, according to Max O'Rell, was "an ignoble mixture of beer and gospelling, of gin and the Bible, of drunkenness and hypocrisy, of unheard-of filth and unrestrained luxury, of misery and prosperity, of poor people frozen to the bone, hungry and abject, and of the insolent rich and happy." Still, the migration figures seemed to show that discontent was less strong in the city than in the countryside.

After 1870 some thirty million Europeans moved overseas, four-fifths of them to the United States, where perhaps fewer than ten million in all had crossed to America in the half century after Waterloo. They left not only from highly urbanized nations but also from Italy, Denmark, Sweden, Norway and Greece. In the period 1861–70 most came from Germany and Great Britain, but forty years later it was the Habsburg monarchy, Italy and Russia which accounted for the highest percentages in the massive exodus of the more than nine millions who abandoned their homelands for the New World within a single decade. Urban justice, even in America, might be hard come by; in the agrarian world of European civilization — though not, perhaps, in America — justice was often almost beyond reach.

Some injustices, however, could not be rectified by flight. Not every discontented Central European farmer could pack up for Latin America, or every unemployed worker in the English Midlands take ship for Australia. The old enemies or society who had had to be fought on the home ground spread with the migration, revealing themselves in nativist prejudice and the exploitation of newcomers. "*Oi weh!*" Anzia Yezierska's mother cried on viewing her Manhattan tenement, "where's the sunshine in America? . . . *Gottinieu!* Like in a grave so dark!" America had no monopoly on discrimination; it existed almost everywhere in the Western world. The revival of hatred for the Jews attested to this, stemming from the financial crisis of 1873 and sparked by such sensational pamphlets as Wilhelm Marr's *The Victory of Judaism over Germanism.* In Germany hatred of the Jew was a weapon for embittered capitalists, ruined landowners, persecuted clerics and chauvinist professors. "Every Jew," Paul de Lagarde said, "is proof of the enfeeblement of our national life and of the worthlessness of what we call the Christian religion." Anti-Semitism flourished in Austria-Hungary, produced massacres and state persecution in Russia and motivated assaults upon parliament in France.

Doubtless the case of Captain Dreyfus was a study in mistaken identity; there was no reason to conclude that the whole of the French Army was infected with Edouard Drumont's virulent anti-Semitism. But, as it happened, "reason of state" and the prestige of the army dictated that this Jew be sacrificed to error and incompetence. "But General, he's innocent!" Major Picquart argued. "That is unimportant," was the reply. "That is not a consideration which should be brought into the reckoning." The debate on the prisoner of Devil's Island did not rock all France: "I am bound to admit," Clemenceau wrote, "that the working classes appear to take no interest whatever in the question." But *l'Affaire* penetrated bourgeois society to the core. The case concerned a scandalous miscarriage of justice; the Affair concerned the mirror of anti-Semitism in which a troubled society came face to face with its inner divisions and conflicts. Dreyfus of course was eventually exonerated; anti-Semitism died away or went underground for a time. But the prisoner's ordeal [15], his family's faith and Picquart's struggle remained as testimony to battles that could not be won by escaping to the New World, by agrarian reform, social insurance or the strike.

17. CURRENTS OF OPTIMISM AND PESSIMISM

Probably anti-Semitism did not bulk large. Whatever the prejudices of pastors such as Adolf Stöcker, however mobs howled outside the École Militaire or at Warsaw or Odessa, a sense of general betterment was growing. The bourgeoisie might resist the income tax, that "most demoralizing of all imposts," that "engine of public extravagance" (it was Gladstone's judgment). The massive migrations might constitute a reproach, but the material advances were written in production statistics and the assaults upon disease. From America to Germany a revolution in physics was under way, while chemists created synthetic fibers and new alloys. The steam turbine and the dynamo, canals through Panama and Suez, the railroad sleeping car, the rubber-tired automobile and, finally, the airplane became familiar. By telephone men made direct contact over vast expanses; by radio, still farther. If the massive *Titanic* foundered in the Atlantic icefields, radio saved nearly one-third of those aboard. With the phonograph men could preserve sound; with the kinetoscope, the sight and motion of their times. Optimism was rife. In the person of

Dr. Samuel Smiles it took the form of celebrating hard work and self-reliance ("The world is his, who has patience and industry"); with Herbert Spencer, the dictum that "The poverty of the incapable, the distresses that come upon the imprudent, the starvation of the idle, and those shoulderings aside of the weak by the strong . . . are the decrees of a large, far-seeing benevolence."

But amidst the clamor of Alfred Krupp's foundries and the Dark Satanic Mills, "the confusion which surrounds us on all sides," as Gottfried Keller put it, dissenting voices were heard. Treitschke's jibe that Cobden believed "the cheap production of cotton and quick journeys for commercial travellers were the supreme aims of civilization" was unfair; yet this civilization *was* more concerned with Manchester and machinery than with Cézanne, Robert Koch or Max Planck. "Is it not dreadful and humiliating," the Slavophile poet Constantine Leontiev remarked, "to think that Moses went up to Sinai, the Greeks built their lovely temples, the Romans waged their Punic wars, Alexander . . . fought his battles, apostles preached, martyrs suffered, poets sang, artists painted, knights shone at tournaments—only that some French, German or Russian bourgeois garbed in unsightly and absurd clothes should enjoy life 'individually' or 'collectively' on the ruins of all this vanished splendor?" Others were as gloomy. Arthur Schopenhauer protested against the gospel of success and "the howling colossal suffering" that accompanied it. Nietzsche considered "disintegration" the mark of the age: "All our road is slippery and dangerous, while the ice which still bears us has grown dangerously thin: we all feel the mild and gruesome breath of the thaw-wind — soon, where we are walking, no one will any longer be able to stand." Extremists like Johann-Jakob Bachofen concluded (as early as 1869!) that Europe was finished; only Russia and America would thrive in the century to come. But though the "mindless desolation" George Romanes foresaw was not inevitable, some case was to be made for Jakob Burckhardt's feeling that "world optimism is getting leaky"[16]. What provoked such sentiments differed from case to case, but many sensitive souls reflected this disenchantment in the waning century.

18. PROSPECTS FOR PEACE AND WAR

Not a little of the brooding was the product of war and threat of war. As the years ran out, a doubt might have been observed in that earlier sense of security which had temporarily disguised the eternal human ambivalence toward war and peace. The Enlightenment had been prone to conclude with Accarias de Serionne that "If the spirit of commerce should extend to every quarter, wars will become less frequent in Europe." Kant, the sage of Königsberg, proposed much the same thing. Whether reflecting exhaustion or the peculiar interests of the commercial classes, the first half of the century heard few paeans to war. True that Hegel wrote of states "forever at glorious and bloody war with each other"; but, as in the case of Joseph de Maistre ("as the movement of the winds preserves the sea from the putrefaction to which it would be reduced by a permanent calm"), this conception was peculiarly abstract. The shock of the Revolutionary wars had been substantial. But though, like Thiers, Frenchmen resented the British Mediterranean challenge in 1840, they supported Guizot and humiliation; whoever was bored by Louis Philippe, it was not the peasantry and the plutocracy. Very likely Jefferson's proposition, "Peace is our passion," was something less than the creed of his or any later generation; but the early Victorian era felt closer to Samuel Pufendorff than to Thomas Hobbes when it came to analyzing the state of nature.

Still it was a fact that the spirit of nationalism cut across the general tranquillity. Already there were murmurings about the necessity of war in the just cause. "A new generation," Tocqueville remarked in 1828, "brings with it passions and hopes." After Sadowa, Bismarck said that anyone who had looked into a dying man's eyes would not go lightly to war. "The war with France was a necessary conclusion," he noted later. For his part, Napoleon III had simply turned away in tears from the blackened faces, crawling with flies, lying in the midsummer sun around the fields, roads and ravines of Solferino. "What scoundrels we should be," Cavour confessed, "if we did for ourselves the things we do for Italy." But by then such delicacy was almost out of place. With Winwood Reade, many would still say that "famine, pestilence, and war are no longer essential for the advancement of the human race." Others, with Proudhon and John Ruskin, reflected ambivalently on the "wholesome calamity" of war. Some agreed with Moltke that "Permanent peace is a dream, and not even a beautiful one. War is an essential element of God's scheme of things." This sort of sentiment rose over Europe like the night wind, and yet it was answered from the same quarter. "War is a grand thing to look at from a distance," General Fleury observed after the Italian campaign. ". . . But all this is at the cost of many tears. . . . Butcheries of this sort are not in the spirit of the times."

Throughout the century, though not unbrokenly, peace societies had been formed. Elihu Burritt of Connecticut, Bertha von Suttner of Austria and Frédéric Passy of France contributed importantly to the river of rationalist assault upon war. The fears of Count Witte for the backward Romanov Empire in an armed and highly industrialized world, possibly even the warnings of the Polish banker Ivan Bloch in his six-volume study *The Future of War* ("increased slaughter on so terrible a scale as to render it impossible to get troops to push the battle to a decisive encounter") contributed to the calling of the Hague Peace Conference of 1899. Norman Angell's *The Great Illusion* informed Europe, America and Asia in 1910 that war could not be profitable. Perhaps the proof was irrefutable; the real question was whether it seemed relevant. At all events, the age ended in a cacophony of prescriptions and warnings [17]. "The essence of war is Violence," Admiral Sir John Fisher said. "Moderation is Imbecility. Hit first! Hit hard! and hit *anywhere!*" Bloch, who had not noticeably moved the Peace Conference with his vision of a war of attrition, simply wondered how long the social fabric would remain stable under such conditions.

19. THE FALTERING PROMISE OF AMERICA

A general apprehensiveness in this armed peace may have played some role, but precisely what impelled the ten or so millions who left Europe for the United States in the first fourteen years of the twentieth century no one could say. The blandishments of American railroad and shipping companies were involved; above all there was the hope that America represented to those who came, as the Danish poet Adam Dan said, "not empty-handed" but with "a rich inheritance." On the whole it was, as Goethe had said, better in America. The liberties of Americans, their freedom from military service, their free press and their religious liberty were the envy of many in less happy lands. And yet to some it seemed that the "American Revolution" Benjamin Rush considered unfinished in 1783 was still incomplete. Slavery was gone; civil rights were still withheld from the Negro. The world had moved on since John Adams divided society into "the gentlemen and the simple men," but as Woodrow Wilson put it in 1913, "The evil has come with the good, and much fine gold has been corroded." Manhattan's Lower East Side slums were Murderer's Alley and Misery Row; police brutality, landlord exploitation, traffic in women and children damned the New World as it accused the Old. Nevertheless, a strength of this American society was its forthright self-criticism. Against the Robber Barons were the Muckrakers; against Mark Hanna, Tom Johnson. "All th' pomes by th' lady authoressesses," said Mr. Dooley, "that used to begin: 'Oh, moon, how fair!' now begin: 'Oh, Ogden Armour, how awful!' "

The shame of the great cities in the eastern United States was only part of the story. Many immigrants continued overland toward the Pacific. Before Germany had been made, the railroad in America went through; as William II dropped the old pilot, the U.S. Superintendent of the Census proclaimed the frontier virtually to have vanished. The small prospector of '49 had yielded to the great mining companies, the cowboy on the Great Plains to the farmer. The country had expanded and filled up; the new dynasties of Rockefeller and McCormick rose on the late Victorian horizon. The "general happy mediocrity" of Franklin's America was long since over. In its place was a vastly diversified nation of rich and poor, mobile, uprooted, crushed almost by its own mass and threatening to overwhelm its own structural capacity. "The accumulation of individual wealth," Wisconsin's Chief Justice remarked as early as 1873, "seems to be greater than it ever has been since the downfall of the Roman Empire. . . . For the first time in our politics, money is taking the field as an organized power." To this oligarchy a challenge was thrown out by farmers, trade unionists and journalists [18], and by such as Robert La Follette and Woodrow Wilson. The Progressives converged hopefully in 1913 "to square every process of our national life again," as the President said, "with the standards we so proudly set up at the beginning and have always carried at our hearts."

20. ARISTOCRATIC TWILIGHT

The long road from Madison to Wilson seemed now to represent more than a century's journey. The "fortunate accident," as Tocqueville called it, had occurred: the American democracy had survived war, oligarchy and cultural conflict. What part was owing to "Parson" Weems or Noah Webster, to the doctrine of President Monroe or the firmness of Lincoln, was as indeterminable as were the contributions of Mark Twain, Hull House or the American Federation of Labor. Nineteenth-century America was rich in achievement, though not more so than Europe. Perhaps it was that the United States seemed to have changed as greatly as it had grown; the European transformation sometimes appeared less radical. Where once they had bowed to the former Empress Marie Louise, the citizens of Parma now voted for Giovanni Giolitti, and yet so many promises of the Risorgimento had expired in the paralysis of United Italy. The Bourbons no longer reigned in Naples, but then neither the Habsburg nor the Romanov sovereign was noticeably modern. Universal suffrage prevailed in Germany; no one believed the Reichstag seriously controlled government and policy. Parliament was supreme in France, but amid so many governmental changes politics appeared somewhat static, a complicated game in a closed arena. "But Madame," Aristide Briand once remarked on the subject of ministerial fall from power, "one does not fall. One sits down at the roadside, lights a cigarette, and waits to see the body of one's successor pass by."

All the same, immense changes had occurred. Elementary education, available almost nowhere to the European poor in 1815, had been legislated into compulsory existence ("The opening of every schoolhouse closes a jail," Guizot noted), though Spain defaulted and Belgium lagged. Vienna had grown nearly five-fold, Berlin almost nine, London and Paris more than three. In 1815 no more than 2 percent of Europeans lived in cities larger than 100,000, and by 1914 15 percent did. The age that began in 1815 with an economic depression survived many crises to finish in 1914 with a stupendous productive leap forward. "Today," Jules Simon said with some exaggeration, "we have become accustomed to the luxuries of Capua." No doubt faith in Christian principles had flagged. Europeans believed in national destiny, in the free-enterprise system or the coming triumph of socialism and, above all, in themselves. Europe was expansive and, for all its surviving conventions, free. Art set out to shock the established order. "It takes upon itself," Rémy de Gourmont declared, "no religious, social or moral mission. . . . It wishes to be free, to be useless, to be absurd." Everywhere the search was for speed and size: towering steel structures against the sky, swift liners plowing the Atlantic in a week, long trains crossing continents. It was a middle-class world, and the aristocracy, which in some states still retained social and even political power, surrendered its authority steadily if not altogether quietly [19]. If the world was still for the very few, much in 1914 would have been unrecognizable to the gentlemen of the Congress of Vienna.

21. THE LAMPS GO OUT

They had been agreed that it was middle-class presumption and confidence which spelled ruin. Certainly the West on the eve of 1914 was confident; whether it was fearful is much more in dispute. It had doubled its standing armies in forty-three years and quadrupled its military expenditures, but no overwhelming sense of impending catastrophe was evident. Crises had come and, with conferences and concessions, gone. Undeniably, however, there was an intensification of preparations for war: the relentless naval race between Germany and Great Britain; the lengthening military service in the conscript armies of France and the European empires; the airships, airplanes and submarines that had long since threatened to expand the dimensions of war. Above all, there were the alliances and alignments brought about by fear of isolation. "I have written," Romain Rolland said somewhat ambiguously at the conclusion of *Jean Christophe,* "the tragedy of a generation which is nearing its end."

In a sense, Bismarck had created that fear; he had not on that account been spared its consequences. His choice of Austria-Hungary in the alliance of 1879 was a commitment from which there was to be no retreat for Germany and, as it happened, much of the world. After him, no statesman managed to impose direction upon the international system; no doubt the Iron Chancellor's control had in any event run its course. Thereafter things fell apart. The ideological absurdity of France allying herself with Russia was a military necessity. It freed Europe from the German hegemony; it made 1914 possible. Only the occasion was lacking and the intention of Great Britain uncertain—although her interests were clear. It was her good fortune, and that of France, as it was the misfortune of Habsburg and Hohenzollern, that Germany invaded Belgium and made the cause honorable and apparently clear.

All the work of the peace societies and the individual peace propagandists was lost; the generalized desire of all peoples for peace was swept away. For although some philosophers, political scientists and soldiers had preached war, most voices had been raised against it, and this was true of both those who sought to remake the social order and those who spoke for social conservatism. "War alone," Nicholas' prime minister Peter Stolypin had warned, "can assure the triumph of Revolution; without war it is powerless." Opposed to orthodox Marxians prepared to welcome war as the midwife of revolution, Jean Jaurès rejected the idea of gambling "the certainty of progressive emancipation of the proletariat on this bloody throw of the dice." But national fears and ambitions were to confound such reasoning.

The Moroccan alarms, the Austro-Russian rivalry and the Balkan Wars had accustomed Europe to the notion of constant crisis and an inevitable general war, just as Prussia's lightning sucesses against Denmark, Austria and France nearly half a century earlier had taught the world that wars were won in a sudden clash of arms and morale. "The first great battle will decide the whole war," went the prevailing doctrine, "and wars will be short." Unaware of what an inconclusive first encounter might entail, Europe accepted its fate when the Habsburg monarchy chose to destroy the South Slav nationalism that must otherwise, as it seemed to Franz Josef's servants, spell out the multinational empire's end. While Field Marshal Conrad von Hötzendorf's long advocacy of preventive war against Serbia was finally nearing success, still a mood of determined optimism prevailed in cities far from the hot Bosnian town where the Archduke and his lady had died. "It will be the same as at Agadir," Jaurès insisted as he left the emergency meeting of the Second International's Bureau in Brussels. "There will be ups and downs. But things just cannot not be worked out. I've got two hours before train time. Let's go to the museum to see the Flemish primitives."

But Jaurès himself was assassinated in a café on the Rue Montmartre in Paris at 9:40 on the evening of July 31. The socialist leader's murderer, Raoul Villain, an obscure nationalist hothead, wrote: "I punished him, and my act was the symbol of a new day." It was on the contrary nothing but the fatal absurdity marking the eve of mobilization in Europe as, one by one, the great states followed Austria-Hungary into war, alleging necessity and honor [20]. No man or state could make a gesture to halt this blind procession. On receiving contradictory telegrams from the German Chancellor and the Chief of Staff, Count Berchtold flung out the contemptuous jibe, "What a joke! Who does rule in Berlin then?" It might have done for the whole of Europe. All the century's achievement and all its deepest thought had no more than postponed the struggle for security and power that Prince Metternich and aristocratic Europe once believed they had eliminated in their time. After nearly forty years, it was as if Dostoevsky's dark prescription had come true: "War is indispensable in our time; without it the world would perish or transform itself into dirty mud with festering wounds. . . . War will clear the air which we breathe, the air in which we stifle in helpless rottenness and spiritual narrowness. We need war and victories. With them the new world will come and the new life begin." Half-consciously, imperfectly articulated, in the bright summer sunshine, amidst holiday crowds and a spirit of cheerful patriotism, this troubled and apocalyptic reflection made its way through the streets of a thousand towns and villages of the now condemned nineteenth-century world.

1

Prince Metternich Appeals to "a True Friend to Order and Public Peace"

RIGHTLY or wrongly, the prevailing spirit of the ruling classes in the first generation of the nineteenth century has been associated with Prince Metternich-Winneburg (1773–1859), Chancellor and Foreign Minister of the Austrian empire until his fall from power in 1848. A hard-headed practitioner of international politics, he made himself the principal exponent of the anti-revolutionary impulse after 1815. Powerful but temperamentally paralyzed, he was condemned to watch the approaching storm that finally swept him aside. He died on June 11, 1859, as the Europe he had presided over was passing away.

"Confession of Faith"—Metternich's Secret Memorandum for Alexander I, dated December 15, 1820

" '*L'Europe*,' a celebrated writer has recently said, '*fait aujourd'hui pitié à l'homme d'esprit et horreur à l'homme vertueux*.'" "Europe today causes an intelligent man to feel sorrow, a virtuous man horror."

It would be difficult to comprise in a few words a more exact picture of the situation at the time we are writing these lines!

Kings have to calculate the chances of their very existence in the immediate future, passions are let loose, and league together to overthrow everything which society respects as the basis of its existence;

From Prince Richard Metternich (ed.), MEMOIRS OF PRINCE METTERNICH, 1773–1835 (London, 1880–82), vol. iii, pp. 454–471. Translation by Mrs. Alexander Napier.

religion, public morality, laws, customs, rights, and duties, all are attacked, confounded, overthrown, or called in question. The great mass of the people are tranquil spectators of these attacks and revolutions, and of the absolute want of all means of defense. A few are carried off by the torrent, but the wishes of the immense majority are to maintain a repose which exists no longer, and of which even the first elements seem to be lost.

What is the cause of all these evils? By what methods has this evil established itself, and how is it that it penetrates into every vein of the social body?

Do remedies still exist to arrest the progress of this evil, and what are they?

These are doubtless questions worthy of the solicitude of every good man who is a true friend to order and public peace — two elements inseparable in principle, and which are at once the first needs and the first blessings of humanity.

Has there never been offered to the world an institution really worthy of the name? Has truth been always confounded with error ever since society has believed itself able to distinguish one from the other? Have the experiences bought at the price of so many sacrifices, and repeated at intervals, and in so many different places, been all in error? Will a flood of light be shed upon society at one stroke? Will knowledge come by inspiration? If one could believe in such phenomena it would not be the less necessary, first of all, to assure oneself of their reality. Of all things, nothing is so fatal as error; and it is neither our wish nor our intention ever to give ourselves up to it. Let us examine the matter!

The source of the evil

Man's nature is immutable. The first needs of society are and remain the same, and the differences which they seem to offer find their explanation in the diversity of influences, acting on the different races by natural causes, such as the diversity of climate, barrenness or richness of soil, insular or continental position, &c. &c. These local differences no doubt produce effects which extend far beyond purely physical necessities; they create and determine particular needs in a more elevated sphere; finally, they determine the laws, and exercise an influence even on religions.

It is, on the other hand, with institutions as with everything else.

Vague in their origin, they pass through periods of development and perfection, to arrive in time at their decadence; and, conforming to the laws of man's nature, they have, like him, their infancy, their youth, their age of strength and reason, and their age of decay.

Two elements alone remain in all their strength, and never cease to exercise their indestructible influence with equal power. These are the precepts of morality, religious as well as social, and the necessities created by locality. From the time that men attempt to swerve from these bases, to become rebels against these sovereign arbiters of their destinies, society suffers from a *malaise* which sooner or later will lead to a state of convulsion. The history of every country, in relating the consequences of such errors, contains many pages stained with blood; but we dare to say, without fear of contradiction, one seeks in vain for an epoch when an evil of this nature has extended its ravages over such a vast area as it has done at the present time. The causes are natural.

History embraces but a very limited space of time. It did not begin to deserve the name of history until long after the fall of great empires. There, where it seems to conduct us to the cradle of civilisation, it really conducts us to ruins. We see republics arise and prosper, struggle, and then submit to the rule of one fortunate soldier. We see one of these republics pass through all the phases common to society, and end in almost universal monarchy — that is to say, subjugating the scattered portions of the then civilised world. We see this monarchy suffer the fate of all political bodies: we see its first springs become enfeebled, and finally decay.

Centuries of darkness followed the irruption of the barbarians. The world, however, could not return to barbarism. The Christian religion had appeared; imperishable in its essence, its very existence was sufficient to disperse the darkness and establish civilisation on new foundations, applicable to all times and all places, satisfying all needs, and establishing the most important of all on the basis of a pure and eternal law! To the formation of new Christian States succeeded the Crusades, a curious mixture of good and evil.

A decisive influence was shortly exercised on the progress of civilisation by three discoveries — the invention of printing, that of gunpowder, and the discovery of the New World. Still later came the Reformation — another event which had incalculable effects, on account of its influence on the moral world. From that time the face of the world was changed.

The facilitation of the communication of thoughts by printing; the total change in the means of attack and defence brought about by the invention of gunpowder; the difference suddenly produced in the value of property by the quantity of metals which the discovery of America put in circulation; the spirit of adventure provoked by the chances of fortune opened in a new hemisphere; the modifications in the relations of society caused by so many and such important changes, all became more developed, and were in some sort crowned by the revolution which the Reformation worked in the moral world.

The progress of the human mind has been extremely rapid in the course of the last three centuries. This progress having been accelerated more rapidly than the growth of wisdom (the only counterpoise to passions and to error); a revolution prepared by the false systems, the fatal errors into which many of the most illustrious sovereigns of the last half of the eighteenth century fell, has at last broken out in a country advanced in knowledge, and enervated by pleasure, in a country inhabited by a people whom one can only regard as frivolous, from the facility with which they comprehend and the difficulty they experience in judging calmly.

Having now thrown a rapid glance over the first causes of the present state of society, it is necessary to point out in a more particular manner the evil which threatens to deprive it, at one blow, of the real blessings, the fruits of genuine civilisation, and to disturb it in the midst of its enjoyments. This evil may be described in one word—presumption; the natural effect of the rapid progression of the human mind towards the perfecting of so many things. This it is which at the present day leads so many individuals astray, for it has become an almost universal sentiment.

Religion, morality, legislation, economy, politics, administration, all have become common and accessible to everyone. Knowledge seems to come by inspiration; experience has no value for the presumptuous man; faith is nothing to him; he substitutes for it a pretended individual conviction, and to arrive at this conviction dispenses with all inquiry and with all study; for these means appear too trivial to a mind which believes itself strong enough to embrace at one glance all questions and all facts. Laws have no value for him, because he has not contributed to make them, and it would be beneath a man of his parts to recognise the limits traced by rude and ignorant generations. Power resides in himself; why should he submit himself to that which was only useful for the man deprived of light and knowledge? That which, according to him, was required in an age of weakness cannot be suitable in an age of reason and vigour, amounting to universal perfection, which the German innovators designate by the idea, absurd in itself, of the Emancipation of the People! Morality itself he does not attack openly, for without it he could not be sure for a single instant of his own existence; but he interprets its essence after his own fashion, and allows every other person to do so likewise, provided that other person neither kills nor robs him.

In thus tracing the character of the presumptuous man, we believe we have traced that of the society of the day, composed of like elements, if the denomination of society is applicable to an order of things which only tends in principle towards individualising all the elements of which society is composed. Presumption makes every man the guide of his own belief, the arbiter of laws according to which he is pleased to govern himself, or to allow someone else to govern him and his neighbours; it makes him, in short, the sole judge of his own faith, his own actions, and the principles according to which he guides them.

Is it necessary to give a proof of this last fact? We think we have furnished it in remarking that one of the sentiments most natural to man, that of nationality, is erased from the Liberal catechism, and that where the word is still employed, it is used by the heads of the party as a pretext to enchain Governments, or as a lever to bring about destruction. The real aim of the idealists of the party is religious and political fusion, and this being analysed is nothing else but creating in favour of each individual an existence entirely independent of all authority, or of any other will than his own, an idea absurd and contrary to the nature of man, and incompatible with the needs of human society.

The course which the evil has followed and still follows

The causes of the deplorable intensity with which this evil weighs on society appear to us to be of two kinds. The first are so connected with the nature of things that no human foresight could have prevented them. The second should be subdivided into two classes, however similar they may appear in their effects.

Of these causes, the first are negative, the others positive. We will place among the first the feebleness and the inertia of Governments.

It is sufficient to cast a glance on the course which the Governments followed during the eighteenth century, to be convinced that not one among them was ignorant of the evil or of the crisis towards which the social body was tending. There were, however, some men, unhappily endowed with great talents, who felt their own strength, and were not slow to appraise the progressive course of their influence, taking into account the weakness or the inertia of their adversaries; and who had the art to prepare and conduct men's minds to the triumph of their detestable enterprise — an enterprise all the more odious as it was pursued without regard to results, simply abandoning themselves to the one feeling of hatred of God and of His immutable moral laws.

France had the misfortune to produce the greatest number of these men. It is in her midst that religion and all that she holds sacred, that morality and authority, and all connected with them, have been attacked with a steady and systematic animosity, and it is there that the weapon of ridicule has been used with the most ease and success.

Drag through the mud the name of God and the powers instituted by His divine decrees, and the revolution will be prepared! Speak of a social contract, and the revolution is accomplished! The revolution was already completed in the palaces of Kings, in the drawing-rooms and boudoirs of certain cities, while among the great mass of the people it was still only in a state of preparation.

* * *

Do remedies for this evil exist, and what are they?

We look upon it as a fundamental truth, that for every disease there is a remedy, and that the knowledge of the real nature of the one should lead to the discovery of the other. Few men, however, stop thoroughly to examine a disease which they intend to combat. There are hardly any who are not subject to the influence of passion, or held under the yoke of prejudice; there are a great many who err in a way more perilous still, on account of its flattering and often brilliant appearance: we speak of *l'esprit de système,* that spirit always false, but indefatigable, audacious and irrepressible, is satisfactory to men imbued with it (for they live in and govern a world created by themselves), but it is so much the more dangerous for the inhabitants of the real world, so different from that created by *l'esprit de système.*

There is another class of men who, judging of a disease by its outward appearance, confound the accessory manifestations with the root of the disease, and, instead of directing their efforts to the source of the evil, content themselves with subduing some passing symptoms.

It is our duty to try and avoid both of these dangers.

The evil exists and it is enormous. We do not think we can better define it and its cause at all times and in all places than we have already done by the word "presumption," that inseparable companion of the half-educated, that spring of an unmeasured ambition, and yet easy to satisfy in times of trouble and confusion.

It is principally the middle classes of society which this moral gangrene has affected, and it is only among them that the real heads of the party are found.

For the great mass of the people it has no attraction and can have none. The labours to which this class — the real people — are obliged to devote themselves, are too continuous and too positive to allow them to throw themselves into vague abstractions and ambitions. The people know what is the happiest thing for them: namely, to be able to count on the morrow, for it is the morrow which will repay them for the cares and sorrows of to-day. The laws which afford a just protection to individuals, to families, and to property, are quite simple in their essence. The people dread any movement which injures industry and brings new burdens in its train.

Men in the higher classes of society who join the revolution are either falsely ambitious men or, in the widest acceptation of the word, lost spirits. Their career, moreover, is generally short! They are the first victims of political reforms, and the part played by the small number among them who survive is mostly that of courtiers despised by upstarts, their inferiors, promoted to the first dignities of the State; and of this France, Germany, Italy, and Spain furnish a number of living examples.

We do not believe that fresh disorders with a directly revolutionary end — not even revolutions in the palace and the highest places in the Government — are to be feared at present in France, because of the decided aversion of the people to anything which might disturb the peace they are now enjoying after so many troubles and disasters.

In Germany, as in Spain and Italy, the people ask only for peace and quiet.

In all four countries the agitated classes are principally composed of wealthy men — real cosmopolitans, securing their personal advantage at the expense of any order of things whatever—paid State officials, men of letters, lawyers, and the individuals charged with the public education.

To these classes may be added that of the falsely ambitious, whose number is never considerable among the lower orders, but is larger in the higher ranks of society.

There is besides scarcely any epoch which does not offer a rallying cry to some particular faction. This cry, since 1815, has been *Constitution.* But do not let us deceive ourselves: this word, susceptible of great latitude of interpretation, would be but imperfectly understood if we supposed that the factions attached quite the same meaning to it under the different *régimes.* Such is certainly not the case. In pure monarchies it is qualified by the name of "national representation." In countries which have lately been brought under the representative *régime* it is called "development," and promises charters and fundamental laws. In the only State which possesses an ancient national representation it takes "reform" as its object. Everywhere it means change and trouble.

* * *

Europe thus presents itself to the impartial observer under an aspect at the same time deplorable and peculiar. We find everywhere the people praying for the maintenance of peace and tranquillity, faithful to God and their Princes, remaining proof against the efforts and seductions of the factious who call themselves friends of the people and wish to lead them to an agitation which the people themselves do not desire!

The Governments, having lost their balance, are frightened, intimidated, and thrown into confusion by the cries of the intermediary class of society, which, placed between the Kings and their subjects, breaks the sceptre of the monarch, and usurps the cry of the people—that class so often disowned by the people, and nevertheless too much listened to, caressed and feared by those who could with one word reduce it again to nothingness.

We see this intermediary class abandon itself with a blind fury and animosity which proves much more its own fears than any confidence in the success of its enterprises, to all the means which seem proper to assuage its thirst for power, applying itself to the task of persuading Kings that their rights are confined to sitting upon a throne, while those of the people are to govern, and to attack all that centuries have bequeathed as holy and worthy of man's respect — denying, in fact, the value of the past, and declaring themselves the masters of the future. We see this class take all sorts of disguises, uniting and subdividing as occasion offers, helping each other in the hour of danger, and the next day depriving each other of all their conquests. It takes possession of the press, and employs it to promote impiety, disobedience to the laws of religion and the State, and goes so far as to preach murder as a duty for those who desire what is good.

One of its leaders in Germany defined public opinion as "the will of the strong man in the spirit of the party" — a maxim too often put in practice, and too seldom understood by those whose right and duty it is to save society from its own errors, its own weaknesses, and the crimes which the factious commit while pretending to act in its interests.

The evil is plain; the means used by the faction which causes these disorders are so blameable in principle, so criminal in their application, and expose the faction itself to so many dangers, that what men of narrow views (whose head and heart are broken by circumstances stronger than their calculations or their courage) regard as the end of society may become the first step towards a better order of things. These weak men would be right unless men stronger than they are come forward to close their ranks and determine the victory.

We are convinced that society can no longer be saved without strong and vigorous resolutions on the part of the Governments still free in their opinions and actions.

We are also convinced that this may yet be, if the Governments face the truth, if they free themselves from all illusion, if they join their ranks and take their stand on a line of correct, unambiguous, and frankly announced principles.

By this course the monarchs will fulfil the duties imposed upon them by Him who, by entrusting them with power, has charged them to watch over the maintenance of justice, and the rights of all, to avoid the paths of error, and tread firmly in the way of truth. Placed beyond the passions which agitate society, it is in days of trial chiefly that they are called upon to despoil realities of their false appearances, and to show themselves as they are, fathers invested with the authority belonging by right to the heads of families, to prove that, in days of mourning, they know how to be just, wise, and therefore strong, and that they will not abandon the people whom they ought to govern to be the sport of factions, to error and its consequences, which must involve the loss of society. The moment in which we are putting our thoughts on paper is one of these critical moments. The crisis is great; it will be decisive according to the part we take or do not take.

There is a rule of conduct common to individuals and to States, established by the experience of centuries as by that of everyday life. This rule declares "that one must not dream of reformation while agitated by passion; wisdom directs that at such moments we should limit ourselves to maintaining."

Let the monarchs vigorously adopt this principle; let all their resolutions bear the impression of it. Let their actions, their measures, and even their words announce and prove to the world this determination — they will find allies everywhere. The Governments, in establishing the principle of *stability,* will in no wise exclude the development of what is good, for stability is not immobility. But it is for those who are burdened with the heavy task of government to augment the well-being of their people! It is for Governments to regulate it according to necessity and to suit the times. It is not by concessions, which the factious strive to force from legitimate power, and which they have neither the right to claim nor the faculty of keeping within just bounds, that wise reforms can be carried out. That all the good possible should be done is our most ardent wish; but that which is not good must never be confounded with that which is, and even real good should be done only by those who unite to the right of authority the means of enforcing it. Such should be also the sincere wish of the people, who know by sad experience the value of certain phrases and the nature of certain caresses.

Respect for all that is; liberty for every Government to watch over the well-being of its own people; a league between all Governments against factions in all States; contempt for the meaningless words which have become the rallying cry of the factious; respect for the progressive development of institutions in lawful ways; refusal on the part of every monarch to aid or succour partisans under any mask whatever — such are happily the ideas of the great monarchs: the world will be saved if they bring them into action — it is lost if they do not.

2

Alexis de Tocqueville Seeks "the Image of Democracy Itself"

A GENERATION *younger than Metternich, Count Alexis de Tocqueville (1805–59) was infinitely more aware of the need to come to terms with his times. In 1831 he obtained permission to travel to the United States, ostensibly to inspect the penal system. Out of his famous journey of enquiry into the life of Andrew Jackson's America came the three remarkable volumes of* Democracy in America *(1835–40). A Cassandra forecasting doom before the revolution of February 1848, he had his political career ended by Louis Napoleon's* coup d'état *of December 2, 1851. The last years were given to historical research and writing. He died in Cannes, April 16, 1859, and in the somewhat clamorous era of nationalism his name faded from the public consciousness; his true stature would be recognized a century later.*

Democracy in America

AMONGST the novel objects that attracted my attention during my stay in the United States, nothing struck me more forcibly than the general equality of conditions. I readily discovered the prodigious influence which this primary fact exercises on the whole course of society, by giving a certain direction to public opinion, and a certain tenor to the laws; by imparting new maxims to the governing powers, and peculiar habits to the governed. I speedily perceived that the influence of this fact extends far beyond the political character and the laws of the country, and that it has no less empire over civil society than over the Government; it creates opinions, engenders sentiments, suggests the ordinary practices of life, and modifies whatever it does not produce. The more I advanced in the study of

From Alexis de Tocqueville, DEMOCRACY IN AMERICA *(London, 1875), vol. i, pp. 1–13, 443–445; vol. ii, pp. 302–305. Translation by Henry Reeve, Esq.*

American society, the more I perceived that the equality of conditions is the fundamental fact from which all others seem to be derived, and the central point at which all my observations constantly terminated.

I then turned my thoughts to our own hemisphere, where I imagined that I discerned something analogous to the spectacle which the New World presented to me. I observed that the equality of conditions is daily progressing towards those extreme limits which it seems to have reached in the United States, and that the democracy which governs the American communities appears to be rapidly rising into power in Europe. I hence conceived the idea of the book which is now before the reader.

It is evident to all alike that a great democratic revolution is going on amongst us; but there are two opinions as to its nature and consequences. To some it appears to be a novel accident, which as such may still be checked; to others it seems irresistible, because it is the most uniform, the most ancient, and the most permanent tendency which is to be found in history. . . .

In perusing the pages of our history, we shall scarcely meet with a single great event, in the lapse of seven hundred years, which has not turned to the advantage of equality. The Crusades and the wars of the English decimated the nobles and divided their possessions; the erection of communities introduced an element of democratic liberty into the bosom of feudal monarchy; the invention of firearms equalised the villein and the noble on the field of battle; printing opened the same resources to the minds of all classes; the post was organised so as to bring the same information to the door of the poor man's cottage and to the gate of the palace; and Protestantism proclaimed that all men are alike able to find the road to heaven. The discovery of America offered a thousand new paths to fortune, and placed riches and power within the reach of the adventurous and the obscure. If we examine what has happened in France at intervals of fifty years, beginning with the eleventh century, we shall invariably perceive that a twofold revolution has taken place in the state of society. The noble has gone down on the social ladder, and the *roturier* has gone up; the one descends as the other rises. Every half-century brings them nearer to each other, and they will very shortly meet.

Nor is this phenomenon at all peculiar to France. Whithersoever we turn our eyes we shall witness the same continual revolution throughout the whole of Christendom. The various occurrences of national existence have everywhere turned to the advantage of democracy; all men have aided it by their exertions: those who have intentionally laboured in its cause, and those who have served it unwittingly; those who have fought for it and those who have declared themselves its opponents, have all been driven along in the same track, have all laboured to one end, some ignorantly and some unwillingly; all have been blind instruments in the hands of God.

The gradual development of the equality of conditions is therefore a providential fact, and it possesses all the characteristics of a Divine decree: it is universal, it is durable, it constantly eludes all human interference, and all events as well as all men contribute to its progress. Would it, then, be wise to imagine that a social impulse which dates from so far back can be checked by the efforts of a generation? Is it credible that the democracy which has annihilated the feudal system and vanquished kings will respect the citizen and the capitalist? Will it stop now that it has grown so strong and its adversaries so weak? None can say which way we are going, for all terms of comparison are wanting: the equality of conditions is more complete in the Christian countries of the present day than it has been at any time or in any part of the world; so that the extent of what already exists prevents us from foreseeing what may be yet to come.

The whole book which is here offered to the public has been written under the impression of a kind of religious dread produced in the author's mind by the contemplation of so irresistible a revolution, which has advanced for centuries in spite of such amazing obstacles, and which is still proceeding in the midst of the ruins it has made. It is not necessary that God himself should speak in order to disclose to us the unquestionable signs of His will; we can discern them in the habitual course of nature, and in the invariable tendency of events: I know, without a special revelation, that the planets move in the orbits traced by the Creator's finger. If the men of our time were led by attentive observation and by sincere reflection to acknowledge that the gradual and progressive development of social equality is at once the past and future of their history, this solitary truth would confer the sacred character of a Divine decree upon the change. To attempt to check democracy would be in that case to resist the will of God; and the nations would then be constrained to make the best of the social lot awarded to them by Providence.

The Christian nations of our age seem to me to present a most alarming spectacle; the impulse which is bearing them along is so strong that it cannot be stopped, but it is not yet so rapid that it cannot be guided: their fate is in their hands; yet a little while and it may be so no longer. The first duty which is at this time imposed upon those who direct our affairs is to educate the democracy; to warm its faith, if that be possible; to purify its morals; to direct its energies; to substitute a knowledge of business for its inexperience, and an acquaintance with its true interests for its blind propensities; to adapt its government to time and place, and to modify it in compliance with the occurrences and the actors of the age. A new science of politics is indispensable to a new world. This, however, is what we think of least; launched in the middle of a rapid stream, we obstinately fix our eyes on the ruins which may still be descried upon the shores we have left, whilst the current sweeps us along, and drives us backwards toward the gulf. . . .

But the scene is now changed . . . ; the divisions which once severed mankind are lowered; property is divided, power is held in common, the light of intelligence spreads, and the capacities of all classes are equally cultivated; the State becomes democratic, and the empire of democracy is slowly and peaceably introduced into the institutions and the manners of the nation. . . .

. . . The nation, taken as a whole, will be less brilliant, less glorious, and perhaps less strong; but the majority of the citizens will enjoy a greater degree of prosperity, and the people will remain quiet, not because it despairs of amelioration, but because it is conscious of the advantages of its condition. If all the consequences of this state of things were not good or useful, society would at least have appropriated all such as were useful and good; and having once and forever renounced the social advantages of aristocracy, mankind would enter into possession of all the benefits which democracy can afford. . . .

We have, then, abandoned whatever advantages the old state of things afforded, without receiving any compensation from our present condition; we have destroyed an aristocracy, and we seem inclined to survey its ruins with complacency, and to fix our abode in the midst of them.

The phenomena which the intellectual world presents are not less deplorable. The democracy of France, checked in its course or abandoned to its lawless passions, has overthrown whatever crossed its path, and has shaken all that it has not destroyed. Its empire on society has not been gradually introduced or peaceably established, but it has constantly advanced in the midst of disorder and the agitation of a conflict. In the heat of the struggle each partisan is hurried beyond the limits of his opinions by the opinions and the excesses of his opponents, until he loses sight of the end of his exertions, and holds a language which disguises his real sentiments or secret instincts. Hence arises the strange confusion which we are witnessing. I cannot recall to my mind a passage in history more worthy of sorrow and of pity than the scenes which are happening under our eyes; it is as if the natural bond which unites the opinions of man to his tastes and his actions to his principles was now broken; the sympathy which has always been acknowledged between the feelings and the ideas of mankind appears to be dissolved, and all the laws of moral analogy to be abolished.

Zealous Christians may be found amongst us whose minds are nurtured in the love and knowledge of a future life, and who readily espouse the cause of human liberty as the source of all moral greatness. Christianity, which has declared that all men are equal in the sight of God, will not refuse to acknowledge that all citizens are equal in the eye of the law. But, by a singular concourse of events, religion is entangled in those institutions which democracy assails, and it is not unfrequently brought to reject the equality it loves, and to curse that cause of liberty as a foe which it might hallow by its alliance.

By the side of these religious men I discern others whose looks are turned to the earth more than to Heaven; they are the partisans of liberty, not only as the source of the noblest virtues, but more especially as the root of all solid advantages; and they sincerely desire to extend its sway, and to impart its blessings to mankind. It is natural that they should hasten to invoke the assistance of religion, for they must know that liberty cannot be established without morality, nor morality without faith; but they have seen religion in the ranks of their adversaries, and they inquire no further; some of them attack it openly, and the remainder are afraid to defend it.

In former ages slavery has been advocated by the venal and slavish-minded, whilst the independent and the warm-hearted were struggling without hope to save the liberties of mankind. But men of high and generous characters are now to be met with, whose opinions are at variance with their inclinations, and who praise that servility which they have themselves never known. Others, on the contrary, speak in the name of liberty, as if they were able to feel its sanctity and its majesty, and loudly claim for humanity those rights which they have always disowned. There are virtuous and peaceful individuals whose pure morality, quiet habits, affluence, and talents fit them to be the leaders of the surrounding population; their love of their country is sincere, and they are prepared to make the greatest sacrifices to its welfare, but they confound the abuses of civilization with its benefits, and the idea of evil is inseparable in their minds from that of novelty.

Not far from this class is another party, whose object is to materialize mankind, to hit upon what is expedient without heeding what is just, to acquire knowledge without faith, and prosperity apart from virtue; assuming the title of the champions of modern civilization, and placing themselves in a station which they usurp with insolence, and from which they are driven by their own unworthiness. Where are we then? The religionists are the enemies of liberty, and the friends of liberty attack religion; the high-minded and the noble advocate subjection, and the meanest and most servile minds preach independence; honest and enlightened citizens are opposed to all progress, whilst men without patriotism and without principles are the apostles of civilization and of intelligence. Has such been the fate of the centuries which have preceded our own? and has man always inhabited a world like the present, where nothing is linked together, where virtue is without genius, and genius without honour; where the love of order is confounded with a taste for oppression, and the holy rites of freedom with a contempt of law; where the light thrown by conscience on human actions is dim, and where nothing seems to be any longer forbidden or allowed, honourable or shameful, false or true? I cannot, however, believe that the Creator made man to leave him in an endless struggle with the intellectual miseries which surround us: God destines a calmer and a more certain future to the communities of Europe; I am unacquainted with His designs, but I shall not cease to believe in them because I cannot fathom them, and I had rather mistrust my own capacity than His justice.

There is a country in the world where the great revolution which I am speaking of seems nearly to have reached its natural limits; it has been effected with ease and simplicity, say rather that this country has attained the consequences of the democratic revolution which we are undergoing without having experienced the revolution itself. The emigrants who fixed themselves on the shores of America in the beginning of the seventeenth century severed the democratic principle from all the principles which repressed it in the old communities of Europe, and transplanted it unalloyed to the New World. It has there been allowed to spread in perfect freedom, and to put forth its consequences in the laws by influencing the manners of the country.

It appears to me beyond a doubt that sooner or later we shall arrive, like the Americans, at an almost complete equality of conditions. But I do not conclude from this that we shall ever be necessarily led to draw the same political consequences which the Americans have derived from a similar social organization. I am far from supposing that they have chosen the only form of government which a democracy may adopt; but the identity of the efficient cause of laws and manners in the two countries is sufficient to account for the immense interest we have in becoming acquainted with its effects in each of them. . . .

. . . I confess that in America I saw more than America; I sought the image of democracy itself, with its inclinations, its character, its prejudices, and its passions, in order to learn what we have to fear or to hope from its progress. . . .

* * *

It must not, then, be imagined that the impulse of the British race in the New World can be arrested. The dismemberment of the Union, and the hostilities which might ensue, the abolition of republican institutions, and the tyrannical government which might succeed it, may retard this impulse, but they cannot prevent it from ultimately fulfilling the destinies to which that race is reserved. No power upon earth can close upon the emigrants that fertile wilderness which offers resources to all industry and a refuge from all want. Future events, of whatever nature they may be, will not deprive the Americans of their climate or of their inland seas, of their great rivers or of their exuberant soil. Nor will bad laws, revolutions, and anarchy, be able to obliterate that love of prosperity and that spirit of enterprise which seem to be the distinctive characteristics of their race, or to extinguish that knowledge which guides them on their way.

Thus, in the midst of the uncertain future, one event at least is sure. At a period which may be said to be near (for we are speaking of the life of a nation), the Anglo-Americans will alone cover the immense space contained between the Polar regions and the Tropics, extending from the coasts of the Atlantic to the shores of the Pacific Ocean. The territory which will probably be occupied by the Anglo-Americans at some future time, may be computed to equal three-quarters of Europe in extent. The climate of the Union is upon the whole preferable to that of Europe, and its natural advantages are not less great; it is therefore evident that its population will at some future time be proportionate to our own. Europe, divided as it is between so many different nations, and torn as it has been by incessant wars and the barbarous manners of the Middle Ages, has notwithstanding attained a population of 410 inhabitants to the square league. What cause can prevent the United States from having as numerous a population in time? . . .

The time will therefore come when one hundred and fifty millions of men will be living in North America, equal in condition, the progeny of one race, owing their origin to the same cause, and preserving the same civilisation, the same language, the same religion, the same habits, the same manners, and imbued with the same opinions, propagated under the same forms. The rest is uncertain, but this is certain; and it is a fact new to the world—a fact fraught with such portentous consequences as to baffle the efforts even of the imagination.

There are, at the present time, two great nations in the world which seem to tend towards the same end, although they started from different points: I allude to the Russians and the Americans. Both of them have grown up unnoticed; and whilst the attention of mankind was directed elsewhere, they have suddenly assumed a most prominent place amongst the nations; and the world learned their existence and their greatness at almost the same time.

All other nations seem to have nearly reached their natural limits, and only to be charged with the maintenance of their power; but these are still in the act of growth; all the others are stopped, or continue to advance with extreme difficulty; these are proceeding with ease and with celerity along a path to which the human eye can assign no term. The American struggles against the natural obstacles which oppose him; the adversaries of the Russian are men; the former combats the wilderness and savage life; the latter, civilisation with all its weapons and its arts: the conquests of the one are therefore gained by the ploughshare; those of the other by the sword. The Anglo-American relies upon personal interest to accomplish his ends, and gives free scope to the unguided exertions and common sense of the citizens; the Russian centres all the authority of society in a single arm: the principal instrument of the former is freedom; of the latter, servitude. Their starting-point is different, and their courses are not the same; yet each of them seems to be marked out by the will of Heaven to sway the destinies of half the globe.

* * *

Before I close for ever the theme that has detained me so long, I would fain take a parting survey of all the various characteristics of modern society, and appreciate at last the general influence to be exercised by the principle of equality upon the fate of mankind; but I am stopped by the difficulty of the task, and in presence of so great an object my sight is troubled, and my reason fails. The society of the modern world which I have sought to delineate, and which I seek to judge, has but just come into existence. Time has not yet shaped it into perfect form: the great revolution by which it has been created is not yet over: and amidst the occurrences of our time, it is almost impossible to discern what will pass away with the revolution itself, and what will survive its close. The world which is rising into existence is still half encumbered by the remains of the world which is waning into decay; and amidst the vast perplexity of human affairs, none can say how much of ancient institutions and former manners will remain, or how much will completely disappear. Although the revolution which is taking place in the social condition, the laws, the opinions and the feelings of men, is still very far from being terminated, yet its results already admit of no comparison with anything that the world has ever before witnessed. I go back from age to age up to the remotest antiquity; but I find no parallel to what is occurring before my eyes: as the past has ceased to throw its light upon the future, the mind of man wanders in obscurity.

Nevertheless, in the midst of a prospect so wide, so novel and so confused, some of the more prominent characteristics may already be discerned and pointed out. The good things and the evils of life are more equally distributed in the world: great wealth tends to disappear, the number of small fortunes to increase; desires and gratifications are multiplied, but extraordinary prosperity and irremediable penury are alike unknown. The sentiment of ambition is universal, but the scope of ambition is seldom vast. Each individual stands apart in solitary weakness; but society at large is active, provident, and powerful: the performances of private persons are insignificant, those of the State immense. There is little energy of character; but manners are mild, and laws humane. If there be few instances of exalted heroism or of virtues of the highest, brightest, and purest temper, men's habits are regular, violence is rare, and cruelty almost unknown. Human existence becomes longer, and property more secure: life is not adorned with brilliant trophies, but it is extremely easy and tranquil. Few pleasures are either very refined or very coarse; and highly-polished manners are as uncommon as great brutality of tastes. Neither men of great learning, nor extremely ignorant communities, are to be met with; genius becomes more rare, information more diffused. The human mind is impelled by the small efforts of all mankind combined together, not by the strenuous activity of certain men. There is less perfection, but more abundance, in all the productions of the arts. The ties of race, of rank, and of country are relaxed; the great bond of humanity is strengthened. If I endeavour to find out the most general and the most prominent of all these different characteristics, I shall have occasion to perceive, that what is taking place in men's fortunes manifests itself under a thousand other forms. Almost all extremes are softened or blunted: all that was most prominent is superseded by some mean term, at once less lofty and less low, less brilliant and less obscure, than what before existed in the world.

When I survey this countless multitude of beings, shaped in each other's likeness, amidst whom nothing rises and nothing falls, the sight of such universal uniformity saddens and chills me, and I am tempted to regret that state of society which has ceased to be. When the world was full of men of great importance and extreme insignificance, of great wealth and extreme poverty, of great learning and extreme ignorance, I turned aside from the latter to fix my observation on the former alone, who gratified my sympathies. But I admit that this gratification arose from my own weakness: it is because I am unable to see at once all that is around me, that I am allowed thus to select and separate the objects of my predilection from among so many others. Such is not the case with that Almighty and Eternal Being, whose gaze necessarily includes the whole of created things, and who surveys distinctly, though at once, mankind and man. We may naturally believe that it is not the singular prosperity of the few, but the greater well-being of all, which is most pleasing in the sight of the Creator and Preserver of men. What appears to me to be man's decline, is to His eye advancement; what afflicts me is acceptable to Him. A state of equality is perhaps less elevated, but it is more just; and its justice constitutes its greatness and its beauty. I would strive then to raise myself to this point of the Divine contemplation, and thence to view and to judge the concerns of men.

No man, upon the earth, can as yet affirm absolutely and generally, that the new state of the world is better than its former one; but it is already easy to perceive that this state is different. Some vices and some virtues were so inherent in the constitution of an aristocratic nation, and are so opposite to the character of a modern people, that they can never be infused into it; some good tendencies and some bad propensities which were unknown to the former, are natural to the latter; some ideas suggest themselves spontaneously to the imagination of the one, which are utterly repugnant to the mind of the other. They are like two distinct orders of human beings, each of which has its own merits and defects, its own advantages and its own evils. Care must therefore be taken not to judge the state of society, which is now coming into existence, by notions derived from a state of society which no longer exists; for as these states of society are exceedingly different in their structure, they cannot be submitted to a just or fair comparison. It would be scarcely more reasonable to require of our own contemporaries the peculiar virtues which originated in the social condition of their forefathers, since that social condition is itself fallen, and has drawn into one promiscuous ruin the good and evil which belonged to it. . . .

For myself, who now look back from this extreme limit of my task, and discover from afar, but at once, the various objects which have attracted my more attentive investigation upon my way, I am full of apprehensions and of hopes. I perceive mighty dangers which it is possible to ward off—mighty evils which may be avoided or alleviated; and I cling with a firmer hold to the belief, that for democratic nations to be virtuous and prosperous they require but to will it.

. . . Providence has not created mankind entirely independent or entirely free. It is true that around every man a fatal circle is traced, beyond which he cannot pass; but within the wide verge of that circle he is powerful and free: as it is with man, so with communities. The nations of our time cannot prevent the conditions of men from becoming equal; but it depends upon themselves whether the principle of equality is to lead them to servitude or freedom, to knowledge or barbarism, to prosperity or to wretchedness.

3

Lord Ashley on the "Spectacles of Suffering and Oppression" in Industrial England

NOWHERE more than in England was the cost of industrialism brought to public attention. The Tory aristocrat Anthony Ashley Cooper, later 7th Earl of Shaftesbury (1801–85), was foremost in interesting the nation in the plight of the "wage-slaves." An opponent of the Reform Bill of 1832 and of socialism and trade unions, he was narrow in his views but a true humanist. The following extracts from two speeches in the Commons, in 1840 and 1844, illustrate the evidence which finally moved the House to enact protective legislation. Sir James Graham (1792–1861), free-trader, and many times a Cabinet minister, expressed the opposition to government regulation feared by the manufacturing classes.

a House of Commons: August 4, 1840

EMPLOYMENT of children] Lord *Ashley* spoke as follows: "It is, Sir, with feelings somewhat akin to despair, that I now rise to bring before the House, the motion of which I have given notice. When I consider the period of the Session, the long discussions that have already taken place to-day, the scanty attendance of Members, and the power which any Member possesses of stopping me midway in my career, I cannot but entertain misgivings, that I shall not be able to bring, under the attention of the House, this subject, which has now occupied so large a portion of my public life, and in which are now concentrated, in one hour, the labours of years. Sir, I must assure the House, that this motion has not been conceived, nor will it be introduced, in any hostile spirit towards her Majesty's Ministers; quite the reverse. I do indeed trust, nay more, I have reason to be-

From HANSARD'S PARLIAMENTARY DEBATES (London), 3rd Series, vol. 55 (August 4, 1840), cols. 1259–1274; vol. 73 (March 15, 1844), cols. 1073–1110.

lieve, that I shall obtain their hearty and effectual support. Sir, I know well that I owe an apology and an explanation to the House for trespassing on their patience at so late a period — my explanation is this: I have long been taunted with narrow and exclusive attention to the children in the factories alone; I have been told, in language and writing, that there [are] other cases fully as grievous, and not less numerous; that I was unjust and inconsiderate in my denouncement of the one, and my omission of the other. I have, however, long contemplated this effort which I am now making; I had long resolved that, so soon as I could see the factory children, as it were, safe in harbour, I would undertake a new task. The committee of this Session on mills and factories, having fully substantiated the necessity, and rendered certain the amendment of the law, I am now endeavouring to obtain an inquiry into the actual circumstances and condition of another large part of our juvenile population. Sir, I hardly know whether any argument is necessary to prove that the future hopes of a country must, under God, be laid in the character and condition of its children; however right it may be to attempt, it is almost fruitless to expect, the reformation of its adults; as the sapling has been bent, so will it grow. To ensure a vigorous and moral manhood, we must train them aright from their earliest years, and so reserve the full development of their moral and physical energies for the service hereafter of our common country. Now, Sir, whatever may be done or proposed in time to come, we have, I think, a right to know the state of our juvenile population; the House has a right, the country has a right. How is it possible to address ourselves to the remedies of evils which we all feel, unless we have previously ascertained both the nature and the cause of them? The first step towards a cure is a knowledge of the disorder. We have asserted these truths in our factory legislation; and I have on my side, the authority of all civilized nations of modern times; the practice of this House; the common sense of the thing; and the justice of the principle. Sir, I may say with Tacitus, "*opus adgredior, optimum casibus . . . ipsâ etiam pace sœvum:*" to give but an outline of all the undertaking, would occupy too much of your time and patience; few persons, perhaps, have an idea of the number and variety of the employments which demand and exhaust the physical energies of young children, or of the extent of suffering to which they are exposed. It is right, Sir, that the country should know at what cost its pre-eminence is purchased,

"Petty rogues submit to fate,
That great ones may enjoy their state."

The number I cannot give with any degree of accuracy, though I may venture to place them as many-fold the numbers of those engaged in the factories — the suffering I can exhibit, to a certain degree, in the documents before me. . . .

Now, Sir, will the House allow me to set before them, in a few cases, the evidence I have been able to obtain illustrative of the nature and effects of these several departments of industry? The first I shall take is the manufacture of tobacco, a business of which, perhaps, but little is generally known; in this I find that —

> "Children are employed twelve hours a-day. They go as early as seven years of age. The smell in the room is very strong and offensive. They are employed in spinning the twist tobacco; in the country, the children work more hours in the day, being frequently until nine and ten o'clock at night. Their opportunities for education are almost none, and their appearance altogether sickly."

The next department I shall take is that of bleaching. In bleaching —

> "Children are employed at eleven, and oftentimes younger. They go to work at any time of the day or night, when they have a deal of work. The same children labour all night for two or three nights in a week. Their opportunities for education very few, except in a Sunday school."

Now, here let the House observe the extent of toil and of watchfulness oftentimes imposed on children of very tender years. During two or three nights in a week, they are deprived altogether of their natural rest; a demand so severe on the bodily powers, that, when exacted of the police and soldiery of this metropolis, it has been found most pernicious to their physical constitution. From the Potteries, Mr. Spencer (a factory Commissioner) reported, in 1833: —

> "The plate-makers of most works employ boys, often their own, to be their assistants; their occupation is to remove the plates to the drying houses, which are heated to 120 degrees; and in this occupation, in which the boy is kept on the run, he is laboriously employed from six o'clock in the morning till

seven in the evening, excepting the intervals of breakfast and dinner. (Again), In other works some of the children called cutters, in attendance upon the printer, appear to me to suffer from a prolonged attendance at the factory. They are compelled to attend in the morning an hour before the printer, to light fires and prepare his apartment, and often wait in the evening for some time after the rest have departed, to prepare for the ensuing day. (Again), When there is a fair demand, the plate-makers and their assistants, work three or four nights per week till ten, and sometimes as late as eleven." . . .

Sir, there is another department of industry called card-setting, in which children are employed to make part of the machinery of the cotton-mills. In answer to some questions I put to a gentleman resident in the neighborhood of some card-setting establishments, he says: —

"Children are employed from five years old and upwards; their length of labour extends from five or six o'clock in the morning to eight at night."

I will now, Sir, exhibit the state of the collieries, and I cannot well imagine any thing worse than these painful disclosures. In reference to this, I will read an abstract of evidence collected from three witnesses by Mr. Tuffnell, in 1833: —

"Labour very hard, nine hours a-day regularly, sometimes twelve, sometimes above thirteen hours; stop two or three minutes to eat; some days nothing at all to eat, sometimes work and eat together; have worked a whole day together without stopping to eat; a good many children in the mines, some under six years of age; sometimes can't eat, owing to the dust, and damp, and badness of the air; sometimes it is as hot as an oven, sometimes so hot as to melt a candle. A vast many girls in the pits go down just the same as the boys, by ladders or baskets; the girls wear breeches; beaten the same as the boys; many bastards produced in the pits; a good deal of fighting amongst them; much crookedness caused by the labour; work by candle-light; exposed to terrible accidents; work in very contracted spaces; children are plagued with sore feet and gatherings." "I cannot but think, (says one witness), that many nights they do not sleep with a whole skin, for their backs get cut and bruised with knocking against the mine, it is so low. It is wet under foot; the water oftentimes runs down from the roof; many lives lost in various ways; and many severely injured by burning; workers knocked up after fifty." "I cannot much err, (says Mr. Commissioner Tuffnell), in coming to the conclusion, both from what I saw, and the evidence of witnesses given on oath above, that it must appear to every impartial judge of the two occupations, that the hardest labour, in the worst room, in the worst conducted factory, is less hard, less cruel, and less demoralizing, than the labour of the best of coal mines."

Now, Sir, the next is a trade to which I must request the particular attention of the House. The scenes it discloses are really horrible; and all who hear me will join in one loud and common condemnation. I speak of the business of pinmaking. . . . .

One witness a pin-header, aged twelve, said: —

"I save seen the children much beaten ten times a-day, so that with some the blood comes, many a time; none of the children where I work can read or write." . . . "Each child (reports Mr. Commissioner Tufnell), is in a position continually bent in the form of the letter C, its head being about eight inches from the table. My inquiries (he adds), fully corroborated the account of its being the practice of parents to borrow sums of money on the credit of their children's labour, and then let them out to pin heading till it is paid. One woman had let out both her children for ten months, and another had sold her's for a year."

Now I must entreat the attention of hon. Members to this system of legalized slavery; and I cannot better invite it, than by reading an extract from a letter which I have lately received: —

"You also know (says my informant), the practice of the masters in securing the services of these little slaves. One man in this town employs from four to five hundred of them. A very ordinary practice is, for the master to send for the parents or guardians, offer them an advance of money, an irresistible temptation, and then extract a bond, which the magistrates enforce, that the repayment of the loan shall be effected through the labour of the child. A child of tender age can rarely earn more than from 9*d.* to 1*s.* a-week. Thus the master becomes bodily possessor of the children as his *bonâ fide* slaves, and works them according to his pleasure."

And now mark this; —

"If he continues, with the employment to pay wages, and keep the loan hanging over the head of the parents, who do not refuse to take the wages, yet cannot repay the loan, the master may keep possession of the child as his slave, for an indefinite time. This is done to a great extent; the relieving-officer has tried in vain to break through the iniquitous practice; but it seems that the magistrates have not power to do it."

Now, Sir, may I ask, is this not a system of legalized slavery? Is not this a state of things which demands the interposition of Parliament, or at least an investigation, that we may know to what an extent these horrid practices have been carried? Surely the House will not now be astonished at the concluding remark of Mr. Tuffnell's report: —

"Knowing (says he), the cruelties that are sometimes practised, in order to keep those infants at work, I was not surprised at being told by a manufacturer, that he had left the trade, owing to the disgust he felt at this part of the business." . . .

Sir, the next and last trade which I shall now describe, is the calico printing; a business which demands the labour of several thousand children. . . .

A person, whose name is not given, states, that: —

"Being frequently detained in his counting-house late at night, till twelve or one o'clock, he has often, in going home in the depth of winter, met mothers taking their children to the neighbouring printworks, the children crying."

All this I can confirm and exceed, by the statements of a letter I hold in my hand, from a medical gentleman, living in the very centre of print works. I wish there were time to read the whole of it, but I fear I have already fatigued the House by the number of my extracts: —

"Many children (he writes), are only six years of age; one-half of them, he believes, are under nine; the labour of children is not only harder, but of longer duration. During night-work the men are obliged to shake their teerers to keep them awake, and they are not seldom aroused by blows. This work is very fatiguing to the eyes; their sight consequently fails at a very early age. They have to clean the blocks; this is done at the margin of the brook, on which the works stand. I often see these little creatures standing up to the calves of their legs in the water, and this, even in the severest weather, after being kept all day in rooms heated to a most oppressive degree. The injurious effect of this close and heated atmosphere is much aggravated by the effluvia of the colours; these are in most cases metallic salts, and . . . very noxious. The atmosphere of the room is consequently continually loaded with poisonous gases of different kinds."

Sir, these are a few facts, and only a few, of the many that I could adduce for your consideration, were I not afraid of being wearisome to the House. But I think I have sufficiently proved, that there prevails a system of slavery under the sanction of law; that parents sell the services of their children, even of the tenderest years, for periods of long and most afflicting duration; that, in many instances, children of not more than five or six years old are employed in these trades from twelve to sixteen hours a-day, of course deprived of all means of education, while their health is undermined, or utterly destroyed. If the inquiry I move for be granted, it will develope [sic], I am sure, cases far more numerous, and quite as painful, as those I have been able to produce. Now, Sir, I may be called upon to suggest a remedy; Sir, I am not yet prepared to do so, but I will state my objects, and the motives of my proposition. My first and great object is to place, if possible, the children of this land in such a position, and under such circumstances, as to lay them open to what Dr. Chalmers would call "an aggressive movement" for education; to reserve and cherish their physical energies, to cultivate and improve their moral part, both of which, be they taken separately or conjointly, are essential to the peace, security, and progress of the empire. Sir, we have had the honour of setting the example in these things, and other nations of the world have begun to follow that example; we must not now fall back into the rear, and become the last where once we were first. . . .

Sir, I next desire to remove these spectacles of suffering and oppression from the eyes of the poorer classes, or at least to ascertain if we can do so: these things perplex the peaceable, and exasperate the discontented; they have a tendency to render capital odious, for wealth is known to them only by its oppressions; they judge of it by what they see immediately around them; they know but little beyond their own narrow sphere; they do not extend their view over the whole surface of the land, and so perceive and understand the compensating advantages that wealth and poverty bestow on the community at large. Sir, with so much ignorance on one side, and so much oppression on the other, I have never wondered that perilous errors and bitter hatreds have prevailed; but I have wondered much, and been very thankful that they have prevailed so little. . . .

Next, Sir, I hope to trace some of the secret and efficient causes of crime and pauperism; and by learning the causes, to ascertain the remedy. It is very curious and very instructive to observe how we compel, as it were, vice and misery with one hand, and endeavour to repress them with the other; but the whole course of our manufacturing system tends to these results: you engage children from their earliest and tenderest years in these long, painful, and destructive occupations; when they have approached to manhood, they have outgrown their employments, and they are turned upon the world without moral, without professional education; the business they have learned, avails them nothing; to what can they turn their hands for a maintenance? the children, for instance, who have been taught to make pins, having reached fourteen or fifteen years of age, are unfit to make pins any longer; to procure an honest livelihood then becomes to them almost impossible; the governors of prisons will tell you, the relieving-officers will tell you, that the vicious resort to plunder and prostitution; the rest sink down into a hopeless pauperism. . . . And now, Sir, to conclude this long, and, I fear, wearisome address — my first grand object, as I have already said, is to bring these children within the reach of education; it will then be time enough to fight about the mode. Only let us exhibit these evils — there is wit enough, experience enough, activity enough, and principle enough in the country, to devise some remedy. I am sure that the exhibition of the peril will terrify even the most sluggish, and the most reluctant, into some attempt at amendment; but I hope for far better motives. For my own part I will say, though possibly I may be charged with cant and hypocrisy, that I have been bold enough to undertake this task, because I must regard the objects of it as beings created, as ourselves, by the same Maker, redeemed by the same Saviour, and destined to the same immortality; and it is, therefore, in this spirit, and with these sentiments, which, I am sure, are participated by all who hear me; that I now venture to entreat the countenance of this House, and the cooperation of her Majesty's Ministers; first to investigate, and ultimately to remove, these sad evils, which press so deeply and so extensively on such a large and such an interesting portion of the human race."

b House of Commons: March 15, 1844

HOURS of labour in factories] House in Committee on the Factories Bill.

Lord *Ashley* rose to propose the amendment of which he had given notice. . . .

"Now, I would say with a view to conciliate opposition, that though I shall be ready to propose, as I intend to do, to limit the labour of all young persons and children to ten hours in each day, I am yet willing to obtain that object in parts and by degrees; that is, I propose to limit the hours of labour for such persons to eleven hours a day from the 1st of October in the present year, and ten hours a day from the 1st of October, 1845."

[Passing to the question of female labor, Lord Ashley then discoursed on the evils of attendant alcoholism.]

Mr. Braidley, when boroughreeve of Manchester, stated, "that in one gin shop, during eight successive Saturday evenings, from seven till ten o'clock, he observed, on an average rate, 412 persons enter by the hour, of which the females were 60 per cent." Many females state, that the labour induces "an intolerable thirst; they can drink, but not eat." I do not doubt that several of the statements I have read, will create surprise in the minds of many hon. Members; but if they were to converse with operatives who are acquainted with the practical effects of the system, they would cease to wonder at the facts I have detailed. I might detain the House by enumerating the evils which result from the long working of males and females together in the same room. I could show the many and painful effects to which females are exposed, and the manner in which they lament and shrink from the inconveniences of their situation. I have letters from Stockport and Manchester, from various individuals, dwelling on the mischievous consequences which arise from the practice of modest women working so many hours together with men, and not being able to avail themselves of those opportunities which would suggest themselves to every one's mind without particular mention. Many mills, I readily admit, are admirably regulated, but they are yet in a minority — were all of such a description as several that I have seen, they might not, perhaps, require any enactments. But, to return, Mr. Rayner, the medical officer of Stockport, says: —

> "It has been the practice in mills, gradually to dispense with the labour of males, but particularly grown-up men, so that the burthen of maintaining the family has rested almost exclusively on the wife and children, while the men have to stay at home, and look after household affairs, or ramble about the streets unemployed."

But listen to another fact, and one deserving of serious attention; that the females not only perform the labour, but occupy the places of men; they are forming various clubs and associations, and gradually acquiring all those privileges which are held to be the proper portion of the male sex. These female clubs are thus described: — Fifty or sixty females, married and single, form themselves into clubs, ostensibly for protection; but, in fact, they meet together, to drink, sing, and smoke; they use, it is stated, the lowest, most brutal, and most disgusting language imaginable." Here is a dialogue which occurred in one of these clubs, from an ear witness: — "A man came into one of these club-rooms, with a child in his arms; 'Come lass,' said he, addressing one of the women, 'come home, for I cannot keep this bairn quiet, and the other I have left crying at home.' 'I won't go home, idle devil,' she replied, 'I have thee to keep, and the bairns too, and if I can't get a pint of ale quietly, it is tiresome. This is only the second pint that Bess and me have had between us; thou make sup if thou likes, and sit thee down, but I won't go home yet.' " Whence is it that this singular and unnatural change is taking place? Because that on women are imposed the duty and burthen of supporting their husbands and families, a perversion as it were of nature, which has the inevitable effect of introducing into families disorder, insubordination, and conflict. . . .

"I met," says an informant of mine, "with a mother of factory workers, who told me that all the churches and chapels were useless places, and so was all the talk about education, since the young and old were unable to attend, either in consequence of the former being imprisoned in the mills so many hours, and being in want of rest the little time they were at home; and the latter being compelled to live out of the small earnings of their children, and cannot get clothing, so they never think of going to churches or chapels. She added, 'when you get up to London, tell them we'll turn out the next time (meaning the women), and let the soldiers fire upon us if they dare, and depend upon it there will be a break out, and a right one, if that House of Commons don't alter things, for they can alter if they will, by taking mothers and daughters out of the factories, and sending the men and big lads in.' ". . .

This will conclude the statement that I have to make to the House—and now, Sir, who will assert that these things should be permitted to exist? Who will hesitate to apply the axe to the root of the tree, or, at least, endeavour to lop off some of its deadliest branches? What arguments from general principles will they adduce against my proposition? What, drawn from peculiar circumstances? . . .

No, Sir, these sources of mischief must be dried up; every public consideration demands such an issue; the health of the females; the care of their families; their conjugal and parental duties; the comfort of their homes; the decency of their lives; the rights of their husbands; the peace of society; and the laws of God— and, until a vote shall have been given this night, which God avert, I never will believe that there can be found in this House one individual man who will deliberately and conscientiously inflict, on the women of England such a burthen of insufferable toil. . . .

We ask but a slight relaxation of toil, a time to live, and a time to die; a time for those comforts that sweeten life, and a time for those duties that adorn it; and, therefore, with a fervent prayer to Almighty God that it may please him to turn the hearts of all who hear me to thoughts of justice and of mercy, I now finally commit the issue to the judgment and humanity of Parliament. . . .

Sir *J. Graham*] . . . The noble Lord said, the time is come when, in his opinion, it is necessary to lay the axe to the root of the tree. Before we do this let me entreat the Committee carefully to consider what is that tree which we are to lay prostrate. If it be, as I suppose, the tree of the commercial greatness of this country, I am satisfied that although some of its fruits may be bitter, yet upon the whole it has produced that greatness, that wealth, that prosperity, which make these small islands most remarkable in the history of the civilized world, which upon the whole, diffuse happiness amidst this great community, and render this nation one of the most civilised, if not the most civilised, and powerful on the face of the globe. My noble Friend begs us also not to turn a deaf ear to the cry of distress from the working classes. I entreat this House, indeed I need not urge it upon them, having seen the attention with which they listened to the remarks which my noble Friend made—I entreat the House carefully to weigh the subject now brought under discussion. . . .

. . . My noble Friend drew a comparison between agricultural and manufacturing labourers, and he did not, I am sure, draw that comparison invidiously. I must, however, express some doubt as to the physical fact stated by my noble Friend. I believe, when you take into consideration the exposure to the inclemency of the weather, and other disadvantageous circumstances which fall upon the agricultural labourer, that it may very fairly be doubted, whether on account of the vicissitudes he encounters, the chances are not, upon the whole, against the agricultural labourer, on the score of health, as compared with the manufacturer. But the House will consider whether it be of any practical advantage to discuss that point now. We have arrived at a state of society when without commerce and manufactures this great community cannot be maintained. Let us, as far as we can, mitigate the evils arising out of this highly artificial state of society; but let us take care to adopt no step that may be fatal to commerce and manufactures. . . .

. . . You are now discussing whether you shall abridge by one-sixth the period of time in which capital is to be replaced, all interest upon it paid, and the original outlay restored. Such an abridgment would render it impossible that capital with interest should be restored. Then in the close race of competition which our manufacturers are now running with foreign competitors, it must be considered what effect this reduction of one-sixth of the hours of labour would have upon them. The question in its bearing upon competition must be carefully considered; and I have been informed that in that respect such a step would be fatal to many of our manufacturers. A feather would turn the scale: an extra pound weight would lose the race. But that would not be the first effect. The first effect would fall upon the operative. It is notorious that a great part of the power of the mill-owners, a power which alone justifies such legislation as this, arises from the redundant supply of labour. It follows that when a master is pressed upon by your legislation, he will compensate himself by forcing upon those in his employ a decrease of wages. . . .

. . . The question then arises, whether you shall create in the manufacturing districts one sudden general fall of wages to the amount of 25 per cent.? I believe that the adoption of the Motion of my noble Friend would produce that effect. Though I am most anxious to take every precaution with regard to infant labour—though I am as firmly resolved as my noble Friend to urge upon the House to put a limit upon female labour, still, upon the whole, I cannot recommend the House to adopt an enactment which limits the labour of young persons to a shorter period than twelve hours. . . .

. . . I believe, moreover, so far from being advantageous to the working classes, my noble Friend's proposition would be ruinous to their interests, and fatal to our commercial prosperity, and though my feelings and wishes are with him, my sense of duty never more clearly pointed out the course I ought to take, in reluctantly, but firmly, resisting his proposition.

4

Marx and Engels: "Let the Ruling Classes Tremble. . . ."

MANY CRITICS were more radical than Ashley. Among them the intellectual partnership of Karl Marx (1818–83) and Friedrich Engels (1820–95) was perhaps the most important and disturbing of the age. The son of a Christianized Jewish lawyer in Trier, Marx took up journalism after philosophical studies in the Young Hegelian circle. Removing to Paris in 1843, he met young Engels, son of a wealthy cotton-spinner from Barmen, whose social concerns appeared in his book on The Condition of the Working Classes in England in 1844. *Thereafter the two men spent their lives in cooperative analysis of the human condition. In Brussels, December 1847, at the request of the Communist League, they wrote a brief survey of the working-class problem, the celebrated* Communist Manifesto. *As exiles in England they elaborated their thesis, commented publicly on their times, and came to lead the First International. One of the major interpretations of Western history, theirs was the most compelling prophecy of the age of the common man, and became the most powerful militant ideology of our times.*

a *Manifesto of the Communist Party*

A SPECTRE is haunting Europe—the spectre of communism. All the powers of old Europe have entered into a holy alliance to exorcise this spectre: Pope and tsar, Metternich and Guizot, French radicals and German police-spies.

Where is the party in opposition that has not been decried as communistic by its opponents in power? Where is the opposition that has not hurled back the branding reproach of communism, against the more advanced opposition parties, as well as against its reactionary adversaries?

From SELECTED WORKS OF KARL MARX AND FRIEDRICH ENGELS *(London, 1942), vol. i, pp. 204–206, 241, 162–166, 181–186. Reprinted by permission of Lawrence & Wishart and International Publishers Co., Inc.*

Two things result from this fact:

I] Communism is already acknowledged by all European powers to be itself a power.

II] It is high time that Communists should openly, in the face of the whole world, publish their views, their aims, their tendencies, and meet this nursery tale of the spectre of communism with a manifesto of the party itself.

To this end, Communists of various nationalities have assembled in London, and sketched the following manifesto, to be published in the English, French, German, Italian, Flemish and Danish languages.

I] *Bourgeois and proletarians*[1]

The history of all hitherto existing society is the history of class struggles.

Freeman and slave, patrician and plebeian, lord and serf, guild-master and journeyman, in a word, oppressor and oppressed stood in constant opposition to one another, carried on an uninterrupted, now hidden, now open fight, a fight that each time ended, either in a revolutionary reconstitution of society at large, or in the common ruin of the contending classes.

In the earlier epochs of history, we find almost everywhere a complicated arrangement of society into various orders, a manifold gradation of social rank. In ancient Rome we have patricians, knights, plebeians, slaves; in the Middle Ages, feudal lords, vassals, guild-masters, journeymen, apprentices, serfs; in almost all of these classes, again, subordinate gradations.

The modern bourgeois society that has sprouted from the ruins of feudal society has not done away with class antagonisms. It has but established new classes, new conditions of oppression, new forms of struggle in place of the old ones.

Our epoch, the epoch of the bourgeoisie, possesses, however, this distinctive feature: It has simplified the class antagonisms. Society as a whole is more and more splitting up into two great hostile camps, into two great classes directly facing each other — bourgeoisie and proletariat.

* * *

The Communists turn their attention chiefly to Germany, because that country is on the eve of a bourgeois revolution that is bound to be carried out under more advanced conditions of European civilisation and with a much more developed proletariat than that of England was in the seventeenth, and of France in the eighteenth century, and because the bourgeois revolution in Germany will be but the prelude to an immediately following proletarian revolution.

In short, the Communists everywhere support every revolutionary movement against the existing social and political order of things.

In all these movements they bring to the front, as the leading question in each, the property question, no matter what its degree of development at the time.

Finally, they labour everywhere for the union and agreement of the democratic parties of all countries.

The Communists disdain to conceal their views and aims. They openly declare that their ends can be attained only by the forcible overthrow of all existing social conditions. Let the ruling classes tremble at a communist revolution. The proletarians have nothing to lose but their chains. They have a world to win.

Workingmen of all countries, unite!

b *Socialism: Scientific and Utopian*

. . . THE CLASS struggle between proletariat and bourgeoisie came to the front in the history of the most advanced European countries, in proportion to the development there, on the one hand, of large-scale industry, and on the other, of the newly-won political domination of the bourgeoisie. Facts more and more forcibly stamped as lies the teachings of bourgeois economics as to the identity of the interests of capital and labour, as to the universal harmony and universal prosperity that free competition brings. All these things could no longer be ignored, any more than the French and English socialism which was their theoretical, even though extremely imperfect, expression. But the old idealist conception of history, which was not yet displaced, knew nothing of class struggles based on material interests, in fact knew nothing at all of material interests; production and all economic relations appeared in it only as incidental, subordinate elements in the "history of civilisation."

The new facts made imperative a new examination of all past

history, and then it was seen that *all* past history, with the exception of primitive conditions, was the history of class struggles, that these warring classes of society are always the products of the conditions of production and exchange, in a word, of the *economic* conditions of their time; that therefore the economic structure of society always forms the real basis from which, in the last analysis, is to be explained the whole superstructure of legal and political institutions, as well as of the religious, philosophical, and other conceptions of each historical period. Hegel had freed the conception of history from metaphysics, he had made it dialectical—but his conception of history was essentially idealistic. Now idealism was driven from its last refuge, the philosophy of history; now a materialist conception of history was propounded, and the way was found to explain man's consciousness by his being, instead of, as heretofore, his being by his consciousness.

Henceforward socialism no longer appeared as the accidental discovery of this or that brilliant mind, but as the necessary outcome of the struggle between two historically developed classes—the proletariat and the bourgeoisie. Its task was no longer to manufacture a system of society as perfect as possible, but to investigate the historical, economic succession of events from which these classes and their antagonism had of necessity sprung and to discover in the economic position thus created the means for solving the conflict. But the socialism of earlier days was just as incompatible with this materialist conception of history as the French materialist conception of nature was with dialectics and modern natural science. It is true that the earlier socialism criticised the existing capitalist mode of production and its consequences, but it could not explain them, and so also could not get the mastery over them; it could only simply reject them as evil. The more violently it denounced the exploitation of the working class, which was inseparable from it, the less was it in a position to state clearly wherein this exploitation consists and how it arises. But what had to be done was to show this capitalist mode of production on the one hand in its historical sequence and in its inevitability for a definite historical period, and therefore also the inevitability of its downfall; and on the other hand also to lay bare its essential character, which was still hidden. This was done by the discovery of *surplus value*. It was shown that the appropriation of unpaid labour is the basic form of the capitalist mode of production and of the exploitation of the worker effected through it; that even if the capitalist buys the labour power of his labourer at its full value as a commodity on the market, he yet extracts more value from it than he paid for; and that in the ultimate analysis this surplus value forms those sums of value from which are heaped up the constantly increasing masses of capital in the hands of the possessing classes. The process both of capitalist production and of the production of capital was explained.

These two great discoveries, the materialist conception of history and the revelation of the secret of capitalist production by means of surplus value, we owe to Marx. With these discoveries socialism became a science, which had in the first place to be developed in all its details and relations.

The materialist conception of history starts from the principle that production, and with production the exchange of its products, is the basis of every social order; that in every society which has appeared in history the distribution of the products, and with it the division of society into classes or estates, is determined by what is produced and how it is produced, and how the product is exchanged. According to this conception, the ultimate causes of all social changes and political revolutions are to be sought, not in the minds of men, in their increasing insight into eternal truth and justice, but in changes in the mode of production and exchange; they are to be sought not in the *philosophy* but in the *economics* of the epoch concerned. The growing realisation that existing social institutions are irrational and unjust, that reason has become nonsense and good deeds a scourge, is only a sign that changes have been taking place quietly in the methods of production and forms of exchange, with which the social order, adapted to previous economic conditions, is no longer in accord. This also involves that the means through which the abuses that have been revealed can be got rid of must likewise be present, in more or less developed form, in the altered conditions of production. These means are not to be *invented* by the mind, but *discovered* by means of the mind in the existing material facts of production.

Where then, on this basis, does modern socialism stand?

The existing social order, as is now fairly generally admitted, is the creation of the present ruling class, the bourgeoisie. The mode of production peculiar to the bourgeoisie — called, since Marx, the capitalist mode of production — was incompatible with the local privileges and the privileges of birth as well as with the reciprocal personal ties of the feudal system; the bourgeoisie shattered the feudal system, and on its ruins established the bourgeois social order, the realm of free competition, freedom of movement, equal rights for commodity owners, and all the other bourgeois glories. The capitalist mode of production could now develop freely. From the time when steam and the new tool-making machinery had begun to transform the former manufacture into large-scale industry, the productive forces evolved under bourgeois direction developed at a pace that was previously unknown and to an unprecedented degree. But just as manufacture, and the handicraft industry which had been further developed under its influence, had previously come into conflict with the feudal fetters of the guilds, so large-scale industry, as it develops more fully, comes into conflict with the barriers within which the capitalist mode of production holds it confined. The new forces of production have already outgrown the bourgeois form of using them; and this conflict between productive forces and mode of production is not a conflict which has arisen in men's heads, as for example the conflict between original sin and divine justice; but it exists in the facts, objectively, outside of us, independently of the will or purpose even of the men who brought it about. Modern socialism is nothing but the reflex in thought of this actual conflict, its ideal reflection in the minds first of the class which is directly suffering under it—the working class.

* * *

By more and more transforming the great majority of the population into proletarians, the capitalist mode of production brings into being the force which, under penalty of its own destruction, is compelled to carry out this revolution. By more and more driving towards the conversion of the vast socialised means of production into state property, it itself points the way for the carrying through of this revolution. *The proletariat seizes the state power and transforms the means of production in the first instance into state property.* But in doing this, it puts an end to itself as the proletariat, it puts an end to all class differences and class antagonisms; it puts an end also to the state as the state. Former society, moving in class antagonisms, had need of the state, that is, an organisation of the exploiting class at each period for the maintenance of its external conditions of production; that is, therefore, for the forcible holding down of the exploited class in the conditions of oppression (slavery, villeinage or serfdom, wage labour) determined by the existing mode of production. The state was the official representative of society as a whole, its embodiment in a visible corporation; but it was this only in so far as it was the state of that class which itself, in its epoch, represented society as a whole; in ancient times, the state of the slave-owning citizens; in the Middle Ages, of the feudal nobility; in our epoch, of the bourgeoisie. When ultimately it becomes really representative of society as a whole, it makes itself superfluous. As soon as there is no longer any class of society to be held in subjection, as soon as, along with class domination and the struggle for individual existence based on the former anarchy of production, the collisions and excesses arising from these have also been abolished, there is nothing more to be repressed which would make a special repressive force, a state, necessary. The first act in which the state really comes forward as the representative of society as a whole—the taking possession of the means of production in the name of society—is at the same time its last independent act as a state. The interference of the state power in social relations becomes superfluous in one sphere after another, and then ceases of itself. The government of persons is replaced by the administration of things and the direction of the processes of production. The state is not "abolished," *it withers away.* It is from this standpoint that we must appraise the phrase "free people's state"—both its justification at times for agitational purposes, and its ultimate scientific inadequacy—and also the demand of the so-called anarchists that the state should be abolished overnight.

Since the emergence in history of the capitalist mode of production, the taking over of all means of production by society has often been dreamed of, by individuals as well as by whole sects, more or less vaguely and as an ideal of the future. But it could only become possible, it could only become a historical necessity, when the material conditions for its realisation had come into existence. Like every other social progress, it becomes realisable not through the perception that the existence of classes is in contradiction with justice, equality, etc., not through the mere will to abolish these classes, but through certain new economic conditions. The division of society into an exploiting and an exploited class, a ruling and an oppressed class, was the necessary outcome of the low development of production hitherto. So long as the sum of social labour yielded a product which only slightly exceeded what was necessary for the bare existence of all; so long, therefore, as all or almost all the time of the great majority of the members of society was absorbed in labour, so long was society necessarily divided into classes. Alongside of this great majority exclusively absorbed in labour there developed a class, freed from direct productive labour, which managed the general business of society: the direction of labour, affairs of state, justice, science, art and so forth. It is therefore the law of the division of labour which lies at the root of the division into classes. But this does not mean that this division into classes was not established by violence and robbery, by deception and fraud, or that the ruling class, once in the saddle, has ever failed to strengthen its domination at the cost of the working class and to convert its social management into the exploitation of the masses.

But if, on these grounds, the division into classes has a certain historical justification, it has this only for a given period of time, for given social conditions. It was based on the insufficiency of production; it will be swept away by the full development of the modern productive forces. And in fact the abolition of social classes has as its presupposition a stage of historical development at which the existence not merely of some particular ruling class or other but of any ruling class at all, that is to say, of class difference itself, has become an anachronism, is out of date. It therefore presupposes that the development of production has reached a level at which the appropriation of means of production and of products, and with these, of political supremacy, the monopoly of education and intellectual leadership by a special class of society, has become not only superfluous but also economically, politically and intellectually a hindrance to development.

This point has now been reached. Their political and intellectual bankruptcy is hardly still a secret to the bourgeoisie themselves, and their economic bankruptcy recurs regularly every ten years. In each crisis society is smothered under the weight of its own productive forces and products of which it can make no use, and stands helpless in face of the absurd contradiction that the producers have nothing to consume because there are no consumers. The expanding force of the means of production bursts asunder the bonds imposed upon them by the capitalist mode of production. Their release from these bonds is the sole condition necessary for an unbroken and constantly more rapidly progressing development of the productive forces, and therewith of a practically limitless growth of production itself. Nor is this all. The appropriation by society of the means of production will put an end not only to the artificial restraints on production which exist today, but also to the positive waste and destruction of productive forces and products which is now the inevitable accompaniment of production and reaches its zenith in crises. Further, it sets free for society as a whole a mass of means of production and products by putting an end to the senseless luxury and extravagance of the present ruling class and its political representatives. The possibility of securing for every member of society, through social production, an existence which is not only fully sufficient from a material standpoint and becoming richer from day to day, but also guarantees to them the completely unrestricted development and exercise of their physical and mental faculties — this possibility now exists for the first time, but it does exist.

The seizure of the means of production by society puts an end to commodity production, and therewith to the domination of the product over the producer. Anarchy in social production is replaced by conscious organisation on a planned basis. The struggle for individual existence comes to an end. And at this point, in a certain sense, man finally cuts himself off from the animal world, leaves the conditions of animal existence behind him and enters conditions which are really human. The conditions of existence forming man's environment, which up to now have dominated man, at this point pass under the dominion and control of man, who now for the first time becomes the real conscious master of nature, because and in so far as he has become master of his own social organization. The laws of his own social activity, which have hitherto confronted him as external, dominating laws of nature, will then be applied by man with complete understanding, and hence will be dominated by man. Men's own social organisation, which has hitherto stood in opposition to them as if arbitrarily decreed by nature and history, will then become the voluntary act of men themselves. The objective, external forces which have hitherto dominated history, will then pass under the control of men themselves. It is only from this point that men, with full consciousness, will fashion their own history; it is only from this point that the social causes set in motion by men will have, predominantly and in constantly increasing measure, the effects willed by men. It is humanity's leap from the realm of necessity into the realm of freedom.

Note by F. Engels to the English Edition of 1888

1. By bourgeoisie is meant the class of modern capitalists, owners of the means of social production and employers of wage labour. By proletariat, the class of modern wage labourers who, having no means of production of their own, are reduced to selling their labour power in order to live.

5

Mazzini: "The Map of Europe Has to Be Re-Made"

OF ALL the romantic exiles, none had a more tragic destiny than Giuseppe Mazzini (1805–72). This Genoese physician's son committed himself to the liberation of Italy from parochial division and Habsburg dominion. A revolutionary propagandist and inciter to popular insurrection against tyranny, he was expelled from Piedmont, France and Switzerland, and was fated to see Italians united under the Sardinian monarchy rather than under the democratic republic whose champion he was. He died in obscurity and disenchantment on March 10, 1872. Possibly the greatest prophet of liberal nationalism, he singled out the Italian people for a special role in the reformation of mankind. The essay below appeared in the Westminster Review, *April 2, 1852.*

Europe: Its Condition and Prospects

THE LITERATURE of the Continent during the last few years has been essentially political, revolutionary, and warlike. Out of ten historical works, seven at least speak to us, from a favourable point of view or otherwise, of a revolution now extinct; out of ten polemical, political, economical, or other works, seven at least proclaim or combat a revolution about to take place. The first bear the impress of terror; the last are full of gigantic hopes, though most imperfectly defined. Calm has fled from the minds of Continental writers. Poetry is silent, as if frightened by the storm now gathering in the hearts of men. Romance becomes rarer every day; it would find no readers. Pure art is a myth. Style itself is changed; when it is not commonplace, when it retains something of that individual originality which every style ought to have, it is sharp, cutting, biting.

From William Clark (ed.), ESSAYS: SELECTED FROM THE WRITINGS, LITERARY, POLITICAL AND RELIGIOUS OF JOSEPH MAZZINI *(London, n.d.), pp. 261–294.*

The pen seems, as it were, sword-shaped; all the world thinks and writes as if it felt itself on the eve of a battle.

From the midst of this tempest, which I point out, because to sleep is to perish amid the storm, voices are heard exclaiming, "Beware! Society is in danger. Anarchy threatens us. The barbarians are at our gates. Revolutions destroy all the guarantees of order; from change to change we are rushing into nothingness. We have conceded too much; we must retrace our steps and strengthen power at all price." Other voices reply to them, — "It is too late, your society is dead, corrupted; hasten to bury it. The salvation of the world is in *us,* in an entirely new order of things, in a society founded upon a basis diametrically opposed to yours." Flags are raised on high in infinite variety: *Liberty, Authority, Nationality,* 1815, *Labour, Property, Rights, Duties, Association, Individualism* — all these devices are displayed aloft. It is the night of the Brocksberg — a sort of intellectual and moral chaos, to which scarcely anything analogous is to be found, unless we go back some eighteen centuries in the history of the world, to the fall of the Roman Empire; when the ancient gods were dying; when the human mind was wavering between the sceptical epicureanism of the masters, and the aspiration of the slaves to the UNKNOWN GOD; when the earth trembled under the steps of unknown races, impelled by a mysterious irresistible power towards the centre of European society.

What is the signification of a crisis thus prolonged, notwithstanding all the efforts which are made to overcome it? Have these *barbarians* of our days a *Rome* in which great destinies are to be accomplished, and towards which, like Attila and his hordes, they are impelled by an invisible hand; or do they march onward to lose themselves in deserts; without a purpose, without a tomb, without leaving any useful memorable trace in history? Are we advancing towards anarchy or toward a new mode of things, — towards dissolution or towards a transformed life? All ask themselves this question; all could resolve it, if the point of view of each man were not narrowed by his position in some one of the adverse camps; by the now prevailing habit of judging of the depth, the intensity, and the direction of the European current by the passing ebullitions of the surface; and by a prejudice, presently to be defined, which for half-a-century has influenced almost all appreciations of the political situation.

And yet this question *must* be solved. It is a vital one. It necessarily contains a rule for our actions. A law of Solon decreed that those who in an insurrection abstained from taking part on one side or the other should be degraded. It was a just and holy law, founded on the belief,—then instinctive in the heart of Solon, but now comprehended and expressed in a thousand formulæ,—in the solidarity of humanity. It would be just now more than ever. What! you are in the midst of the uprising, not of a town, but of the whole human race; you see brute force on the one side, and right on the other; you march between proscription and martyrdom; between the scaffold and the altar; whole nations are struggling under oppression; generations are proscribed; men slaughter each other at your very doors; they die by hundreds, by thousands, fighting for or against an idea; this idea is either good or evil; and you, continuing the while to call yourselves men and Christians, would claim the right of remaining neutral? You cannot do so without moral degradation. Neutrality, that is to say, indifference between good and evil, the just and the unjust, liberty and oppression, is simply Atheism.

Let us, then, endeavour to distinguish all that there is of permanent from all that is merely accessory and transitory in the crisis; all that will remain, and which demands satisfaction, from that which is only a momentary ebullition, the dross or scum of metal in fusion. The question now is, how to carry forward the balance of the past half-century to the credit of the half-century to come. I shall endeavour to do this as rapidly as possible; not as summarily, however, as their Excellencies the ambassadors of France, Austria, Russia, and of the thirty-five or thirty-six States of Germany.

Their Excellencies have very recently made a discovery which would remarkably simplify our solution if we could believe them upon their word. According to them, there are in London four or five persons who are the cause of all the disturbances of the Continent. They walk abroad, and all Europe is agitated; they associate themselves for an object, whatever it may be, and the whole of Europe associates itself with them. England has only to abandon her noblest privilege, that of exercising a free hospitality, and to drive these men across the ocean, and Europe would sleep in peace under the bâton of Austria, the knout of Russia, the *cavalletto* of the Pope. Pity that Lord Granville[1] should not have reached to the height of their Excellencies! Pity that for such a peace he should scruple to violate English law and English honour.

No; the agitation in Europe is not the work of a few individuals, of a few refugees, be they who they may; and there is something in this opinion sad and ridiculous at the same time: I say sad, because it evidently shows the inability of the "masters of the world" to comprehend and to abridge the crisis. Individuals are only powerful at the present day, so far as they are the exponents of the condition and collective aspirations of large bodies of men. For sixty years Europe has been convulsed by a series of political struggles which have assumed all aspects by turns; which have raised every conceivable flag, from that of pure despotism to that of anarchy; from the organisation of the *bourgeoisie* in France and elsewhere as the dominant caste, to the *jacqueries* [peasant uprisings] of the peasants of Gallicia. Thirty revolutions have taken place. Two or three royal dynasties have been engulfed in the abyss of popular fury. Nations have risen, like Greece, from the tomb where they had been for ages buried; others, like Poland, have been erased from the map. Forgotten, almost unknown races, the Sclavonian race, the Roumaine race, silent until now, have disinterred their traditionary titles, and demanded to be represented in the Congress of Nations. Kings and Queens have gone to die in exile. The Austrian Empire, the China of Europe, has been on the brink of destruction. A Pope, drawn along by the popular current, has been obliged to bless a national insurrection, and then to fly in disguise from the capital of the Christian world. Vienna has twice been covered with barricades. Rome has seen the republican banner float above the Vatican. Governments, attacked and overthrown, have ten or twenty times recovered strength, drawn closer their alliances, overrun the half of Europe with their armies, annihilated revolutions, effaced entire generations of revolutionary spirits by the sword, the scaffold, exile, or imprisonment, and crushed, as they term it, the hydra of disorder and anarchy. The heads of the hydra have sprung up again fifty for one; the struggle has recommenced at the foot of the scaffold of those who initiated it; the idea has gained strength beneath the hammer on the anvil; we are now, three years after an European restoration, three months after the *triumph of order* in France, calculating upon and arming for new struggles; and we are told that all this is the work of a few individuals, transmitting from one to another, every ten years, the inheritance of a subversive idea! As well might the conquest of the world by Christianity be attributed to the underground labour of a secret society. Christian truth emerged from the catacombs, *because the whole world was thirsting for it.* The ancient unity was broken; a new one was necessary. Between these two unities chaos reigned, in which humanity cannot live. It reigns now, because amidst the ruins of an unity in which mankind no longer has faith, a new unity is being elaborated. If a few men have power with the multitudes, it is because these men embody this unity in themselves better than others do. And though you may destroy them to-day, others will replace them to-morrow.

Europe no longer possesses unity of faith, of mission, or of aim. Such unity is a necessity in the world. Here, then, is the secret of the crisis. It is the duty of every one to examine and analyse calmly and carefully the probable elements of this new unity. But those who persist in perpetuating, by violence or by Jesuitical compromise, the external observance of the old unity, only perpetuate the crisis and render its issue more violent.

Europe — I might say the world, for Europe is the lever of the world — no longer believes in the sanctity of royal races; she may still accept them here and there as a guarantee of stability, as a defence against the encroachments of some other dangerous element; but she no longer believes in the *principle,* in any special virtue residing in them, in a divine right consecrating and protecting them. Wherever they reign despotically, she conspires against them; wherever liberty exists under their sway, in however small a degree, she supports them under a brevet of impotence. She has invented the political axiom, "Kings reign without governing"; wherever they govern, and govern badly, she overthrows them.

Europe no longer believes in aristocracy, the royalty of several; she no longer believes in the inevitable physical transmission, in the perpetual inheritance of virtue, intelligence, and honour; she believes in it no longer, either scientifically or practically. Wherever an aristocracy acts well — if that ever happens to be the case — she follows its lead; not as an aristocracy, but as a doer of good: wherever it drags itself along in the pride of its old traditions — idle, ignorant, and decayed — she rids herself of it; she destroys it, either by revolutions or by ridicule. The carnival on the Continent looks to the historical order of patricians for its masks.

Europe no longer believes in the Papacy; she no longer believes that it possesses the right, mission, or capacity of spiritual education or guidance; she no longer believes in the immediate revelation, in the direct transmission of the designs and laws of Providence, by virtue of election, to any individual whatsoever; five years ago she was seized with enthusiasm for a Pope[2] who seemed disposed to bless the progress of the human race, and to constitute himself the representative of the most advanced ideas of his age; she despised him as soon as he retraced his steps and recommenced the brutal career of his predecessors.

Europe no longer believes in privilege, be it what it may; except in that which no one can destroy, because it comes from God—the privilege of genius and virtue; she desires wealth, but she despises or hates it in the persons of those who possess it, when it is not the price of labour, or when it arrogates to itself rights of political monopoly.

Now look at the actual organisation of Europe—is it not altogether based upon privilege, by whatever name it may be known? How, then, can one wonder at the struggle which is engendered within it?

Let it, then, be openly declared by every honest man, that this struggle is sacred; sacred as liberty, sacred as the soul which creates to itself a body; the idea which makes for itself a habitation. The Utopist may see afar from the lofty hill the distant land which will give to society a virgin soil, a purer air; his duty is to point it out with a gesture and a word to his brothers; but he cannot take humanity in his arms, and carry it there with a single bound; even if this were in his power, humanity would not therefore have progressed.

Progress is the consciousness of progress. Man must attain it step by step, by the sweat of his brow. The transformation of the *medium* in which he lives only takes place in proportion as he merits it; and he can only merit it by struggle; by devoting himself and purifying himself by good works and holy sorrow. He must not be taught to enjoy, but rather to suffer for others; to combat for the salvation of the world. It must not be said to him, *Enjoy; life is the right to happiness;* but rather, *Work; life is a duty, do good without thinking of the consequences to yourself.* He must not be taught, *To each according to his wants,* or *To each according to his passions,* but rather, *To each according to his love.* To invent formulæ and organisations, and neglect the internal man, is to desire to substitute the frame for the picture. Say to men, *Come, suffer; you will hunger and thirst; you will, perhaps, be deceived, be betrayed, cursed; but you have a great duty to accomplish:* they will be deaf, perhaps, for a long time, to the severe voice of virtue; but on the day that they do come to you, they will come as heroes, and will be invincible. Say to them, *Arise, come and enjoy; the banquet of life awaits you; overthrow those who would prevent you from entering:* you will make egotists who would desert you at the first musket-shot, such as those who, the day after having cried *Vive la République,* vote for Louis Napoleon, if he but makes them tremble, or if he promises them to mingle a few grains of socialism with his despotism.

It is the instinctive belief in these things which renders the cause of the Nationalities powerful and sacred. It is by this worship of the idea, of the true, of the morally just, that the initiative of European progress belongs to them.

It was not for a material interest that the people of Vienna fought in 1848; in weakening the empire they could only lose power. It was not for an increase of wealth that the people of Lombardy fought in the same year; the Austrian Government had endeavoured in the year preceding to excite the peasants against the landed proprietors, as they had done in Gallicia; but everywhere they had failed. They struggled, they still struggle, as do Poland, Germany, and Hungary, for country and liberty; for a word inscribed upon a banner, proclaiming to the world that they also live, think, love, and labour for the benefit of all. They speak the same language, they bear about them the impress of consanguinity, they kneel beside the same tombs, they glory in the same tradition; and they demand to associate freely, without obstacles, without foreign domination, in order to elaborate and express their idea; to contribute their stone also to the great pyramid of history. It is something moral which they are seeking; and this moral something is in fact, even politically speaking, the most important question in the present state of things. It is the organisation of the European task. It is no longer the savage, hostile, quarrelsome nationality of two hundred years ago which is invoked by these peoples. The nationality which Ancillon[3] founded upon the following principle: — *Whichever people, by its superiority of strength, and by its geographical position, can do us an injury, is our natural enemy; whichever cannot do us an injury, but can by the amount of its force and by its position injure our enemy, is our natural ally,* — is the princely nationality of aristocracies or royal races. This nationality of the peoples has not these dangers; it can only be founded by a common effort and a common movement; sympathy and alliance will be its result. In principle, as in the ideas formerly laid down by the men influencing every national party, nationality ought only to be to humanity that which the division of labour is in a workshop — the recognised symbol of association; the assertion of the individuality of a human group called by its geographical position, its traditions, and its language, to fulfil a special function in the European work of civilisation.

The map of Europe has to be re-made. This is the key to the present movement; herein lies the initiative. Before acting, the instrument for action must be organised; before building, the ground must be one's own. The social idea cannot be realised under any form whatsoever before this reorganisation of Europe is effected; before the peoples are free to interrogate themselves; to express their vocation, and to assure its accomplishment by an alliance capable of substituting itself for the absolutist league which now reigns supreme.

Take the map of Europe. Study it synthetically in its geographical structure, in the great indications furnished by the lines of mountains and rivers, in the symmetrical arrangement of its parts. Compare the previsions of the future which this examination suggests, with the existing collocation of the principal races and idioms. Open the page of history, and seek for the signs of vitality in the different populations, resulting from the *ensemble* of their traditions; listen, in short, to the cry which rises from the conscience of these populations through their struggles and their martyrs. Then observe the official governmental map, such as has been sanctioned by the treaties of 1815. In the contrast between the two, you will find the definitive answer to the terrors and complaints of diplomatists. Here is the secret of the *conspiracy* which they are endeavouring to destroy, and which will destroy them. Here also is the secret of the future world.

It is in these thirteen or fourteen groups, now dismembered into fifty divisions, almost all weak and powerless in comparison with five of them possessing an irresistibly preponderating force. It is in this Germany, now divided into thirty-five or thirty-six States; a prey alternately to the ambition of Prussia and Austria, and which acknowledges no other divisions than those of pure Teutonic nationality in the south and of Saxony in the north, united on the line of the Maine. It is in this immense race, whose outposts extend as far as Central Germany in Moravia, which has not yet uttered its national cry to Europe, and which aspires to utter it — in heroic Poland, whom we have so much admired only to forget her at the moment of her downfall — in the Sclavonia of the south, extending its branches along the Danube, and destined to rally itself in a vast confederation, probably under the initiative of Hungary — in the Roumaine race, an Italian colony planted by Trajan in the lower basin of the Danube, which would appear to be called upon to serve as a bridge of communication between the Sclavonian and the Greco-Latin races. It is in Greece, which has not risen from the tomb where it lay buried for ages to become a petty German viceroyalty,[4] but to become, by extending itself to Constantinople, a powerful barrier against the European encroachments of Russia. It is in Spain and Portugal, destined sooner or later to be united as an Iberian peninsula. It is in the ancient land of Odin, Scandinavia, of which Sweden must some day complete the unity. It is, above all, in Italy, a predestined nation, which cannot resolve the question of its independence without overthrowing the empire and the papacy at the same time, and planting upon the Capitol and the Vatican the banner of the inviolability of the human soul for the whole world.

NOTES

1. Secretary of State for Foreign Affairs in Lord John Russell's Cabinet.

2. Pius IX, whose reputation for liberalism faded with the revolutions of 1848–1849.

3. Johann Peter Friedrich Ancillon, Prussian statesman, minor historian and royal confidant, loyal to Metternich and sympathetic to reaction.

4. Liberated from the Ottoman Empire in 1830, Greece took Prince Otto of Bavaria for her king, but found him illiberal and finally deposed him in 1862.

6

Commodore Perry Knocks at the Door of "a People So Inquisitive and Acute"

OF THE awakened nationalisms, none was to be more fateful than the Japanese. Samuel Wells Williams (1812–84), missionary, diplomat and sinologist, who first went to Canton for the American Board of Commissioners for Foreign Missions in 1833, was invited to accompany Matthew C. Perry's naval expedition as interpreter. The extracts below record his reactions during the two visits, 1853 and 1854, of the squadron to Yedo Bay to deliver President Fillmore's request for a commercial treaty and better relations, and to receive the reply in the form of the Treaty of Kanagawa. Despite the panic at the appearance of these "black ships of evil mien," commercial concessions were not obtained until 1858. But the importance of this first serious contact was sensed by Williams.

A Journal of the Perry Expedition to Japan (1853–1854)

Tuesday, July 14th, 1853] THE SQUADRON was full of bustle this morning, getting arms burnished, boats ready, steam up, men dressed and making all the preparations necessary to go ashore and be prepared for any alternative. About half past seven o'clock the steamers were under weigh, and soon opened the beach around the point and disclosed the preparations made to receive the letters from President Fillmore. The officials, in their boats, were lying off the "Susquehanna"[1] waiting to see the flag hoisted, and about the

From F. W. Williams (ed.), "A Journal of the Perry Expedition to Japan (1853–1854)," TRANSACTIONS OF THE ASIATIC SOCIETY OF JAPAN (Tokyo, 1910), vol. 37, pp. 58–65, 151–152, 221–226. Reprinted by permission of The Asiatic Society of Japan.

time our anchor was down they were alongside. There were two boats carrying six officials dressed in full costume who, when seated on deck, presented a most singularly grotesque and piebald appearance blended with a certain degree of richness from the gay colors they wore. The second officer was a conspicuous member of this party, he not having been aboard before since the first day; his dark face and sharp features contrasting with his yellow robe, and his black socks, hairy bare legs and short trowsers, all showing out from the overalls of his uniform, made him rather an attractive object. I cannot describe the dresses of these men minutely, but the effect was not unpleasant, though in most of them no harmony of colors was aimed at in the uniforms. They all seemed to be in good spirits and amused themselves looking at the officers in their uniforms and other objects.

By ten o'clock the boats had left the steamer and, under the lead of the natives, were pretty much landed before eleven o'clock on the beach at Kuri-hama,[2] opposite the shed erected for our reception and surrounded with striped curtains; Commodore Perry left under a salute and found the escort ready when he landed to conduct him to the house prepared for his audience. There were fifteen boats in all, containing about 300 people, say 112 marines, 40 musicians, 40 officers and a hundred or more sailors. Every one was armed with a sword, a pistol or a musket, and most of the fire-arms were loaded; I borrowed a coat and sword so as to appear like the rest, but my uniform would hardly bear inspection or classification. A jetty had been made of bundles of straw covered with sand and facilitated the landing very greatly. The precaution of bringing down the two steamers to cover the place of meeting made it easy to land from them without exposure to the sun; the bay near shore was deep but full of seaweed growing in long leaves to near the surface, and doubtless full of marine productions.

The place appointed for receiving these letters was a hut set up on the beach, having two small ones behind it, the whole inclosed by white and blue striped curtains hanging from poles; a screen was in front concealing the front of the rooms and a large opening at each end of it, between that and the side curtains, which were prolonged along the beach on each hand for nearly half a mile. The village was in the south of the cove near the corner from whence the "Morrison"[3] was fired at, a poor hamlet of 200 thatched huts, mostly concealed from our view by the curtains and the crowd. The hills rose behind, partly cultivated and looking exceedingly fresh and green, inviting us in vain to explore their slopes, for the ridiculous laws interfere to prevent our trespassing on them. Truly, laws which prevent such things must have been brought about by a hard and dear experience, for it is against nature thus to prohibit intercourse between man and man.

The Japanese had placed a row of armed boats near the ends of the curtains, and detachments of troops were stationed before the curtains in close array, standing to their arms, their pennons flying from the curtains and gradually bending down to meet the boats at each end. Some of these troops were dressed in dirty white, in a manner similar to the troops in Egypt, with full breeches and tight stockings; others resembled Chinese troops, and many were in a tightly fitting habit. Horsemen were placed behind one or two curtains who wore brass cuirasses and metallic helmets or something like it. Their horses were large animals, far beyond the Chinese beasts I have seen, in size, and looking like another race than the little Lewchewan ponies. All these troops (numbering about 5000 men, as one of the Japanese told me,) maintained the utmost order, nor did the populace intrude beyond the guard. A few miserable fieldpieces stood in front, not over 4^{16} or 5^{16}er, I should think; many files had muskets with bayonets, others had spears, and most I could not see. Crowds of women were noticed by some near the markee, but I suspect they were not numerous. Altogether, the Japanese had taken great pains to receive us in style, while each side had provided against surprises from the other and prepared against every contingency.

As soon as Commodore Perry landed all fell into procession; Captain Buchanan, who was the first man ashore, had arranged all in their places so that no hindrance took place. The marines, headed by Major Zeilen, led off, he going ahead with a drawn sword; then half of the sailors with one band playing between the two parties. Two tall blacks heavily armed supported as tall a standard bearer, carrying a commodore's pennant, and went next before two boys carrying the President's letter and the Full Powers in their boxes covered with red baize. The Commodore, supported by Captain Adams and Lieutenant Contee, each wearing chapeaux, then advanced; the interpreters and secretary came next succeeded by Captain Buchanan and the gay-appearing file of officers whose epaulettes, buttons, etc., shone brightly in the sun. A file of sailors and the band, with marines under Captain Slack, finished this remarkable escort. The escort of Von Resanoff[4] at Nagasaki of seven men was denied a landing until they had been stripped of almost everything belonging to a guard of honor; here, fifty years after, a strongly armed escort of 300 Americans do honor to their President's letter at the other end of the empire, the Japanese being anxious only to know the size and arrangement of what they feel themselves powerless to resist. There were fully a thousand charges of ball in the escort besides the contents of the cartridge boxes. Any treachery on their part would have met a serious revenge.

On reaching the front of the markee the two envoys were seen seated on campstools on the left side of a room, twenty feet square or so, matted and covered with red felt; four campstools were ranged on the right side, and a red lacquered box between them. The chief envoy, Toda, Idzu no kami (Toda, prince of Idzu), and his coadjutor, Ido, Iwamè no kami (Ido, prince of Iwamè), rose as the Commodore entered, and the two parties made slight bows to each other. The boys laid the boxes on the floor and the two blacks came in to open them. They were taken out and opened upon the lacquered box, and the packet containing the copies and translations presented by Mr. Contee. Tatsnoske[5] and Yezaimon[6] were both on the floor, and the former commenced the interview by asking if the letters were ready to be delivered. When he made known the reply he put his head nearly to the floor in speaking to Yezaimon who, on his knees, informed the envoy in a whisper. The receipt for them in Dutch and Japanese was then delivered to Mr. Portman, and the originals themselves opened out in the boxes as they lay. Soon after, Commodore Perry said that in two or three days he intended to leave for Lewchew and China, and would take any letters, etc., for the envoys. This produced no acknowledgment on their part, and he then added that there was a revolution in China by insurgents who had taken Nanking and Amoy, and wished to introduce a new religion. "It will be better not to talk about revolutions at this time," was the significant reply, and proper one too, for I thought it very mal-apropos to bring in such a topic. Yet one might regard it with interest as ominous of the important changes which might now be coming on the Japanese, and of which this interview was a good commencement.

Conversation being thus stopped and no signs of any refreshment appearing, there was nothing else to do than to go. The contrast between its interlocutors was very striking. In the front was a group of foreign officers and behind them the picturesque looking, shaven-pated Japanese in relief against the checked screen; on the left a row of full-dressed officers with swords, epaulettes, etc., all in full lustre; on the right the two envoys and a secretary, with two more plainly dressed men on their knees between the two rows. To describe the robes of these two envoys is difficult. The upper mantilla was a slate-colored brocade kind of silk, made stiff at the shoulders so as to stick out squarely; the girdle a brown color, and the overall trowsers of purplish silk; the swords were not very rich-looking. The coat-of-arms was conspicuous on the sleeves, and some of the undergarments appearing, gave a peculiarly harlequin-like look to his dress, to which the other envoy was accordant. They were immovable and never stirred or hardly spoke during the whole interview; one who tarried a little as we came out said that they relaxed in their stiffness as soon as we had gone, apparently glad that all was over. I got the impression that the two high men had pursed themselves up to an attitude, and had taken on this demure look as part of it, but others looked on it as a subdued manner as if afraid. The re-embarkation took place gradually, no one being in much of a hurry, and I began to talk to the people and invited two of them on board to see the steamer and a revolver. One man wished to know if the women in America were white; another, how he could learn strategy, to which I replied, "Only by your going abroad or letting us come here." I asked him why there was no music, to which he answered that it was very poor. Considerable curiosity was manifested in comparing swords, and some exchanges were proposed; altogether, this part of the interview was far the pleasantest to both parties, and I suspect the Japanese were sorry to see the show end so soon. Many picked up shells and pebbles to remember the spot, and by one o'clock everybody was back to his place.

Two boats full of people came alongside soon after and stayed on board while we steamed back to Uraga. Yezaimon especially took much interest in seeing the working of such stupendous machinery and inquiring into the manner of turning the wheels. All was made plain as we could explain it, though I fear the ideas were very crudely expressed, for I did not know their language well enough, and Portman seemed not to know the machine well enough.

One of our visitors was the military commander of Uraga, an open-faced, pleasant man who wished to learn something of tactics and the construction of revolvers. One of the pistols was fired off by Captain Buchanan to gratify him and Saboroske, and they had many measurements to take of the cannon on deck; the latter greatly amused us by going through the manual with a gun he took off the stand, his face pursed up as if he was a valiant hero. This man is altogether the most forward, disagreeable officer we have had on board, and shows badly among the generally polite men we have hitherto had, prying round into everything and turning over all he saw. At our request the party remained on board while we steamed up to Uraga and then bid us good-bye, having made themselves conspicuous in every part of the ship by their parti-colored dresses. Some refreshments were given them in the cabin, and they went off in good humor.

The receipt given by the two envoys was to this purport: "According to Japanese law it is illegal for any paper to be received from foreign countries except at Nagasaki, but as the Commodore has taken much trouble to bring the letter of the President here, it is notwithstanding received. No conversation can be allowed, and as soon as the documents and the copy are handed over you will leave." The Japanese original is written on very thick paper made from the mulberry (Broussonnetià); the last sentence of it intimated they were to make sail immediately.

The four ships now stood up the bay and anchored about where the "Mississippi" had sounded, some twelve miles above Uraga. Erelong, Yezaimon appeared alongside looking sour enough at this his third visit to the "Susquehanna" to-day. His object was soon explained, and we endeavored to ease his mind in respect to surveying the harbor, telling him that we had told him we were not going to sail immediately, but to go about the bay and seek a better anchorage than that off Uraga for placing our ships next year. The extent of the time we should stay could not be stated, but not likely to exceed four days; we would not land, nor would there be any trouble if the Japanese made none, for our boats were strictly ordered to abstain from theirs. I think he himself was satisfied of our intentions, but his superiors were probably alarmed at the risk and sent him to do what he could to prevent further progress. The interview was rather tedious from its being a struggle, and I suspect the interlocutors were all pleased when it was over. Others from the boat came on board and walked through the ship, and I wish there were more who could have seen her. At this visit and the one earlier in the afternoon many things were shown our visitors, such as engravings, daguerreotypes and curiosities of various sorts, which tended to relieve the monotony of the visit as well as instruct them a little. I have now learned more fluency by my practice and did considerable side talking.

At eventide we were left alone and thus closed this eventful day, one which will be a day to be noted in the history of Japan, one on which the key was put into the lock and a beginning made to do away with the long seclusion of this nation, for I incline to think that the reception of such a letter in such a public manner involves its consideration if not its acceptance; at least the prestige of determined seclusion on her part is gone after the meeting at Kuri-hama.

* * *

[Perry left Japan July 17, 1853, and returned in the spring of 1854 for the reply to Fillmore's letter.]

Friday, March 31st, 1854

Last evening Kenzhiro came about eight o'clock with the Chinese version of the Treaty done from the Japanese, and, after some alterations and the correction of one important error respecting the distance allowed for rambling at Simoda, the whole was agreed upon. This morning a fair copy was made, and about a quarter of one o'clock the Commodore left the ship. On meeting the Japanese commissioners, they exhibited three copies of the Japanese version and one each of the Dutch and Chinese, while we had three copies of the English and one each of the Dutch and Chinese. They first opened theirs at the seals to show the rubrics attached to the name of each commissioner, instead of a seal, and then the Commodore signed the three English copies in their presence. The two copies of the Dutch version were then compared and found to be the same, when they were exchanged, one being signed by Yenoske, the other by Mr. Portman. After this, the Chinese copies were compared, and one character erased in one of them, but when I wished them to sign their copy and date it a difficulty arose, for they wished only to date it in Kayei's name and year, while I required both theirs and ours, as in the Dutch. They declined to write the characters for "our Lord Jesus Christ," and the Commodore allowed the omission, after which they dated it, and Matsusake Michitaro[7] signed it with his rubric; and I signed the other and gave it in exchange. Thus completed the negotiations and signing of the Treaty of Kanagawa, the first one ever made by the Japanese. Long may they rejoice over the blessings it will bring them, and may the Disposer of nations and events make it the opening whereby his great Name may be declared unto them. After so many years of seclusion, He has inclined them to listen to this application to loosen the strictness of their laws, and I sincerely hope they will never have occasion to repent of the privileges granted on this day.

* * *

Saturday, June 24th

A supplementary boat went ashore this morning from the "Mississippi" to carry some printed copies of the port regulations and rates of pilotage in Simoda, to leave with the authorities, so that the last visit was on our part, after all, as the first visit last year was on the side of the Japanese. The day began so rainy and the sea was so rough we have lain at anchor all day, no communication being had with each other or the shore. I wished much to take another ramble over the adjacent hills, but there was no chance; they appeared more inviting than ever, and at any time they and the country about this port are not excelled by any harbor we have seen in Japan.

On a review of the proceedings of this Expedition, no one can refuse his assent to the assertion that it has been peculiarly prospered by God, and, so far as we are at liberty to say it, was planned and carried out so as to receive his blessing as a step in his plans for the extension of his kingdom in this land. The appointment of a naval man as the envoy was wise, as it secured unity of purpose in the diplomatic and executive chief, and probably Perry is the only man in our navy capable of holding both positions, which has been proved by the general prudence and decision of his proceedings since he anchored at Uraga last July. It has been favorable to his unbiassed action that he has had no captain under him whose judgment and knowledge entitled him to the least weight in his mind; all, except Buchanan, spent their thoughts in criticising what he did and wishing they were going home. If the Commodore and the Envoy had been two persons, such a state of feeling in the officers might have at last crippled the firmest purposes of the latter and thwarted the whole enterprise. But such a dilemma was avoided, and Perry regarded all under him as only means and agents to serve his purpose, perhaps too often disregarding wishes and opinions of a comparatively trifling nature. But that extreme is almost unavoidable in minds of strong fibre, and bred for years to command, as he has been, such power has habit.

Further, the remarkable weather experienced since Perry left Macao for Shanghai last April—fair, pleasant and healthy in a degree to draw the attention of all, who have more frequently cried out, "See Perry's luck," than been disposed to acknowledge the hand and favor of God in it — has not a little aided the Expedition. Four or five of the ships have grounded, but none have been injured; . . . It seems to me that he who refuses to recognize the hand and blessing of God in these preservations, and involving his general approval, is unwilling to recognize it anywhere or in anything. . . . The general good health of the 1600 persons in the squadron, destitute as almost all of them have been of fresh provisions since last January, and the good condition of most of the stores brought on, calls for particular mention, as the converse might have hampered the whole enterprise. The Japanese could not easily collect fresh provisions for so large a body of people, and the extremity of sickness might have driven us to the extremity of forcibly supplying ourselves with food at some rate, even if the alternative was instant hostilities and the attack of Yedo itself. Such a procedure, necessary as we might have deemed it for our own preservation, and not to be thought of in almost any position, might have been resorted to by some one less patient, and (I can conceive) might have removed the peaceful opening of Japan to an indefinite period. Now, not a shot has been fired, not a man wounded, not a piece of property destroyed, not a boat sunk, nor a Japanese to be found who is the worse, so far as we know, for the visit of the American Expedition.

Some will ask what has been gained or done by this Expedition at all commensurate with the cost it has been to the United States. What ultimate results will be seen must indeed be estimated, and can only be, when time has disclosed them, both in respect to trade between the two countries and intercourse between their people, in respect to the facilities Japanese coal can give to connecting California and Asia, in that of supplying whalers and other vessels with provisions and retreat from storms. But in the higher benefits likely to flow to the Japanese by their introduction to the family of civilized nations through the Treaty of Kanagawa, increased by the additional regulations signed at Simoda, I see a hundred-fold return for all the additional expense the American government has been at in sending out this Expedition, and a mode of expending her income which will redound greatly to her credit. By permission of the Commodore, I drew up a paper of a general character which was sent to Lin last evening by Moriyama. In it, I endeavored to show how Japan could learn much which would be of enduring benefit to her by adopting the improvements of western lands, and allowing her people to visit them and see for themselves; adding that it was to set before them the most useful and curious specimens of western art that the President had sent out to them such things as a steam engine, a telegraphic apparatus, a daguerreotype, all sorts of agricultural implements, books and drawings explaining these and other things, and not merely curious articles or eatables or arms, from which they might learn to make such, or obtain the assistance of those who could instruct them. The great change in the policy of western nations from what it was two hundred years ago was referred to as removing all grounds for fear of any evil consequences resulting to them by a greater extension of the liberty now granted, and that no one could wish them to do aught which would be injurious or hazardous. The paper closed with a hint respecting the danger, if Americans were followed by spies and officials wherever they went, and that all that was necessary was to have those who did wrong accused and properly punished.

Whatever results may ensue from this and many other hints given to the Japanese since we reached the Bay of Yedo, I think that on the whole the impression left on the people by the squadron has been favorable. More intimate acquaintance would show more good and evil traits in our character, and they have now probably seen a fair average. Erelong I hope and pray that the gracious designs of Providence in thus favoring this Expedition will be still further developed, and the light of revealed truth be permitted to shine upon the benighted and polluted minds of this people. The glorious promises, yet unfulfilled, of the days of gospel liberty are evidences enough of what forms, at least a part of, God's plans in opening the way as has now been done. Among a people so inquisitive and acute, it cannot be long before some will be able to break away from the trammels which now bind them to Japan, and see, for as long as they wish, what Christianity has done for other lands, and what it will do for their own. The day of God's visitation will be one of love, till the ignorant and degraded have had the paths of knowledge and purity laid open for them and the page of Revelation put before them in their own tongue. In all this I see a vast reward for the expenses of this Expedition, and a gain to the cause of humanity and goodness beyond calculation in paltry gold or silver or traffic.

NOTES

1. Perry's flagship.
2. About 40 miles south of Yedo or Tokio.
3. C. W. King, an American businessman in Canton, tried to repatriate shipwrecked Japanese sailors on a goodwill voyage in the *Morrison,* 1825; the hostile reception caused him to return with the castaways to China.
4. Special ambassador from Alexander I, 1804–05, von Resanoff was kept waiting only to receive the message from the Emperor: "Your voyages and your labors are . . . useless."
5. Japanese interpreter.
6. Governor of Utaga.
7. Japanese Commissioner.

7

Flaubert: "Oh, if Ever I Produce a Good Book I'll Have Worked for It!"

LIKE THE *search for new experiences and new markets, the pursuit of truth was incessant. There was no better symbol of dedication to a literary ideal than the novelist Gustave Flaubert (1821–80). Writing in the family house at Croisset, on the banks of the Seine near Rouen, he put everything aside in 1852 for what was to be his most famous book,* Madame Bovary. *Its serial publication in the* Revue de Paris *created a sensation, bringing praise and condemnation, and an abortive state prosecution for immorality. If the theme of adultery, disillusion and suicide was banal, the honesty of its treatment and the extreme pains Flaubert took with it marked it out as a masterpiece of realist literature and social commentary. Flaubert died prematurely on May 8, 1880, leaving behind in his letters to the Provençal poet Louise Colet a glimpse into the process by which his work was put together.*

Letters

To Louise Colet

[Croisset,] Saturday night,
February 1, 1852

BAD WEEK. Work didn't go; I had reached a point where I didn't know what to say. It was all shadings and refinements; I was completely in the dark: it is very difficult to clarify by means

From Francis Steegmuller (ed.), THE SELECTED LETTERS OF GUSTAVE FLAUBERT (London, 1954), pp. 132–135, 140–141, 143, 146, 149–150, 153, 156–157, 162, 168–169, 177–178. Translated and with an introduction by Francis Steegmuller. Reprinted by permission of Farrar, Straus & Cudahy, Inc., and Brandt and Brandt.

of words what is still obscure in your thoughts. I made outlines, spoiled a lot of paper, floundered and fumbled. Now I shall perhaps find my way again. Oh, what a rascally thing style is! I think you have no idea of what kind of a book I am writing. In my other books I was slovenly; in this one I am trying to be impeccable, and to follow a geometrically straight line. No lyricism, no comments, the author's personality absent. It will make sad reading; there will be atrociously wretched and sordid things. Bouilhet, who arrived last Sunday at three just after I had written you, thinks the tone is right and hopes the book will be good. May God grant it! But it promises to take up an enormous amount of time. I shall certainly not be through by the beginning of next winter. I am doing no more than five or six pages a week.

Saturday, 1 A.M.
[*Croisset, March 20–21, 1852*]

The entire value of my book, if it has any, will consist of my having known how to walk straight ahead on a hair, balanced above the two abysses of lyricism and vulgarity (which I seek to fuse in analytical narrative). When I think of what it can be I am dazzled. But then, when I reflect that so much beauty has been entrusted to me, I am so terrified that I am seized with cramps and long to rush off and hide — anywhere. I have been working like a mule for fifteen long years. All my life I have lived with a maniacal stubbornness, keeping all my other passions locked up in cages and visiting them only now and then, for diversion. Oh, if ever I produce a good book I'll have worked for it! Would to God that Buffon's blasphemous words were true.[1] I should certainly be among the foremost.

Saturday, 12:30 A.M.
[*Croisset, March 27, 1852*]

Tonight I finished scribbling the first draft of my young girl's dreams. I'll spend another fortnight sailing on these blue lakes, after which I'll go to a ball and then spend a rainy winter, which I'll end with a pregnancy. And about a third of my book will be done.

Saturday night
[*Croisset, April 24, 1852*]

If I haven't written sooner in reply to your sorrowful and discouraged-sounding letter, it is because I have been in a great fit of work.

The day before yesterday I went to bed at five in the morning and yesterday at three. Since last Monday I have put everything else aside, and have done nothing all week but sweat over my *Bovary,* disgruntled at making such slow progress. I have now reached my ball, which I will begin Monday. I hope that may go better. Since you last saw me I have written 25 pages in all (25 pages in six weeks). They were tough. Tomorrow I shall read them to Bouilhet. As for myself, I have gone over them so much, recopied them, changed them, handled them, that for the time being I can't make head or tail of them. But I think they will stand up. You speak of your discouragements: if you could see mine! Sometimes I don't understand why my arms don't drop from my body with fatigue, why my brains don't melt away. I am leading a stern existence, stripped of all external pleasure, and am sustained only by a kind of permanent rage, which sometimes makes me weep tears of impotence but which never abates. I love my work with a love that is frenzied and perverted, as an ascetic loves the hair shirt that scratches his belly. Sometimes, when I am empty, when words don't come, when I find I haven't written a single sentence after scribbling whole pages, I collapse on my couch and lie there dazed, bogged in a swamp of despair, hating myself and blaming myself for this demented pride which makes me pant after a chimera. A quarter of an hour later everything changes; my heart is pounding with joy. Last Wednesday I had to get up and fetch my handkerchief; tears were streaming down my face. I had been moved by my own writing; the emotion I had conceived, the phrase that rendered it, and the satisfaction of having found the phrase—all were causing me to experience the most exquisite pleasure. At least I believe that all those elements were present in this emotion, which after all was predominantly a matter of nerves. There exist even higher emotions of this same kind: those which are devoid of the sensory element. These are superior, in moral beauty, to virtue—so independent are they of any personal factor, of any human implication. Occasionally (at great moments of illumination) I have had glimpses, in the glow of an enthusiasm that made me thrill from head to foot, of such a state of mind, superior to life itself, a state in which fame counts for nothing and even happiness is superfluous. If everything around us, instead of permanently conspiring to drown us in a slough of mud, contributed rather to keep our spirits healthy, who can tell whether we might not be able to do for aesthetics what stoicism did for morals? . . .

Thursday, 4 A.M.
[*Croisset, July 22, 1852*]

I am in the process of copying and correcting the entire first part of *Bovary.* My eyes are smarting. I should like to be able to read these 158 pages at a single glance and grasp them with all their details in a single thought. A week from Sunday I shall read the whole thing to Bouilhet, and a day or two later you will see me. What a bitch of a thing prose is! It is never finished; there is always something to be done over. Still, I think it is possible to give it the consistency of verse. A good prose sentence should be like a good line of poetry—*unchangeable,* just as rhythmic, just as sonorous. Such, at least, is my ambition (I am sure of one thing: no one has ever conceived a more perfect type of prose than I; but as to the execution, how weak, how weak, oh God!). Nor does it seem to me impossible to give psychological analysis the swiftness, clarity, and impetus of a strictly dramatic narrative. That has never been attempted, and it would be beautiful. Have I succeeded a little in this? I have no idea. At this moment I have no definite opinion about my work.

Monday, 1 A.M.
[*Croisset, July 27, 1852*]

Yes, it is a strange thing, the relation between one's writing and one's personality. Is there anyone more in love with antiquity than I, anyone more haunted by it, anyone who has made a greater effort to understand it? And yet in my books I am as far from antiquity as possible. From my appearance one would think me a writer of epic, drama, brutally factual narrative; whereas actually I feel at home only in analysis—in anatomy, if I may call it such. By natural disposition I love what is vague and misty; and it is only patience and study that have rid me of all the white fat that clogged my muscles. The books I most long to write are precisely those for which I am least endowed. *Bovary,* in this sense, is an unprecedented tour de force (a fact of which I alone shall ever be aware): its subject, characters, effects, etc.—all are alien to me. It should make it possible for me to take a great step forward later. Writing this book I am like a man playing the piano with leaden balls attached to his fingers. But once I have mastered my technique, and find a piece that's to my taste and that I can play at sight, the result will perhaps be good. In any case, I think I am doing the right thing. What one does is not for one's self, but for others. Art is not interested in the personality of the artist. So much the worse for him if he doesn't like red or green or yellow: all colours are beautiful, and his task is to use them. . . .

Sunday, 11 P.M.
[*Croisset, September 19, 1852*]

What trouble my *Bovary* is giving me! Still, I am beginning to see my way a little. Never in my life have I written anything more difficult than what I am doing now—trivial dialogue. . . . I have to portray, simultaneously and in the same conversation, five or six characters who speak, several others who are spoken about, the scene, and the whole town, giving physical descriptions of people and objects; and in the midst of all that I have to show a man and a woman who are beginning (through a similarity of tastes) to fall in love with each other. If only I had space! But the whole thing has to be swift without being dry, and well worked out without taking up too much room; and many details which would be more striking here I have to keep in reserve for use elsewhere. I am going to put the whole thing down quickly, and then proceed by a series of increasingly drastic revisions; by going over and over it I can perhaps pull it together. The language itself is a great stumbling-block. My characters are completely commonplace, but they have to speak in a literary style, and politeness of language takes away so much picturesqueness from any speech!

Saturday night, 3 o'clock
[*Croisset, January 15, 1853*]

The beginning of the week was frightful, but things have been going better since Thursday. I still have six to eight pages to do before reaching a break, and then I'll come to see you. I think that will be in a fortnight. Bouilhet will probably come with me. His reason for not writing you more often is that he has nothing to report or has no time. Do you realize that the poor devil has to give eight hours of lessons a day? . . .

Last week I spent *five days writing one page,* and I dropped everything else for it—my Greek, my English; I gave myself up to it entirely. What worries me in my book is the element of *entertainment.* That side is weak; there is not enough action. I maintain, however, that *ideas* are action. It is more difficult to hold the reader's interest with them, I know, but this is a problem for style to solve. I now have fifty pages in a row without a single event. It is an uninterrupted portrayal of a bourgeois existence and of a love that remains inactive—a love all the more difficult to depict because it is timid and deep, but alas! lacking in inner turbulence, because my gentleman has a sober nature. I had something similar in the first part: the husband loves his wife in somewhat the same fashion as her lover. Here are two mediocrities in the same milieu, and I must differentiate between them. If I bring it off it will be a great achievement, I think, for it will be like painting in monotone without contrasts—not easy. But I fear that all these subtleties will be wearisome, and that the reader will long for more movement. But one must be loyal to one's conception. If I tried to insert action I should be following a rule and would spoil everything. One must sing with one's own voice: and mine will never be dramatic or attractive. Besides, I am convinced that everything is a question of style, or rather of form, of presentation.

Wednesday night, midnight
[*Croisset, April 6, 1853*]

What is making me go so slowly is that nothing in this book is derived from myself; never has my personality been of less use to me. Later I may be able to produce things that are better (I certainly hope so); it is difficult for me to imagine that I will ever write anything more carefully calculated. Everything is deliberate. If it's a failure, it will at least have been good practice. What is natural for me is unnatural for others—I am at home in the realm of the extraordinary and the fantastic, in flights of metaphysics and mythology. *Saint Antoine* didn't demand a quarter of the mental tension that *Bovary* is causing me. It was an outlet for my feelings; I had only pleasure in writing it, and the eighteen months spent writing its five hundred pages were the most deeply voluptuous of my entire life. Think of me now: having constantly to be in the skins of people for whom I feel aversion. For six months I have been a platonic lover, and at this very moment the sound of church bells is causing me Catholic raptures and I feel like going to confession!

Saturday night, 1 A.M.
[*Croisset, June 25–26, 1853*]

At last I have finished the first section of my second part. I have now reached the point I should have reached before our last meeting at Mantes—you see how far behind I am. I shall spend another week reading it over and copying it, and a week from tomorrow shall spew it all out to Bouilhet. If it is all right it will be a great worry off my mind and a considerable accomplishment, I assure you, for I had very little to go on. But I think that this book will have a great defect: namely, a want of proportion between its various parts. I have so far 260 pages containing only preparations for action—more or less disguised expositions of character (some of them, it is true, more developed than others), of landscapes and of places. My conclusion, which will be the account of my little lady's death and funeral and of her husband's grief, will be sixty pages long at least. That leaves, for the body of the action itself, 120 to 160 pages at the most. Isn't this a real defect? What reassures me (though not completely) is that the book is a biography rather than a fully developed story. It is not essentially dramatic; and if the dramatic element is well submerged in the general tone of the book the lack of proportion in the development of the various parts may pass unnoticed. But then isn't life a little like this? An act of coition lasts a minute, and it has been anticipated for months on end. Our passions are like volcanoes; they are continually rumbling, but they erupt only from time to time.

Friday night, 1 A.M.
[*Croisset, July 15, 1853*]

. . . I have been in excellent form this week. I have written eight pages, all of which I think can stand pretty much as they are. Tonight I have just outlined the entire big scene of the Agricultural Show. It will be colossal—thirty pages at least. Against the background of this rustico-municipal celebration, with all its details (all my secondary characters will be shown in action), there will be continuous dialogue between a gentleman and the lady he is doing his best to seduce. Moreover, somewhere in the middle I have a solemn speech by a counsellor of the prefecture, and at the end (this I have already finished) a newspaper article written by my pharmacist, who gives an account of the celebration in fine philosophical, poetical, progressive style. You see it is no small chore. I am sure of my local colour and of many of my effects; but it's a hideous job to keep it from getting too long—especially since this sort of thing shouldn't be skimpy. Once this is behind me I shall soon reach my scene of the lovers in the autumn woods, with their horses cropping the leaves beside them; and then I think I'll have clear sailing — I'll have passed Charybdis, at least, even though Scylla still remains to be negotiated.

Friday night, 2 A.M.
[*Croisset, December 23, 1853*]

I must love you to write you tonight, for I am *exhausted.* My head feels as though it were being squeezed in an iron vice. Since two o'clock yesterday afternoon (except for about twenty-five minutes for dinner), I have been writing *Bovary.* I am in the midst of love-making; I am sweating and my throat is tight. This has been one of the rare days of my life passed completely in illusion from beginning to end. At six o'clock this evening, as I was writing the word 'hysterics,' I was so swept away, was bellowing so loudly and feeling so deeply what my little Bovary was going through, that I was afraid of having hysterics myself. I got up from my table and opened the window to calm myself. My head was spinning. Now I have great pains in my knees, in my back, and in my head. I feel like a man who has ——ed too much (forgive me for the expression) — a kind of rapturous lassitude. And since I am in the midst of love it is only proper that I should not fall asleep before sending you a caress, a kiss, and whatever thoughts are left in me. Will what I write be good? I have no idea — I am hurrying a little, to be able to show Bouilhet a complete section when he comes to see me. What is certain is that my book has been going at a lively rate for the past week. May it continue so, for I am weary of my usual snail's pace. But I fear the awakening, the disillusion that may come from the recopied pages. No matter; it is a delicious thing to write, whether well or badly — to be no longer yourself but to move in an entire universe of your own creating. Today, for instance, man and woman, lover and beloved, I rode in a forest on an autumn afternoon under the yellow leaves, and I was also the horse, the leaves, the wind, the words my people spoke, even the red sun that made them half-shut their love-drowned eyes. Is this pride or piety? Is it a silly overflow of exaggerated self-satisfaction, or is it really a vague and noble religious instinct? But when I think of these marvellous pleasures I have enjoyed I am tempted to offer God a prayer of thanks — if only I knew he could hear me! Praised be the Lord for not creating me a cotton merchant, a vaudevillian, a wit, etc.! Let us sing to Apollo like the ancient bards, and breathe deeply of the cold air of Parnassus; let us strum our guitars and clash our cymbals, and whirl like dervishes in the eternal pageant of Forms and Ideas.

Friday night, midnight
[Croisset, April 7, 1854]

I have just made a fresh copy of what I have written since New Year, or rather since the middle of February, for on my return from Paris I burned all my January work. It amounts to thirteen pages, no more, no less, thirteen pages in seven weeks. However, they are in shape, I think, and as perfect as I can make them. There are only two or three repetitions of the same word which must be removed, and two turns of phrase that are still too much alike. At last something is completed. It was a difficult transition: the reader had to be led gradually and imperceptibly from psychology to action. Now I am about to begin the dramatic, eventful part. Two or three more big pushes and the end will be in sight. By July or August I hope to tackle the denouement. What a struggle it has been! My God, what a struggle! Such drudgery! Such discouragement! I spent all last evening frantically poring over surgical texts. I am studying the theory of clubfeet. In three hours I devoured an entire volume on this interesting subject and took notes. I came upon some really fine sentences. 'The maternal breast is an impenetrable and mysterious sanctuary, where . . . etc.' An excellent treatise, incidentally. Why am I not young? How I should work! One ought to know everything, to write. All of us scribblers are monstrously ignorant. If only we weren't so lacking in stamina, what a rich field of ideas and similes we could tap! Books that have been the source of entire literatures, like Homer and Rabelais, contain the sum of all the knowledge of their times. They knew everything, those fellows, and we know nothing. Ronsard's poetics contains a curious precept: he advises the poet to become well versed in the arts and crafts — to frequent blacksmiths, goldsmiths, locksmiths, etc. — in order to enrich his stock of metaphors. And indeed that is the sort of thing that makes for rich and varied language. The sentences in a book must quiver like the leaves in a forest, all dissimilar in their similarity.

* * *

To Madame Maurice Schlesinger

Paris,
January 14, 1857

How touched I was by your kind letter, dear Madame! I can give you full answers to the questions you ask concerning the author and the book. Here is the whole story:

The *Revue de Paris,* in which I published my novel (in instalments from October 1 to December 15), had previously received two warnings—being an anti-government organ. The authorities thought that it would be a clever move to suppress it entirely, on the grounds of immorality and atheism; and quite at random they picked out some passages from my book which they called licentious and blasphemous. I was summoned before the investigating magistrate and the proceedings began. But friends made strenuous efforts on my behalf, sloshing about for me in the most exalted filth of the capital. Now I am assured that everything has been stopped, though I have heard nothing official. I have no doubts of my success; the whole thing has been too stupid. Consequently, I shall be able to publish my novel in book form. You will receive it in about six weeks, I think, and for your amusement I will mark the incriminated passages. One of them, a description of Extreme Unction, is nothing but a page from the *Rituel de Paris,* put into decent French; but the noble guardians of our religion are not very well versed in catechism.

Still, I might very well have been convicted and despite everything sentenced to a year of imprisonment, not to mention a fine of a thousand francs. In addition, each new volume by your friend would have been severely scrutinized by the gentlemen of the police, and a second offence would have put me in a dungeon for five years: in short, I'd have been unable to print a line. Thus, I have learned: (1) that it is extremely unpleasant to be involved in a political affair; (2) that social hypocrisy is a serious matter. But this time it was so stupid that it grew ashamed of itself, loosened its grip, and crawled back into its hole.

As for the book itself, which is moral, ultra-moral, and which might well be awarded the Montyon prize were it a little less frank (an honour which I covet but little), it has had as much success as a novel can have in a magazine.

The literary world has paid me some pretty compliments—whether sincere or not I do not know. I am even told that Monsieur de Lamartine is loudly singing my praises—which surprises me very much, for everything in my book must annoy him! The *Presse* and the *Moniteur* have made me some very substantial offers. I have been asked to write a comic (!) opera and my *Bovary* has been discussed in various publications large and small. And that, dear Madame, with no modesty whatever, is the balance sheet of my fame. Have no worry about the critics—they will treat me kindly, for they well know that I have no desire to compete with them, in any way; on the contrary, they will be charming—it is so pleasant to have new idols with which to overturn the old.

So I shall resume my dull life, so calm and flat, in which sentences are adventures and the only flowers I gather are metaphors. I shall write as in the past, solely for the pleasure of writing, for myself alone, with no thought of money or publicity. Apollo will doubtless set this to my credit, and one day perhaps I shall succeed in producing something good. For do not persistence and energy overcome all obstacles? Every dream finds its form in the end; there are waters for all thirsts, there is love for all hearts. And then there is no better way of getting through life than to be incessantly preoccupied by an idea—by an ideal, as the grisettes say. . . . Since all alternatives are absurd, let us choose the noblest. Since the sun is beyond our reach, let us stop by our windows and set the lights blazing in our room. . . .

NOTE

1. *La génie est une longue patience* [Genius consists in having a great deal of patience].

8

Renan on "the Founder of the Eternal Religion of Humanity"

THE SKEPTICISM of the Enlightenment ran through the nineteenth century, and materialism chipped away at Christian orthodoxy. Humanism never ceased gaining strength and converts. Inevitably the analysis of Christ given by the French Orientalist Ernest Renan (1823–92) seemed blasphemous and his Life of Jesus *(1863) was anathema. Appointed to the Chair of Hebrew at the Collège de France (despite the Empress's opposition), he lost it with his opening lecture, when he characterized Christ as "an incomparable man, the founder of the eternal religion of humanity, the religion of the spirit." Emile Faguet remarked unkindly that he had made Christ "a little like Renan," but Maurice Barrès was more just in concluding that Renan felt his task to be the conciliation of "religious feeling and scientific analysis."*

Life of Jesus

THAT HE had no knowledge of the general state of the world is evident from every feature of his most authentic discourses. To him the earth appeared to be still divided into kingdoms warring with one another; he seemed to be ignorant of the "Roman Peace" and the new state of society which was inaugurated in his time. He had no precise idea of the Roman power; the name of "Cæsar" alone reached him. He saw, in course of construction, in Galilee or its environs, Tiberias, Julias, Diocæsarea, Cæsarea, stately works of the Herods who sought, by erecting these magnificent buildings, to prove their admiration for Roman civilisation, and their devotion towards the members of the family of Augustus, whose names, by a caprice of

From Ernest Renan, LIFE OF JESUS (London, n.d.), pp. 25–28, 81–82, 166–175, 267–272, 282–284, 288–289. Translated and with an introduction by William G. Hutchinson.

fate, now serve, grotesquely altered, to designate miserable Bedouin hamlets. . . .

What he loved were his Galilean villages, confused masses of huts, of nests and holes cut in the rocks, of wells, of tombs, of fig-trees, and of olives. He always clung close to nature. The courts of kings appeared to him as places where people wear fine clothes. The charming impossibilities of which his parables are full, when he brings kings and the mighty ones of the earth into the story, prove that he never conceived of aristocratic society, save as a young villager who sees the world through the prism of his simplicity.

Still less had he any knowledge of the new idea, created by Hellenic science, and fully confirmed by modern thought, which is the basis of all philosophy, to wit, the exclusion of the supernatural forces, to which the simple belief of early times attributed the government of the universe. Almost a century before him, Lucretius had admirably expressed the immutability of the general system of nature. The negation of miracle—the idea that everything in the world is caused by laws in which the personal intervention of higher beings has no part—was universally admitted in the great schools of all the countries which had accepted Greek science. Perhaps even Babylon and Persia were not strangers to it. Of this progress Jesus knew nothing. Although born at a time when the principles of positive science had already been proclaimed, he lived entirely in supernatural ideas. Never, perhaps, had the Jews been more possessed with the thirst for the marvellous. Philo, who dwelt in a great intellectual centre and had received a very thorough education, possessed only a chimerical and valueless knowledge of science.

On this point Jesus differed in no respect from his countrymen. He believed in the devil, whom he figured as a kind of evil genius, and he imagined, like everybody else, that nervous diseases were caused by demons who possessed the patient and agitated him. To him the marvellous was not the exceptional but the normal state of things. The idea of the impossibilities of the supernatural is coincident with the beginnings of the experimental science of nature. The man who is destitute of any notion of physical laws, who believes that by praying he can change the clouds in their courses, stay disease and even death, finds nothing extraordinary in miracle, since to him the whole course of things is the result of the free will of the Deity. This intellectual state was that of Jesus during all his life. But in his great soul such a belief produced effects altogether opposed to those produced on men of vulgar mind. In the latter, belief in the special intervention of God caused a foolish credulity and the deceptions of charlatans. In his case it led to a profound conception of the close relations of man with God, and to an exaggerated belief in the power of man — beautiful delusions, which were the secret of his strength; for, if they were one day to be the means of laying him open to the criticism of the physicist and the chemist, they gave him an influence over his own age such as no individual before his time had, or since has, possessed.

His distinctive character showed itself while he was still very young. Legend delights to reveal him, even in his childhood, in revolt against paternal authority, and forsaking the commonplace ways of life to fulfil his mission. It is at least certain that relations of kinship were of little account to him. His family do not seem to have loved him and at times he appears to have been harsh towards them. Jesus, like all men exclusively possessed by one idea, came to think lightly of the ties of blood. The bond of thought is the only one recognized by natures such as his. "Behold my mother and my brethren!" he said, stretching forth his hand towards his disciples; "For whosoever shall do the will of my Father which is in heaven, he is my brother and sister and mother."[1] The simple people did not understand his meaning thus, and one day a woman passing near him cried out, "Blessed is the womb that bare thee, and the breasts which thou didst suck." But he said, "Yea, rather blessed are they that hear the word of God, and keep it."[2] Soon, in his bold revolt against nature, he was to go still further; and we shall see him trampling under foot all that is human — ties of blood, love, and country, keeping soul and heart only for the idea which presented itself to him as the absolute form of righteousness and truth.

* * *

. . . Jesus, at the same time that he announced an unparalleled revolution in human affairs, proclaimed the principles upon which society has rested for eighteen hundred years.

That indeed which distinguishes Jesus from the agitators of his own time, and from those of all ages, is his perfect idealism. Jesus was, in some respects, an anarchist, for he had no idea of civil government. That government seemed to him purely and simply an abuse. He spoke of it in vague terms, and as a man of the people with no idea of politics. Every magistrate appeared to him a natural enemy of the people of God; he predicted that his disciples would be in conflict with the civil powers, without thinking for a moment that there was anything of which to be ashamed in this. But he never showed any desire to put himself in the place of the rich and the mighty. He desired to annihilate riches and power, but not to seize them for himself. He predicted that his disciples would suffer persecution and all manner of punishments; but never once did the thought of armed resistance manifest itself. The idea of being all-powerful by suffering and resignation, and of triumphing over force by purity of heart, is indeed an idea peculiar to Jesus. Jesus was not a dualist, for to him everything tended to a concrete realisation; he had not the least notion of a soul separated from the body. But he was a perfect idealist, matter being to him only the outward manifestation of the idea, and the real, the living expression of that which is invisible.

* * *

Many circumstances moreover seem to indicate that Jesus only became a thaumaturgist late in life and against his own inclinations. Frequently he works his miracles with reluctance, only after he has been besought to do so, reproaching those who ask for them with grossness of mind. . . .

It would show lack of a good historical method to attach overmuch importance to our personal prejudices on this point. The essential condition of true criticism is to understand the great diversity of view between different ages, and to free one's self from the instinctive habits due to a purely rational education. To avoid the objections which might be raised against the character of Jesus, we ought not to suppress facts which, in the eyes of his contemporaries, were of the highest importance. It would be easy to say that these are the additions of disciples far inferior to their Master, who, being unable to appreciate his true grandeur, have sought to magnify him by feats of illusion unworthy of him. But the four narrators of the life of Jesus are unanimous in extolling his miracles; one of them, Mark, the interpreter of the apostle Peter, insists so strongly on this point, that, were we to trace the character of Christ from his Gospel exclusively, we should represent him as an exorcist in possession of charms of rare efficacy, as a very powerful and awe-inspiring sorcerer such as people prefer to avoid. We will admit then, without hesitation, that acts which would now be considered characteristic of illusion or madness occupied a large place in the life of Jesus. Is the sublime aspect of such a life to be sacrificed to these uninviting features? By no means. A mere sorcerer would not have brought about a moral revolution like that effected by Jesus. If the thaumaturgist had in Jesus effaced the moralist and the religious reformer, he would have been the founder, not of Christianity, but of a school of theurgy.

The problem, moreover, similarly presents itself in the case of all saints and religious founders. Things now considered morbid, such as epilepsy and hallucinations, were formerly marks of power and greatness. Physicians have a name for the disease which made the fortune of Mahomet. Almost in our own days the men who have done most for their kind (the excellent Vincent de Paul himself!) were, whether they desired it or not, thaumaturgists. If we proceed from the principle that every historical person to whom have been attributed acts which we in the nineteenth century hold to be irrational or suggestive of quackery, was either a madman or a charlatan, all criticism is nullified. The school of Alexandria was a noble school, yet nevertheless it gave itself up to the practice of an extravagant theurgy. Socrates and Pascal were not exempt from hallucinations. Facts must be explained by proportionate causes. Weak points in the human mind only engender weakness; great things always have great causes in man's nature, although they are often developed amidst a number of petty features which, to superficial minds, eclipse their grandeur.

In a general sense therefore it may be truly said that Jesus was only a thaumaturgist and exorcist in spite of himself. As always happens in great and divine careers, he accepted miracles exacted by public opinion rather than performed them. Miracles are usually the work of the public, and not of him to whom they are attributed. Jesus persistently refused to work miracles which the multitude would have created for him; the greatest miracle would have been his refusal to perform any; never would the laws of history and popular psychology have suffered a greater derogation. He was no more free than St. Bernard or St. Francis of Assisi to moderate the thirst of the multitude and his disciples for the marvellous. The miracles of Jesus were a violence done him by his age, a concession forced from him by passing necessity. Exorcist and thaumaturgus have alike fallen from their high place; but the religious reformer will live eternally.

Even those who did not believe in him were impressed by these acts and sought to witness them. The pagans and people unacquainted with him had a feeling of dread, and would fain have driven him out of their district. Many thought perhaps of bringing his name into ill repute by connecting it with seditious movements. But the purely moral tendency of the character of Jesus and his aloofness from politics saved him from such entanglements. His kingdom was in the circle of child-like men, whom the same freshness of imagination, the same foretaste of heaven, had grouped and kept steadfast around him.

* * *

The fundamental idea of Jesus from his earliest days was the establishment of the kingdom of God. But this kingdom of God, as we have already said, appears to have been understood by Jesus in very diverse senses. At times he might be taken for a democratic leader, desiring nothing more than the triumph of the poor and the outcast. At other times, the kingdom of God is the literal consummation of apocalyptic visions relating to the Messiah. Lastly, the kingdom of God is often the spiritual kingdom, and the deliverance at hand is a deliverance of the soul. The revolution desired by Jesus in this last sense is the one which has really taken place, the foundation of a new worship, purer than that of Moses. All these thoughts appear to have existed simultaneously in the mind of Jesus. The first however — that of a temporal revolution — does not appear to have impressed him greatly. He never considered the earth, or the riches of the earth, or material power, as being worth any thought; he had no worldly ambition. At times, as a natural consequence, his great religious importance was in danger of being transformed into a social importance. Men came asking him to act as judge and arbitrator in questions affecting their material interests. Jesus haughtily rejected such proposals, treating them almost as insults. Thinking only of his heavenly ideal, he never abandoned his disdainful poverty. As to the other two conceptions of the kingdom of God, Jesus always appears to have held them simultaneously. Had he been only an enthusiast, led astray by the apocalypses on which popular imagination was nourished, he would have remained an obscure sectary, inferior to those ideas he followed. Had he only been a puritan, a sort of Channing[a] or "Savoyard vicar,"[b] he would undoubtedly have had no success. The two parts of his system, or rather his two conceptions of the kingdom of God, lean on each other; and this mutual support has been the cause of his incomparable success. The earliest Christians were dreamers, moving in a circle of ideas which we should call visionary; but, at the same time, they were the heroes of that social war which culminated in the enfranchisement of the conscience and in the establishment of a religion from which the pure worship proclaimed by the founder will finally proceed.

The apocalyptic ideas of Jesus in their completest form may be thus summed up. The actual state of mankind is nearing its end. This end will be an immense revolution, "an anguish" like the pains of child-birth, a *palingenesis,* or, in the words of Jesus himself, a "new birth," preceded by dark calamities and heralded by strange phenomena. On the great day the sign of the Son of man will shine forth in the heavens; it will be a startling and luminous vision like that of Sinai, a mighty storm rending the clouds, a fiery meteor flashing in the twinkling of an eye from east to west. The Messiah will appear in the clouds, clad in glory and majesty, to the sound of trumpets, and surrounded by angels. His disciples will be seated on thrones beside him. Then the dead will rise and the Messiah proceed to judgment.

At this judgment men will be divided into two classes according to their works, and the angels will execute the sentences. The elect will enter into a delightful place of sojourn which has been prepared for them from the beginning of the world; there they will be seated, clothed with light, at a feast presided over by Abraham, the patriarchs, and the prophets. They will be the smaller number. The rest will depart into *Gehenna.* Gehenna was the valley to the west of Jerusalem. There, at various times, the worship of fire had been practised, and the place had become a sort of sewer. Gehenna, therefore, in the ideas of Jesus, was a gloomy, filthy valley, a subterranean gulf full of fire. Those excluded from the kingdom shall there be burnt and devoured by the undying worm, in the company of Satan and his rebel angels. There shall there be weeping and gnashing of teeth. The kingdom of heaven will be as a closed room, lighted from within, in the midst of a world of darkness and torments.

This new order of things will be eternal. Paradise and Gehenna will be without end. An impassable abyss divides one from the other. The Son of man, seated at the right hand of God, will rule over this final condition of the world and mankind.

That all this was taken literally by the disciples, and, at certain moments by the Master himself, appears absolutely clear from the writings of the time. If the first Christian generation possessed one profound and constant belief, it was that the end of the world was near, and that the great "revelation" of Christ was about to take place. The startling proclamation, "The time is at hand,"[3] which opens and closes the Apocalypse; the incessantly reiterated appeal, "He that hath ears to hear, let him hear!"[4] were rallying cries of hope for the whole apostolic age. A Syrian expression, "*Maran atha,*"[5] "Our Lord cometh!" became a sort of password, which believers employed amongst themselves to strengthen their faith and hopes. The Apocalypse, written in the year 68 of our era, declares that the end will come in three years and a half, and the "Ascension of Isaiah" adopts a closely similar calculation.

Jesus never indulged in such precision of detail. When he was questioned as to the time of his advent, he always refused to reply; indeed, he declared that the date of the great day was known only by the Father, who had revealed it neither to the angels nor to the Son. He said that the time when the kingdom of God was most anxiously expected was just that at which it would not appear. He constantly repeated that his coming would be a surprise, as in the days of Noah and of Lot; that we must be on our guard, always ready to set out; that each one must watch and keep his lamp trimmed as for a wedding procession, which arrives unexpectedly; that the Son of man would come like a thief, at an hour when men would not expect him; that he would appear as a great flash of light, running from one end of the heavens to the other. But his declarations on the proximity of the catastrophe leave no room for any equivocation. "This generation," he says, "shall not pass away, till all things be accomplished."[6] ". . . There be some of them that stand here, which shall in no wise taste of death, till they see the kingdom of God."[7] He reproaches those who do not believe in him, for not being able to read the signs of the kingdom to come. "When it is evening, ye say, It will be fair weather: for the heaven is red. And in the morning, It will be foul weather to-day; for the sky is red and lowering. Ye know how to discern the face of the heaven; but ye cannot discern the signs of the times."[8] By an illusion common to all great reformers, Jesus imagined the end to be much nearer than it actually was; he did not take into account the sluggishness of human movements; he thought to realise in a single day that which, eighteen centuries later, has still to be achieved. . . .

[*Concerning the Resurrection, Renan wrote:*]

On the Sunday morning the women, Mary Magdalen being the first, came at a very early hour to the tomb. The stone had been removed from the opening, and the body was no longer in the place where it had been laid. At the same time, the strangest rumours began to spread in the Christian community. The cry, "He is risen!" quickly ran from disciple to disciple. Love caused it to find ready credence everywhere. What had taken place? In treating of the history of the apostles we shall have to examine this point, and to inquire into the origin of the legends relating to the resurrection. For the historian, the life of Jesus finishes with his last breath. But such was the impression he had left in the heart of his disciples and of a few devoted women, that during some weeks more it was as though he were still alive and consoling them. By whom had his body been taken away? Under what conditions did enthusiasm, always prone to credulity, create the group of narratives by which faith in the resurrection was established? In the absence of contradictory documents this can never be ascertained. Let us say, however, that the strong imagination of Mary Magdalen played an important part in the matter. Divine power of love! Sacred moments in which the passion of one possessed gave to the world a resuscitated God!

* * *

Let us place then the personality of Jesus on the highest summit of human greatness. Let us not be misled by exaggerated doubts in the presence of a legend which forever imprisons us in a superhuman world. The life of Francis of Assisi is also but a tissue of miracles. And yet has the existence of Francis of Assisi, and of the part he played, ever been held in doubt? Let us say no longer that the glory of the foundation of Christianity belongs to the multitude of the early Christians, and not to him whom legend has deified. The inequality of men is much more marked in the East than amongst us. There it is no uncommon thing to see arise, in the midst of a general atmosphere of wickedness, characters whose greatness causes us wonderment. Far from Jesus having been created by his disciples, he shows himself in all things superior to his disciples. The latter, with the exception of St. Paul and perhaps of St. John, were men lacking both invention and genius. St. Paul himself bears no comparison with Jesus, and as to St. John, he has only shown in his Apocalypse how much the poetry of Jesus inspired him. Hence the great superiority of the Gospels amidst the writings of the New Testament. Hence the painful fall we experience in passing from the history of Jesus to that of the apostles. Even the evangelists themselves, who have bequeathed the image of Jesus to us, are so far beneath him of whom they speak that they constantly misrepresent him, from their inability to attain to his height. Their writings are full of errors and misconceptions. At every line we feel that a discourse of divine beauty has been transcribed by narrators who do not understand it, and substitute their own ideas for those which they only half comprehend. On the whole, the character of Jesus, far from having been embellished by his biographers, has been lowered by them. Criticism, to find what he really was, must discard a series of misconceptions resulting from his disciples' inferiority. These painted him as they conceived of him, and frequently, while thinking to raise him, have in reality degraded him.

I know that our modern ideas are more than once offended in this legend, conceived by another race, under another sky, and in the midst of other social needs. There are virtues which, in some respects, conform better with our taste. The good and mild Marcus Aurelius, the humble and gentle Spinoza, since they had no belief in their power to perform miracles, were free from some errors in which Jesus shared. Spinoza, in his profound obscurity, had an advantage which Jesus did not seek. By our extreme discretion in the employment of means of conviction, by our absolute sincerity, and by our disinterested love of the pure idea, we have founded—all we who have devoted our lives to science—a new ethical ideal. But the judgments of general history should not be restricted to considerations of personal merit. Marcus Aurelius and his noble teachers have had no permanent influence on the world. Marcus Aurelius left behind him beautiful books, an execrable son, and a decaying nation. Jesus remains for mankind an inexhaustible principle of moral regeneration. Philosophy does not suffice for the multitude. They must have sanctity. . . .

Let us abstain then from mutilating history in order to satisfy our petty susceptibilities. Which of us, pigmies as we are, could do what the extravagant Francis of Assisi, or the hysterical saint Theresa has done? Let medicine have names to express these great eccentricities of human nature; let it maintain that genius is a disease of the brain; let it see, in a certain moral sensitiveness, the commencement of consumption; let it class enthusiasm and love as nervous symptoms — it matters little. "Healthy" and "diseased" are entirely relative terms. Who would not rather be diseased like Pascal than healthy like the common herd? The narrow ideas about madness which are prevalent in our time very seriously mislead our historical judgments in questions of this order. A state in which a man says things of which he is not conscious, in which thought is produced without the summons and control of the will, now makes him liable to be confined as a lunatic. . . .

This sublime being, who, day by day, still presides over the destiny of the world, we may call divine, not in the sense that Jesus has absorbed all divinity, or has been identical with it, but in the sense that Jesus is he who has caused his fellow-men to make the greatest step towards the divine. Mankind in its totality offers to view an assemblage of low and egoistic beings only superior to the animal in that their selfishness is more reflective. But from the midst of this uniform vulgarity there are columns rising towards heaven and bearing witness to a nobler destiny. Jesus is the highest of these columns which show to man whence he comes and whither he must go. In him was concentrated all that is good, all that is lofty in our nature. He was not sinless; he conquered these same passions that we fight against; no angel of God comforted him save his own good conscience; no Satan tempted him save that which every man bears in his heart. Just as many of his great qualities have been lost to us through the intellectual failings of his disciples, so it is probable that many of his faults have been concealed. But never has any man so much as he made the interests of humanity predominate in his life over the pettiness of self-love. Unreservedly bound to his mission, he subordinated all things to that mission so entirely that, towards the end of his life, the universe no longer existed for him. It was by this intensity of heroic will that he conquered heaven. There never was a man, Sakyamunni[c] perhaps excepted, who has to this degree trampled under foot, family, the joys of the world, and all temporal cares. Jesus lived only for his Father and for the divine mission which he believed himself fated to fulfil.

As for us, eternal children, fated to be powerless as we are, we who labour without reaping, we who will never see the fruit of that which we have sown, let us bow down before these demi-gods. They were able to do that which we cannot do: to create, to affirm, to act. Will great originality be born again, or will the world be content henceforth to follow the paths opened by the bold creators of distant ages? We know not. But whatever the unexpected phenomena of the future, Jesus will never be surpassed. His worship will constantly renew its youth, the legend of his life will bring ceaseless tears, his sufferings will soften the best hearts; all the ages will proclaim that, amongst the sons of men, none has been born who is greater than Jesus.

NOTES

1. Matt. XII. 49, 50.
2. Luke XI. 27, 28.
3. Revelations I. 3, XXII. 10.
4. Matt. XI. 15, XIII. 9, 43; Mark IV. 9, 23, VII. 16; Luke VIII. 8, XIV. 35; Revelations II. 7, 11, 27, 29, III. 6, 13, 22, XIII. 9.
5. I Cor. XVI. 22.
6. Matt. XXIV. 34; Mark XIII. 30.
7. Matt. XVI. 28, XXIII. 36, 39.
8. Matt. XVI. 2–4; Luke XII. 54–56.

EDITOR'S NOTES

a. William Ellery Channing, American divine, opponent of slavery and Unitarian champion of intellectual and spiritual freedom.

b. The *Profession of Faith of the Savoyard Vic* by the eighteenth century *philosophe* Jean-Jacques Rousseau expounded a highly personal "natural religion."

c. The Buddha Sakyamunni, worshipped as "the eternal omnipresent Buddha mind" by the Nichiren sect in Japan.

9

The "Highly Distasteful" Conclusions of Charles Darwin

STILL MORE *sensational were the writings of the naturalist Charles Darwin* (1809–82). *Influencd by the pessimistic views of the Rev. Thomas Malthus's* An Essay on the Principle of Population (1798) *with its embryonic doctrine of the struggle for survival in the world, and by the notions of the antiquity of the earth he obtained from Sir* Charles Lyell's Principles of Geology (1830–33), *Darwin moved—at the same time as* Alfred Wallace—*toward a full statement of his views. They finally appeared in November* 1859 *in* On The Origin of Species by Means of Natural Selection. *The work aroused a storm, colliding as it did with fundamentalist Christian teaching on the origin of man, although its general argument was eventually to find support even among those circles at first most hostile. The following passages are from a later work first published in* 1871.

The Descent of Man and Selection in Relation to Sex

General summary and conclusion

MANY OF THE views which have been advanced are highly speculative, and some no doubt will prove erroneous; but I have in every case given the reasons which have led me to one view rather than to another. It seemed worth while to try how far the principle of evolution would throw light on some of the more complex problems in the natural history of man. False facts are highly injurious to the progress of science, for they often endure long; but false views, if supported by some evidence, do little harm, for every one takes a salutary pleasure in proving their falseness; and when

From Charles Darwin, THE DESCENT OF MAN AND SELECTION IN RELATION TO SEX *(New York, 1896), pp. 606–613, 617–619.*

this is done, one path toward error is closed and the road to truth is often at the same time opened.

The main conclusion here arrived at, and now held by many naturalists who are well competent to form a sound judgment, is that man is descended from some less highly organised form. The grounds upon which this conclusion rests will never be shaken, for the close similarity between man and the lower animals in embryonic development, as well as in innumerable points of structure and constitution, both of high and of the most trifling importance, — the rudiments which he retains, and the abnormal reversions to which he is occasionally liable, — are facts which cannot be disputed. They have long been known, but until recently they told us nothing with respect to the origin of man. Now when viewed by the light of our knowledge of the whole organic world, their meaning is unmistakable. The great principle of evolution stands up clear and firm, when these groups of facts are considered in connection with others such as the mutual affinities of the members of the same group, their geographical distribution in past and present times, and their geological succession. It is incredible that all these facts should speak falsely. He who is not content to look, like a savage, at the phenomena of nature as disconnected, cannot any longer believe that man is the work of a separate act of creation. He will be forced to admit that the close resemblance of the embryo of man to that, for instance, of a dog — the construction of his skull, limbs and whole frame on the same plan with that of other mammals, independently of the uses to which the parts may be put — the occasional re-appearance of various structures, for instance of several muscles, which man does not normally possess, but which are common to the Quadrumana — and a crowd of analogous facts — all point in the plainest manner to the conclusion that man is the co-descendant with other mammals of a common progenitor.

We have seen that man incessantly presents individual differences in all parts of his body and in his mental faculties. These differences or variations seem to be induced by the same general causes, and to obey the same laws as with the lower animals. In both cases similar laws of inheritance prevail. Man tends to increase at a greater rate than his means of subsistence; consequently he is occasionally subjected to a severe struggle for existence, and natural selection will have effected whatever lies within its scope. A succession of strongly-marked variations of a similar nature is by no means requisite; slight fluctuating differences in the individual suffice for the work of natural selection; not that we have any reason to suppose that in the same species, all parts of the organisation tend to vary to the same degree. We may feel assured that the inherited effects of the long-continued use or disuse of parts will have done much in the same direction with natural selection. Modifications formerly of importance, though no longer of any special use, are long-inherited. When one part is modified, other parts change through the principle of correlation, of which we have instances in many curious cases of correlated monstrosities. Something may be attributed to the direct and definite action of the surrounding conditions of life, such as abundant food, heat or moisture; and lastly, many characters of slight physiological importance, some indeed of considerable importance, have been gained through sexual selection.

No doubt man, as well as every other animal, presents structures, which seem to our limited knowledge, not to be now of any service to him, nor to have been so formerly, either for the general conditions of life, or in the relations of one sex to the other. Such structures cannot be accounted for by any form of selection, or by the inherited effects of the use and disuse of parts. We know, however, that many strange and strongly-marked peculiarities of structure occasionally appear in our domesticated productions, and if their unknown causes were to act more uniformly, they would probably become common to all the individuals of the species. . . . In general we can only say that the cause of each slight variation and of each monstrosity lies much more in the constitution of the organism, than in the nature of the surrounding conditions; though new and changed conditions certainly play an important part in exciting organic changes of many kinds.

Through the means just specified, aided perhaps by others as yet undiscovered, man has been raised to his present state. But since he attained to the rank of manhood, he has diverged into distinct races, or as they may be more fitly called, sub-species. Some of these, such as the Negro and European, are so distinct that, if specimens had been brought to a naturalist without any further information, they would undoubtedly have been considered by him as good and true species. Nevertheless all the races agree in so many unimportant details of structure and in so many mental peculiarities, that these can be accounted for only by inheritance from a common progenitor; and a progenitor thus characterised would probably deserve to rank as man.

It must not be supposed that the divergence of each race from the other races, and of all from a common stock, can be traced back to any one pair of progenitors. On the contrary, at every stage in the process of modification, all the individuals which were in any way better fitted for their conditions of life, though in different degrees, would have survived in greater numbers than the less well-fitted. The process would have been like that followed by man, when he does not intentionally select particular individuals, but breeds from all the superior individuals, and neglects the inferior. He thus slowly but surely modifies his stock, and unconsciously forms a new strain. So with respect to modifications acquired independently of selection, and due to variations arising from the nature of the organism and the action of the surrounding conditions, or from changed habits of life, no single pair will have been modified much more than the other pairs inhabiting the same country, for all will have been continually blended through free intercrossing.

By considering the embryological structure of man, — the homologies which he presents with the lower animals, — the rudiments which he retains, — and the reversions to which he is liable, we can partly recall in imagination the former condition of our early progenitors; and can approximately place them in their proper place in the zoological series. We thus learn that man is descended from a hairy, tailed quadruped, probably arboreal in its habits, and an inhabitant of the Old World. This creature, if its whole structure had been examined by a naturalist, would have been classed amongst the Quadrumana, as surely as the still more ancient progenitor of the Old and New World monkeys. The Quadrumana and all the higher mammals are probably derived from an ancient marsupial animal, and through a long line of diversified forms, from some amphibian-like creature, and this again from some fish-like animal. In the dim obscurity of the past we can see that the early progenitor of all the Vertebrata must have been an aquatic animal, provided with branchiæ, with the two sexes united in the same individual, and with the most important organs of the body (such as the brain and heart) imperfectly or not at all developed. This animal seems to have been more like the larvæ of the existing marine Ascidians than any other known form.

The high standard of our intellectual powers and moral disposition is the greatest difficulty which presents itself, after we have been driven to this conclusion on the origin of man. But every one who admits the principle of evolution, must see that the mental powers of the higher animals, which are the same in kind with those of man, though so different in degree, are capable of advancement. Thus the interval between the mental powers of one of the higher apes and of a fish, or between those of an ant and scale-insect, is immense; yet their development does not offer any special difficulty; for with our domesticated animals, the mental faculties are certainly variable, and the variations are inherited. No one doubts that they are of the utmost importance to animals in a state of nature. Therefore the conditions are favourable for their development through natural selection. The same conclusion may be extended to man; the intellect must have been all-important to him, even at a very remote period, as enabling him to invent and use language, to make weapons, tools, traps, &c., whereby with the aid of his social habits, he long ago became the most dominant of all living creatures.

A great stride in the development of the intellect will have followed, as soon as the half-art and half-instinct of language came into use; for the continued use of language will have reacted on the brain and produced an inherited effect; and this again will have reacted on the improvement of language. As Mr. Chauncey Wright has well remarked, the largeness of the brain in man relatively to his body, compared with the lower animals, may be attributed in chief part to the early use of some simple form of language, — that wonderful engine which affixes signs to all sorts of objects and qualities, and excites trains of thought which would never arise from the mere impression of the senses, or if they did arise could not be followed out. The higher intellectual powers of man, such as those of ratiocination, abstraction, self-consciousness, &c., probably follow from the continued improvement and exercise of the other mental faculties.

The development of the moral qualities is a more interesting problem. The foundation lies in the social instincts, including under this term the family ties. These instincts are highly complex, and in the case of the lower animals give special tendencies towards certain definite actions; but the more important elements are love, and the distinct emotion of sympathy. Animals endowed with the social instincts take pleasure in one another's company, warn one another of danger, defend and aid one another in many ways. These instincts do not extend to all the individuals of the species, but only to those of the same community. As they are highly beneficial to the species, they have in all probability been acquired through natural selection. A moral being is one who is capable of reflecting on his past actions and their motives—of approving of some and disapproving of others; and the fact that man is the one being who certainly deserves this designation, is the greatest of all distinctions between him and the lower animals. But in the fourth chapter I have endeavoured to shew that the moral sense follows, firstly, from the enduring and ever-present nature of the social instincts; secondly, from man's appreciation of the approbation and disapprobation of his fellows; and thirdly, from the high activity of his mental faculties, with past impressions extremely vivid; and in these latter respects he differs from the lower animals. Owing to this condition of mind, man cannot avoid looking backwards and forwards, and comparing past impressions. Hence after some temporary desire or passion has mastered his social instincts, he reflects and compares the now weakened impression of such past impulses with the ever-present social instincts; and he then feels that sense of dissatisfaction which all unsatisfied instincts leave behind them, he therefore resolves to act differently for the future,—and this is conscience. Any instinct, permanently stronger or more enduring than another, gives rise to a feeling which we express by saying that it ought to be obeyed. A pointer dog, if able to reflect on his past conduct, would say to himself, I ought (as indeed we say of him) to have pointed at that hare and not have yielded to the passing temptation of hunting it.

Social animals are impelled partly by a wish to aid the members of their community in a general manner, but more commonly to perform certain definite actions. Man is impelled by the same general wish to aid his fellows; but has few or no special instincts. He differs also from the lower animals in the power of expressing his desires by words, which thus become a guide to the aid required and bestowed. The motive to give aid is likewise much modified in man: it no longer consists solely of a blind instinctive impulse, but is much influenced by the praise or blame of his fellows. The appreciation and the bestowal of praise and blame both rest on sympathy; and this emotion, as we have seen, is one of the most important elements of the social instincts. Sympathy, though gained as an instinct, is also much strengthened by exercise or habit. As all men desire their own happiness, praise or blame is bestowed on actions and motives, according as they lead to this end; and as happiness is an essential part of the general good, the greatest-happiness principle indirectly serves as a nearly safe standard of right and wrong. As the reasoning powers advance and experience is gained, the remoter effects of certain lines of conduct on the character of the individual, and on the general good, are perceived; and then the self-regarding virtues come within the scope of public opinion, and receive praise, and their opposites blame. But with the less civilised nations reason often errs, and many bad customs and base superstitions come within the same scope, and are then esteemed as high virtues, and their breach as heavy crimes.

The moral faculties are generally and justly esteemed as of higher value than the intellectual powers. But we should bear in mind that the activity of the mind in vividly recalling past impressions is one of the fundamental though secondary bases of conscience. This affords the strongest argument for educating and stimulating in all possible ways the intellectual faculties of every human being. No doubt a man with a torpid mind, if his social affections and sympathies are well developed, will be led to good actions, and may have a fairly sensitive conscience. But whatever renders the imagination more vivid and strengthens the habit of recalling and comparing past impressions, will make the conscience more sensitive, and may even somewhat compensate for weak social affections and sympathies.

The moral nature of man has reached its present standard, partly through the advancement of his reasoning powers and consequently of a just public opinion, but especially from his sympathies having been rendered more tender and widely diffused through the effects of habit, example, instruction, and reflection. It is not improbable that after long practice virtuous tendencies may be inherited. With the more civilised races, the conviction of the existence of an all-seeing deity has had a potent influence on the advance of morality. Ultimately man does not accept the praise or blame of his fellows as his sole guide, though few escape this influence, but his habitual convictions, controlled by reason, afford him the safest rule. His conscience then becomes the supreme judge and monitor. Nevertheless the first foundation or origin of the moral sense lies in the social instincts, including sympathy; and these instincts no doubt were primarily gained, as in the case of the lower animals, through natural selection.

The belief in God has often been advanced as not only the greatest, but the most complete of all the distinctions between man and the lower animals. It is however impossible, as we have seen, to maintain that this belief is innate or instinctive in man. On the other hand a belief in all-pervading spiritual agencies seems to be universal; and apparently follows from a considerable advance in man's reason, and from a still greater advance in his faculties of imagination, curiosity and wonder. I am aware that the assumed instinctive belief in God has been used by many persons as an argument for His existence. But this is a rash argument, as we should thus be compelled to believe in the existence of many cruel and malignant spirits, only a little more powerful than man; for the belief in them is far more general than in a beneficent Deity. The idea of a universal and beneficent Creator does not seem to arise in the mind of man, until he has been elevated by long-continued culture.

He who believes in the advancement of man from some low organised form, will naturally ask how does this bear on the belief in the immortality of the soul. The barbarous races of man, as Sir J. Lubbock[1] has shewn, possess no clear belief of this kind; but arguments derived from the primeval beliefs of savages are, as we have just seen, of little or no avail. Few persons feel any anxiety from the impossibility of determining at what precise period in the development of the individual, from the first trace of a minute germinal vesicle, man becomes an immortal being; and there is no greater cause for anxiety because the period cannot possibly be determined in the gradually ascending organic scale.

I am aware that the conclusions arrived at in this work will be denounced by some as highly irreligious; but he who denounces them is bound to shew why it is more irreligious to explain the origin of man as a distinct species by descent from some lower form, through the laws of variation and natural selection, than to explain the birth of the individual through the laws of ordinary reproduction. The birth both of the species and of the individual are equally parts of that grand sequence of events, which our minds refuse to accept as the result of blind chance. The understanding revolts at such a conclusion, whether or not we are able to believe that every slight variation of structure,—the union of each pair in marriage,—the dissemination of each seed,—and other such events, have all been ordained for some special purpose.

* * *

Man scans with scrupulous care the character and pedigree of his horses, cattle, and dogs before he matches them; but when he comes to his own marriage he rarely, or never, takes any such care. He is impelled by nearly the same motives as the lower animals, when they are left to their own free choice, though he is in so far superior to them that he highly values mental charms and virtues. On the other hand he is strongly attracted by mere wealth or rank. Yet he might by selection do something not only for the bodily constitution and frame of his offspring, but for their intellectual and moral qualities. Both sexes ought to refrain from marriage if they are in any marked degree inferior in body or mind; but such hopes are Utopian and will never be even partially realised until the laws of inheritance are thoroughly known. Everyone does good service, who aids towards this end. When the principles of breeding and inheritance are better understood, we shall not hear ignorant members of our legislature rejecting with scorn a plan for ascertaining whether or not consanguineous marriages are injurious to man.

The advancement of the welfare of mankind is a most intricate problem: all ought to refrain from marriage who cannot avoid abject poverty for their children; for poverty is not only a great evil, but tends to its own increase by leading to recklessness in marriage. On the other hand, as Mr. Galton[2] has remarked, if the prudent avoid marriage, whilst the reckless marry, the inferior members tend to supplant the better members of society. Man, like every other animal, has no doubt advanced to his present high condition through a struggle for existence consequent on his rapid multiplication; and if he is to advance still higher, it is to be feared that he must remain subject to a severe struggle. Otherwise he would sink into indolence, and the more gifted men would not be more successful in the battle of life than the less gifted. Hence our natural rate of increase, though leading to many and obvious evils, must not be greatly diminished by any means. There should be open competition for all men; and the most able should not be prevented by laws or customs from succeeding best and rearing the largest number of offspring. Important as the struggle for existence has been and even still is, yet as far as the highest part of man's nature is concerned there are other agencies more important. For the moral qualities are advanced, either directly or indirectly, much more through the effects of habit, the reasoning powers, instruction, religion, &c., than through natural selection; though to this latter agency may be safely attributed the social instincts, which afforded the basis for the development of the moral sense.

The main conclusion arrived at in this work, namely that man is descended from some lowly organised form, will, I regret to think, be highly distasteful to many. But there can hardly be a doubt that we are descended from barbarians. The astonishment which I felt on first seeing a party of Fuegians on a wild and broken shore will never be forgotten by me, for the reflection at once rushed into my mind — such were our ancestors. These men were absolutely naked and bedaubed with paint, their long hair was tangled, their mouths frothed with excitement, and their expression was wild, startled, and distrustful. They possessed hardly any arts, and like wild animals lived on what they could catch; they had no government, and were merciless to every one not of their own small tribe. He who has seen a savage in his native land will not feel much shame, if forced to acknowledge that the blood of some more humble creature flows in his veins. For my own part I would as soon be descended from that heroic little monkey, who braved his dreaded enemy in order to save the life of his keeper, or from that old baboon, who descending from the mountains, carried away in triumph his young comrade from a crowd of astonished dogs — as from a savage who delights to torture his enemies, offers up bloody sacrifices, practises infanticide without remorse, treats his wives like slaves, knows no decency, and is haunted by the grossest superstitions.

Man may be excused for feeling some pride at having risen, though not through his own exertions, to the very summit of the organic scale; and the fact of his having thus risen, instead of having been aboriginally placed there, may give him hope for a still higher destiny in the distant future. But we are not here concerned with hopes or fears, only with the truth as far as our reason permits us to discover it; and I have given the evidence to the best of my ability. We must, however, acknowledge, as it seems to me, that man with all his noble qualities, with sympathy which feels for the most debased, with benevolence which extends not only to other men but to the humblest living creature, with his god-like intellect which has penetrated into the movements and constitution of the solar system — with all these exalted powers — Man still bears in his bodily frame the indelible stamp of his lowly origin.

NOTES

1. Sir John Lubbock, distinguished naturalist, politician, banker, and writer of popular scientific books, created Baron Avebury in 1900.

2. Darwin's cousin, Francis Galton, meteorologist and anthropologist, pioneer in the science of eugenics, knighted in 1909.

10

Lincoln Requests "the Legal Means for Making this Contest a Short and Decisive One"

Such intellectual shocks as Darwin's were paralleled by the most severe political shocks after the mid-century. Perhaps the emergence of United States preponderance in the twentieth century has given the Civil War a magnitude in retrospect it did not then appear to have. But even busy Europeans watched carefully and calculated their own interests and the chances of the contending parties. Explanations of the outbreak have never ceased to differ. Doubtless the view from the White House was not impartial; but Abraham Lincoln (1809–65) gave the Congress on July 4, 1861, as calm an account as any participant could have. Only four months in office, he had now to give the last four years of his life to war: a time of defeat, hesitation, diplomatic crisis and personal trial, followed by confidence, victory and the tragedy at Ford's Theater, April 14, 1865. Mortally wounded, he died early next day.

Message to Congress in Special Session: July 4, 1861

Fellow-citizens of the Senate and House of Representatives]

HAVING been convened on an extraordinary occasion, as authorized by the Constitution, your attention is not called to any ordinary subject of legislation.

At the beginning of the present presidential term, four months ago, the functions of the Federal Government were found to be gen-

From John C. Nicolay and John Hay (eds.), ABRAHAM LINCOLN, COMPLETE WORKS *(New York, 1894), vol. ii, pp. 55–56.*

erally suspended within the several States of South Carolina, Georgia, Alabama, Mississippi, Louisiana, and Florida, excepting only those of the Post-office Department.

Within these States all the forts, arsenals, dockyards, custom-houses, and the like, including the movable and stationary property in and about them, had been seized, and were held in open hostility to this government, excepting only Forts Pickens, Taylor, and Jefferson, on and near the Florida coast, and Fort Sumter, in Charleston Harbor, South Carolina. The forts thus seized had been put in improved condition, new ones had been built, and armed forces had been organized and were organizing, all avowedly with the same hostile purpose.

The forts remaining in the possession of the Federal Government in and near these States were either besieged or menaced by warlike preparations, and especially Fort Sumter was nearly surrounded by well-protected hostile batteries, with guns equal in quality to the best of its own, and outnumbering the latter as perhaps ten to one. A disproportionate share of the Federal muskets and rifles had somehow found their way into these States, and had been seized to be used against the government. Accumulations of the public revenue lying within them had been seized for the same object. The navy was scattered in distant seas, leaving but a very small part of it within the immediate reach of the government. Officers of the Federal army and navy had resigned in great numbers; and of those resigning a large proportion had taken up arms against the government. Simultaneously, and in connection with all this, the purpose to sever the Federal Union was openly avowed. In accordance with this purpose, an ordinance had been adopted in each of these States, declaring the States respectively to be separated from the National Union. A formula for instituting a combined government of these States had been promulgated; and this illegal organization, in the character of confederate States, was already invoking recognition, aid, and intervention from foreign powers.

Finding this condition of things, and believing it to be an imperative duty upon the incoming executive to prevent, if possible, the consummation of such attempt to destroy the Federal Union, a choice of means to that end became indispensable. This choice was made and was declared in the inaugural address. The policy chosen looked to the exhaustion of all peaceful measures before a resort to any stronger ones. It sought only to hold the public places and property not already wrested from the government, and to collect the revenue, relying for the rest on time, discussion, and the ballot-box. It promised a continuance of the mails, at government expense, to the very people who were resisting the government; and it gave repeated pledges against any disturbance to any of the people, or any of their rights. Of all that which a President might constitutionally and justifiably do in such a case, everything was forborne without which it was believed possible to keep the government on foot. . . .

It is thus seen that the assault upon and reduction of Fort Sumter was in no sense a matter of self-defense on the part of the assailants. They well knew that the garrison in the fort could by no possibility commit aggression upon them. They knew — they were expressly notified — that the giving of bread to the few brave and hungry men of the garrison was all which would on that occasion be attempted, unless themselves, by resisting so much, should provoke more. They knew that this government desired to keep the garrison in the fort, not to assail them, but merely to maintain visible possession, and thus to preserve the Union from actual and immediate dissolution — trusting, as hereinbefore stated, to time, discussion, and the ballot-box for final adjustment; and they assailed and reduced the fort for precisely the reverse object — to drive out the visible authority of the Federal Union, and thus force it to immediate dissolution. That this was their object the executive well understood; and having said to them in the inaugural address, "You can have no conflict without being yourselves the aggressors," he took pains not only to keep this declaration good, but also to keep the case so free from the power of ingenious sophistry that the world should not be able to misunderstand it. By the affair at Fort Sumter, with its surrounding circumstances, that point was reached. Then and thereby the assailants of the government began the conflict of arms, without a gun in sight or in expectancy to return their fire, save only the few in the fort sent to that harbor years before for their own protection, and still ready to give that protection in whatever was lawful. In this act, discarding all else, they have forced upon the country the distinct issue, "immediate dissolution or blood."

And this issue embraces more than the fate of these United States. It presents to the whole family of man the question whether a constitutional republic or democracy — a government of the people by the same people — can or cannot maintain its territorial integrity against its own domestic foes. It presents the question whether discontented individuals, too few in numbers to control administration according to organic law in any case, can always, upon the pretenses made in this case, or on any other pretenses, or arbitrarily without any pretense, break up their government, and thus practically put an end to free government upon the earth. It forces us to ask: "Is there, in all republics, this inherent and fatal weakness?" "Must a government, of necessity, be too strong for the liberties of its own people, or too weak to maintain its own existence?"

So viewing the issue, no choice was left but to call out the war power of the government; and so to resist force employed for its destruction, by force for its preservation. . . .

The forbearance of this government had been so extraordinary and so long continued as to lead some foreign nations to shape their action as if they supposed the early destruction of our National Union was probable. While this, on discovery, gave the executive some concern, he is now happy to say that the sovereignty and rights of the United States are now everywhere practically respected by foreign powers; and a general sympathy with the country is manifested throughout the world.

It is now recommended that you give the legal means for making this contest a short and decisive one: that you place at the control of the government for the work at least four hundred thousand men and $400,000,000. That number of men is about one tenth of those of proper ages within the regions where, apparently, all are willing to engage; and the sum is less than a twenty-third part of the money value owned by the men who seem ready to devote the whole. A debt of $600,000,000 now is a less sum per head than was the debt of our Revolution when we came out of that struggle; and the money value in the country now bears even a greater proportion to what it was then than does the population. Surely each man has as strong a motive now to preserve our liberties as each had then to establish them.

A right result at this time will be worth more to the world than ten times the men and ten times the money. The evidence reaching us from the country leaves no doubt that the material for the work is abundant, and that it needs only the hand of legislation to give it legal sanction, and the hand of the executive to give it practical shape and efficiency. One of the greatest perplexities of the government is to avoid receiving troops faster than it can provide for them. In a word, the people will save their government if the government itself will do its part only indifferently well.

It might seem, at first thought, to be of little difference whether the present movement at the South be called "secession" or "rebellion." The movers, however, well understand the difference. At the beginning they knew they could never raise their treason to any respectable magnitude by any name which implies violation of law. They knew their people possessed as much of moral sense, as much of devotion to law and order, and as much pride in and reverence for the history and government of their common country as any other civilized and patriotic people. They knew they could make no advancement directly in the teeth of these strong and noble sentiments. Accordingly, they commenced by an insidious debauching of the public mind. They invented an ingenious sophism which, if conceded, was followed by perfectly logical steps, through all the incidents, to the complete destruction of the Union. The sophism itself is that any State of the Union may consistently with the National Constitution, and therefore lawfully and peacefully, withdraw from the Union without the consent of the Union or of any other State. The little disguise that the supposed right is to be exercised only for just cause, themselves to be the sole judges of its justice, is too thin to merit any notice.

With rebellion thus sugar-coated they have been drugging the public mind of their section for more than thirty years, and until at length they have brought many good men to a willingness to take up arms against the government the day after some assemblage of men have enacted the farcical pretense of taking their State out of the Union, who could have been brought to no such thing the day before.

This sophism derives much, perhaps the whole, of its currency from the assumption that there is some omnipotent and sacred supremacy pertaining to a State — to each State of our Federal Union. Our States have neither more nor less power than that reserved to them in the Union by the Constitution — no one of them ever having been a State out of the Union. The original ones passed into the Union even before they cast off their British colonial dependence; and the new ones each came into the Union directly from a condition of dependence, excepting Texas. And even Texas, in its temporary independence, was never designated a State. The new ones only took the designation of States on coming into the Union, while that name was first adopted for the old ones in and by the Declaration of Independence. Therein the "United Colonies" were declared to be "free and independent States"; but even then the object plainly was not to declare their independence of one another or of the Union, but directly the contrary, as their mutual pledge and their mutual action before, at the time, and afterward, abundantly show. The express plighting of faith by each and all of the original thirteen in the Articles of Confederation, two years later, that the Union shall be perpetual, is most conclusive. Having never been States either in substance or in name outside of the Union, whence this magical omnipotence of "States Rights," asserting a claim of power to lawfully destroy the Union itself? Much is said about the "sovereignty" of the States; but the word even is not in the National Constitution, nor, as is believed, in any of the State constitutions. What is "sovereignty" in the political sense of the term? Would it be far from wrong to define it "a political community without a political superior"? Tested by this, no one of our States except Texas ever was a sovereignty. And even Texas gave up the character on coming into the Union; by which act she acknowledged the Constitution of the United States, and the laws and treaties of the United States made in pursuance of the Constitution, to be for her the supreme law of the land. The States have their status in the Union, and they have no other legal status. If they break from this, they can only do so against law and by revolution. The Union, and not themselves separately, procured their independence and their liberty. By conquest or purchase the Union gave each of them whatever of independence or liberty it has. The Union is older than any of the States, and, in fact, it created them as States. Originally some dependent colonies made the Union, and, in turn, the Union threw off their old dependence for them, and made them States, such as they are. Not one of them ever had a State constitution independent of the Union. Of course, it is not forgotten that all the new States framed their constitutions before they entered the Union—nevertheless, dependent upon and preparatory to coming into the Union.

Unquestionably the States have the powers and rights reserved to them in and by the National Constitution; but among these surely are not included all conceivable powers, however mischievous or destructive, but, at most, such only as were known in the world at the time as governmental powers; and certainly a power to destroy the government itself had never been known as a governmental, as a merely administrative power. This relative matter of national power and State rights, as a principle, is no other than the principle of generality and locality. Whatever concerns the whole should be confided to the whole — to the General Government; while whatever concerns only the State should be left exclusively to the State. This is all there is of original principle about it. Whether the National Constitution in defining boundaries between the two has applied the principle with exact accuracy, is not to be questioned. We are all bound by that defining, without question.

What is now combated is the position that secession is consistent with the Constitution — is lawful and peaceful. It is not contended that there is any express law for it; and nothing should ever be implied as law which leads to unjust or absurd consequences. The nation purchased with money the countries out of which several of these States were formed. Is it just that they shall go off without leave and without refunding? The nation paid very large sums (in the aggregate, I believe, nearly a hundred millions) to relieve Florida of the aboriginal tribes. Is it just that she shall now be off without consent or without making any return? The nation is now in debt for money applied to the benefit of these so-called seceding States in common with the rest. Is it just either that creditors shall go unpaid or the remaining States pay the whole? A part of the present national debt was contracted to pay the old debts of Texas. Is it just that she shall leave and pay no part of this herself?

Again, if one State may secede, so may another; and when all shall have seceded, none is left to pay the debts. Is this quite just to creditors? Did we notify them of this sage view of ours when we borrowed their money? If we now recognize this doctrine by allowing seceders to go in peace, it is difficult to see what we can do if others choose to go or to extort terms upon which they will promise to remain.

The seceders insist that our Constitution admits of secession. They have assumed to make a national constitution of their own, in which of necessity they have either discarded or retained the right of secession as they insist it exists in ours. If they have discarded it, they thereby admit that on principle it ought not to be in ours. If they have retained it by their own construction of ours, they show that to be consistent they must secede from one another whenever they shall find it the easiest way of settling their debts, or effecting any other selfish or unjust object. The principle itself is one of disintegration, and upon which no government can possibly endure.

If all the States save one should assert the power to drive that one out of the Union, it is presumed the whole class of seceder politicians would at once deny the power and denounce the act as the greatest outrage upon State rights. But suppose that precisely the same act, instead of being called "driving the one out," should be called "the seceding of the others from that one," it would be exactly what the seceders claim to do, unless, indeed, they make the point that the one, because it is a minority, may rightfully do what the others, because they are a majority, may not rightfully do. These politicians are subtle and profound on the rights of minorities. They are not partial to that power which made the Constitution and speaks from the preamble calling itself "We, the People."

It may well be questioned whether there is to-day a majority of the legally qualified voters of any State, except perhaps South Carolina, in favor of disunion. There is much reason to believe that the Union men are the majority in many, if not in every other one, of the so-called seceded States. The contrary has not been demonstrated in any one of them. It is ventured to affirm this even of Virginia and Tennessee; for the result of an election held in military camps, where the bayonets are all on one side of the question voted upon, can scarcely be considered as demonstrating popular sentiment. At such an election, all that large class who are at once for the Union and against coercion would be coerced to vote against the Union.

It may be affirmed without extravagance that the free institutions we enjoy have developed the powers and improved the condition of our whole people beyond any example in the world. Of this we now have a striking and an impressive illustration. So large an army as the government has now on foot was never before known, without a soldier in it but who has taken his place there of his own free choice. But more than this, there are many single regiments whose members, one and another, possess full practical knowledge of all the arts, sciences, professions, and whatever else, whether useful or elegant, is known in the world; and there is scarcely one from which there could not be selected a President, a cabinet, a congress, and perhaps a court, abundantly competent to administer the government itself. Nor do I say this is not true also in the army of our late friends, now adversaries in this contest; but if it is, so much better the reason why the government which has conferred such benefits on both them and us should not be broken up. Whoever in any section proposes to abandon such a government would do well to consider in deference to what principle it is that he does it—what better he is likely to get in its stead — whether the substitute will give, or be intended to give, so much of good to the people? There are some foreshadowings on this subject. Our adversaries have adopted some declarations of independence in which, unlike the good old one, penned by Jefferson, they omit the words "all men created equal." Why? They have adopted a temporary national constitution, in the preamble of which, unlike our good old one, signed by Washington, they omit "We, the People," and substitute, "We, the deputies of the sovereign and independent States." Why? Why this deliberate pressing out of view the rights of men and the authority of the people?

This is essentially a people's contest. On the side of the Union it is a struggle for maintaining in the world that form and substance of government whose leading object is to elevate the condition of men — to lift artificial weights from all shoulders; to clear the paths of laudable pursuit for all; to afford all an unfettered start, and a fair chance in the race of life. Yielding to partial and temporary departures, from necessity, this is the leading object of the government for whose existence we contend.

I am most happy to believe that the plain people understand and appreciate this. It is worthy of note that while in this, the government's hour of trial, large numbers of those in the army and navy who have been favored with the offices have resigned and proved false to the hand which had pampered them, not one common soldier or common sailor is known to have deserted his flag.

Great honor is due to those officers who remained true, despite the example of their treacherous associates; but the greatest honor, and most important fact of all, is the unanimous firmness of the common soldiers and common sailors. To the last man, so far as known, they have successfully resisted the traitorous efforts of those whose commands, but an hour before, they obeyed as absolute law. This is the patriotic instinct of the plain people. They understand, without an argument, that the destroying of the government which was made by Washington means no good to them.

Our popular government has often been called an experiment. Two points in it our people have already settled — the successful establishing and the successful administering of it. One still remains — its successful maintenance against a formidable internal attempt to overthrow it. It is now for them to demonstrate to the world that those who can fairly carry an election can also suppress a rebellion; that ballots are the rightful and peaceful successors of bullets; and that when ballots have fairly and constitutionally decided, there can be no successful appeal back to bullets; that there can be no successful appeal, except to ballots themselves, at succeeding elections. Such will be a great lesson of peace: teaching men that what they cannot take by an election, neither can they take it by a war; teaching all the folly of being the beginners of a war.

Lest there be some uneasiness in the minds of candid men as to what is to be the course of the government toward the Southern States after the rebellion shall have been suppressed, the executive deems it proper to say it will be his purpose then, as ever, to be guided by the Constitution and the laws; and that he probably will have no different understanding of the powers and duties of the Federal Government relatively to the rights of the States and the people, under the Constitution, than that expressed in the inaugural address. . . .

It was with the deepest regret that the executive found the duty of employing the war power in defense of the government forced upon him. He could but perform this duty or surrender the existence of the government. No compromise by public servants could, in this case, be a cure; not that compromises are not often proper, but that no popular government can long survive a marked precedent that those who carry an election can only save the government from immediate destruction by giving up the main point upon which the people gave the election. The people themselves, and not their servants, can safely reverse their own deliberate decisions.

As a private citizen the executive could not have consented that these institutions shall perish; much less could he, in betrayal of so vast and so sacred a trust as the free people have confided to him. He felt that he had no moral right to shrink, nor even to count the chances of his own life in what might follow. In full view of his great responsibility he has, so far, done what he has deemed his duty. You will now, according to your own judgment, perform yours. He sincerely hopes that your views and your actions may so accord with his, as to assure all faithful citizens who have been disturbed in their rights of a certain and speedy restoration to them, under the Constitution and the laws.

And having thus chosen our course, without guile and with pure purpose, let us renew our trust in God, and go forward without fear and with manly hearts.

Abraham Lincoln.

July 4, 1861.

11

1870–71: General von Moltke Reports "This Dreadful War"

Terrible though the American conflict was, no political and military event after 1815 was more shattering than the defeat of France by Prussia and her German allies. The bottling up of the main French armies and the swift capture of Napoleon III were followed by the long siege of Paris, where the Republic had been proclaimed. Hoping to starve the capital out rather than assault it, General Helmuth von Moltke (1800–91), the Prussian chief of staff, resisted Bismarck's importunings until the year's end. His letters from the field illustrate his optimism and offer a commentary on the events in the Republic struggling to be born, to fight off the Germans and to remain undivided, all at the same time. For his successes in this war which he had urged upon Bismarck, Moltke was created a Count in late October, and a Field Marshal the following year. He retired in 1888, and died on April 24, 1891.

Letters

To his brother Adolph

Berlin,
18th July, 1870

WHAT A CHANGE has come over the aspect of affairs during the few days that have elapsed since my departure. That profligate adventurer from Boulogne[1] sets two nations against one another in order to save, if he can, the interests of his dynasty. Never before have we on our side waged a more just warfare than this, and we may rely therefore upon God's protection. His ways, however, are not always our ways, and in the progress of the world He sometimes

From MOLTKE'S LETTERS TO HIS WIFE AND OTHER RELATIVES *(London, 1896), vol. ii, pp. 223, 225–234, 236–244.*

accomplishes His ends by lost battles. Nevertheless, we trust to obtain a happy issue; the political situation, too, is a favourable one, since we have good reason for believing that during the beginning, at all events, we shall not have a second enemy at our back.

Ferrière,
21st September, 1870

. . . Paris has since yesterday been completely invested on every side, and for the time being we wait to see how those hundred thousand men of the *gardes mobiles* whom the newspapers talk about, will enjoy this kind of embrace. The march hither from the south met with considerable opposition from the last and still intact French corps, the fourteenth, but the latter was yesterday compelled to fall back upon the forts, losing seven guns in course of doing so. The Vth Army Corps, which occupied the van of our advance, had engagements upon the 17th, 18th, and 19th. *La France qui est plus forte que jamais* (France, which is stronger than ever,) continues, notwithstanding all these circumstances, to use big words. They no longer have such a thing as an army in the field, but they have still M. Rochefort,[2] *professeur de barricades,* and *la poitrine des patriotes invincibles* [the breasts of invincible patriots]. All the same, there appeared yesterday here in the enemy's head-quarters the *République* itself in the person of M. Jules Favre.[3]

22nd.—. . .

M. Favre has not yet returned from Paris, and as he declared but a short while ago that not an inch of French soil nor a single stone of a French fortress will be ceded, and as the Parisians have, during the entire campaign, read absolutely nothing else except reports of victories, it will be somewhat surprising if one does not hear all of a sudden of rather different propositions being made. I should not be the least surprised to hear that they have massacred him. The republic of honest people is threatened with much greater danger by the red republic than by the hostile army; possibly even the latter may have yet to be called in to maintain social order in this capital of the civilized world. At Versailles the Prussians were very well received after two thousand men of the *Gardes mobiles* had delivered up three hundred wretched rifles, and Sèvres actually begged for a garrison. In Paris the gas supply has had to be stopped, and water is only allowed to be taken during restricted hours. All the railway traffic is interrupted. The *bois de Boulogne* [a Paris park] is full of cattle, and from our positions near Meudon and St. Cloud we can at any moment expose them to fire. The promenade of the *beau-* and *demi-monde* [society high and low] has ceased, and this morning the Parisian had to take his coffee without milk. How long he will continue to hold out remains to be seen. . . .

Versailles,
12th October

. . . Nothing seems to enrage Paris so much as the circumstance that we do not take the initiative in anything. Victor Hugo writes, *Nous avons cru voir arriver Arminius, et nous ne voyons que Schinnerhannes* [We expected to see Arminius come, instead we see only Schinnerhannes]. For the present, at all events, as we cannot do more than invest the place, we are in that wretched state of expectation. The process of starving out is, as Metz has shown, a very slow one, but it finally accomplishes its work. Up to the present time all the sallies which have been made have been repulsed, and we, on the other hand, are by no means idle. The hopes of the Parisians are entirely founded upon the army of the Loire, which has been already actually reported to be marching to their relief. That was so far quite correct, but this same army was yesterday utterly routed, and Orleans has been occupied by us. By to-day we shall have taken up our position on yonder side of the river, which, as is well known, has never before been crossed by hostile troops. The government in Tours will have to look about for another place of shelter.

Will this wretched land at last become aware that it has been conquered, and that its situation is growing worse from day to day? And yet I doubt not, they have, even at the present moment, again published some report of a victory! It is indeed remarkable that the *Gaulois,* which at all times has occupied a chief place among lying newspapers, has published the letter of a French officer who has had the extraordinary courage to tell the French the truth. You will find it in one of the next numbers of our *Berliner Zeitung.* More exactly could the situation not possibly be characterized than it has been done by this well-informed and intelligent military man.

That on the 9th inst. before Metz a large sally has again been repulsed, you will no doubt have heard before these lines reach you. Matters there cannot continue in their present state much longer. It is a hard trial of patience for the investing troops, and a harder one still for those who are invested. The perseverance and pertinacity of the French ought to receive due acknowledgment; it must be said to their credit that it appears to them to be utterly incredible that they could possibly be conquered, and yet the superiority of the Germans had been shown in *all* the battles, even in those in which they were opposed to greater numbers, as, for example, was the case on the 16th of August, and here in front of Paris. At the same time the whole operations of this campaign could only be carried out by decidedly superior numbers, for we had in hand at one and the same time the investment of Metz, the siege of Strasbourg, and the march upon Paris. The thoughtless advisers of the emperor, the prattlers of the chambers, and the journalists ought before everything else to have inquired what a united Germany really meant.

The republican authorities in Paris do not dare to lay this question before the country. In the snuff-box of an emissary was discovered the decree signed by Favre and Gambetta[4] which stops the assembly of the *Corps législatif* [lower house of parliament], which had been fixed by their colleague Crémieux[5] to take place on the 16th inst., and which harps with somewhat anxious delicacy upon his arbitrary proceedings. From this one can only conclude that there is no prospect whatever of an authority being formed in France with which one could enter upon serious negotiations. It really is a most wicked treatment to deceive the nation by constant lies about the condition of the country. Should Paris hold out until there is a total exhaustion of provisions the situation may take a turn, the mere thought of which is terrible. If even then peace be concluded and the traffic be fully re-established, how, with the very best endeavours on our side, can subsistence sufficient for the wants of two millions of human beings be brought on here? The environs of this immense town to a distance of ten miles have been completely exhausted, the railways have been completely blocked up by the franc-tireurs, and it will take more than a month to repair the breaches. The only railway which up to the present we have been able to put into a serviceable condition we are using for the transport of our own provisions.

It is dreadful to see the ridiculous way in which the mob, which has obtained the upper hand, has behaved. Along the beautiful roads which lead to the capital the whole pavement has literally been torn up and intersected with trenches, though one can still drive along the good summer path next to it; the beautiful oak trees and genuine chestnuts have all been rooted up and hurled together ready to be chopped up; and the noble arches of the viaducts lie in ruins at the bottom of the river. All these various obstacles would be of some use if they were defended, but these franctireurs have run away from every point, and their work of destruction has delayed our advance guard only a few hours, and the forward march of the general army only a day. Everywhere we found pontoon bridges ready next to the blown-up structures, the reconstruction of which will cost the country several millions of francs. Half of the villages around Paris consist of charming villas and castles. The inhabitants of these, however, were driven out by force, and in cases where they refused to go their houses were set on fire. Naturally enough the soldier breaks open the door which he finds closed, the cellar in which he searches for bread and wine, and the cupboard in which he looks for a napkin or a plate. It is most distressing to see some of these places, compared with the order which prevails where the inhabitants managed to escape this tyranny or where superior officers had been quartered. Here in Versailles, for instance, one would be led to believe that the most serene peace reigned, were it not for the thunder which is heard coming from the guns of Paris. All the shops are open, and the commercial spirit has already led to the exposing for sale of pieces of Prussian uniforms. Jewellers and watchmakers are not afraid to exhibit their precious wares. Orders from head-quarters are stuck up at the corner of the streets prohibiting riding on the footpaths or smoking in the galleries, and in the fields ploughing and sowing are going on without the peasants being in the least afraid that their horses would be unharnessed and taken from them. Of course prices and requisitions continue to be very high, and everybody hopes that all these calamities may soon come to an end.

I at all events wish for this, and frequently do I long for the quiet retirement of the Kapellenberge. The news which I get from my peaceful home is like sun-rays amidst the restless turmoil and the exciting state of expectancy in which we are living here.

To his cousin Ballhorn

Versailles,
26th October, 1870

Many thanks, dear Edward, for their kind congratulations to all who sent them. It is very gratifying to receive news in these times of commotion from the home of peace, which even in this campaign has by God's mercy been kept preserved from all the horrors of a hostile invasion. What that means we see here only too plainly. The inextinguishable spirit of the French seems to find it impossible to recognize that they are conquered and prostrate with the ground. They continue this hopeless struggle, which is assuming in consequence a more and more bitter character. On the occasion of the last fight every single house in Chateaudun had to be taken by storm, and the whole town was destroyed by fire. This unavoidable horrible exhibition has had, however, this result, that Chartres has submitted voluntarily, and will influence other quarters. The finale in Metz appears to be close at hand, of course after a ten weeks' delay; this will probably bring the French leaders to their senses.

It is a remarkable mercy of God that our nearest relations who happen to be in the ranks of the army have, up to the present, remained quite unharmed. For how much mourning has already spread among our families!

At this moment the representatives of the South German princes are assembled here, and it will be seen whether this great time will suffice to outweigh their trifling interests.

Once again sincere thanks. May God grant us a joyful reunion.

To his brother Adolph

Versailles,
27th October

With joy and heartfelt thankfulness did I receive the good wishes from home. A's letter concluded with the wish, may Bazaine[6] glorify the 26th by the surrender of Metz.

Even so has it happened! The capitulation will certainly take place—that is unless quite unforeseen circumstances intervene to prevent it—only this afternoon at five o'clock. Before these lines reach you, the telegraph will no doubt have already announced the great event, and the one hundred and one guns in the Lustgarten will have proclaimed the same news to the population of Berlin. Another hundred and fifty thousand French march into captivity, and the mighty fortress of Metz falls into our hands. Since the Babylonian captivity the world has not heard the like. We now require an army to guard three hundred thousand prisoners of war; France is without an army. And yet we must wait to see whether the Parisians who are now raging in fever heat will cease from their hopeless resistance. Before that I should not like to have recourse to the last sanguinary remedy of a regular attack. The sallies have hitherto been baffled by our outposts. Nowhere were they successful in their efforts to break through our lines. But any pursuit on our part is utterly impossible, and we are daily losing men by the fire of the forts, which continue their tremendous expenditure of ammunition, firing at random, and at distances of eight thousand yards—over three-quarters of a mile [sic]. Each shot costs six thalers, while one of the large steel shells of the navy costs as much as ninety-three thalers. With from sixty to one hundred shots they kill from three or five to twenty of our men, according as good fortune wills it. In part also we are exposed to infantry fire, and one has to be very careful to remove his cap before looking over the top of a wall or a breastwork. All the auxiliary troops from abroad have been beaten and annihilated, but the Government still tries, by means of lying reports and patriotic phrases, to rouse the unfortunate population of the provinces to a new resistance, to put down which will entail the destruction of whole towns. Then, too, the nagging of the franctireurs has to be repaid by bloody reprisals, and the war takes on a more and more violent character. It is bad enough that armies have sometimes to be set to butcher one another; there is no necessity for setting whole nations against each other—that is not progress, but rather a return to barbarism. How little can even the rising *en masse* of a nation, even so brave as this one, do against the smallest but well-trained division of troops! Of this our journalists, who keep constantly preaching about arming the populace, might have seen an instance in this campaign.

There is nothing else left for us to do, so long as no really supreme authority, one, too, duly acknowledged by the nation, is constituted in France, except to spread the devastations of war to an even greater extent. . . .

To his cousin Ballhorn

8 A.M., 28th October

Just received telegram from Metz. Fortress has capitulated. Three marshals, six thousand officers, and altogether one hundred and seventy-three thousand men prisonsers of war. Only sixteen thousand on sick list.

23rd November

I have not written for a long time. When one is compelled to follow out but one idea day and night for months, it becomes almost a torture, and yet it is difficult to tear one's mind away from it.

After Sedan and Metz, it appeared, no doubt, in Berlin as if all was at an end. We have had since, however, to pass through a most anxious time. The greater part of our fighting forces was stopped before Paris, and the obstinate and lengthy resistance of the army of Bazaine, whom they now declare to be a traitor, prevented us from getting reinforcements for a long time. Meanwhile the terrorism of the lawyer government enabled them to profit by all the good and bad qualities of the French nation, their patriotism, their courage, their vanity, and their ignorance. Surrounded on the outside by armed bands, we had at the same time to face on the inside the most desperate sallies, and on the outside treachery and attacks. Although the entire French army has wandered off in captivity to Germany, there are nevertheless at present more armed men opposed to us in France than there were at the beginning of the war. Belgium, England, and America supply arms in abundance, and if to-day a million weapons were to arrive, in a few days hence we should have another million of armed Frenchmen to fight against. In the next place, this government of terrorism has called out all men up to forty-six years of age from house and farm, from family and home, to follow the standards. That such a warfare is a cruelty to the country, and one which wounds her to the core, is of but very little consequence to these men, whose only desire is to secure to themselves a power, about the legality of which they dare not ask the nation. It can never be sufficiently widely published that we have always expressed ourselves as willing to approve of free elections, the freest certainly that France has ever yet had, in those parts of the country which are in our occupation, and that without any armistice or other condition whatever. One could wish, speaking from a general humanitarian point of view, to see it proved that the firm resolution of an entire nation renders its subjection impossible, and that the army of the people, as is constantly advocated by our liberals, suffices to protect a country. The state of matters in our country is certainly quite different, and we hope to be able to prove that the rising even of a nation, which possesses such inexhaustible supplies and such patriotism as the French has, cannot hold out against a well-trained and valiant army; and, in the case of such a recklessly provoked war of attack, cosmopolitan and philanthropist alike can find consolation in the fact. Now we have all our fighting forces at the front, and can accept the challenge. More important results will doubtless have been obtained by the time you receive this letter. The only way, however, to bring about a final decision now is by the exercise of unmerciful strictness. Fouqué tells about a knight who used to invariably appear wherever help and protection was required; but all fled when he came, because great calamities were generally found to follow close in his footsteps. Such is also the fate of the towns here under their protectors, the national guard and the volunteers. The inhabitants of a fort cannot complain of their lot, but when a town like Chateaudun among others has been almost destroyed in consequence of the useless attempts of its protectors to defend themselves in it, it can only be considered as a cruelty on their part. The towns, which were fortunate enough not to possess such protectors, are all right. In Rheims we have repaired railways and canals in order to re-open the supply of coal to forty thousand factory work people. The abundant wine harvest has been gathered in without the slightest interference, and the making of champagne is in full swing. Here in Versailles all the shops are open, the market overflows with provisions, and on the fields the peasant may be seen peaceably guiding his plough team. Yonder, where our outposts are stationed, you may see a self-made wilderness of abandoned houses, ruined villas, mansions which have been burned down after being set on fire by shells, and forests which have been cut down. The chief thing, however, is that a throng of armed men is far from being an army, and that it is a piece of barbarity to lead such into battle. The war is becoming more embittered and hateful the longer it lasts. Nobody can wish for peace more heartily than I do, but never could I bring myself to vote for a peace which did not secure to Germany the existence which she has obtained through such great sacrifices.

In this matter much depends upon Germany herself. The discussions of the Reichstag will become very interesting when the South German question is made the order of the day. . . .[7]

The general desire for the conclusion of this dreadful war makes our people at home forget that it is only five months since it began. Everything is expected from a bombardment of Paris; and that this has not already been proceeded with is ascribed to considerations of delicacy for the Parisians or to the influence of some high personages, whereas as a matter of fact, all that is really kept in view here is military practicability and possibility. From three different quarters already have the following verses been forwarded to me—

"Guter Moltke, gehst so stumm, immer um das Ding herum;
Bester Moltke, sei nicht dumm, mach' doch endlich: Bumm, bumm, bumm."

("Good Moltke, you always go too quietly and slowly about the matter; dearest Moltke, don't be silly, but finish it up with boom, boom, boom.")

What it really means to attack a fortress, for whose defence a whole army is arrayed, one might have learned from the case of Sebastopol. Sebastopol only became a fortress during the progress of the attack. All its supplies could be brought by sea. The preparations lasted ten months. The first assault cost ten, the second thirteen thousand men.

Before we can bombard Paris we must have the forts in our possession. Nothing has been neglected which might simplify the application of these means of compulsion. I expect much more result, however, from the slow but surely acting "hunger."

We know that for some weeks past there have been only a few gaslights burning in Paris, and that in most of the houses, notwithstanding the unusually early and severe winter, people have to do without fires, owing to a total want of coal. A letter of General V. to his wife, which was captured in a balloon, gives the following prices—one kilo of butter twenty francs, one fowl, twenty francs "*une dinde, non truffée, bien entendu*" ("a turkey—not truffled, of course") from sixty to seventy francs. He describes his supper very neatly. Herring with mustard sauce, besides a delicious little "*filet de bœuf, dont on faisait fête. Paul le cuisinier avait fait des bassesses pour l'avoir; il a promis au boucher M. et à Madame M. un sauf conduit pour un des forts pour tâcher de voir les Prussiens.*" ("A delicious filet de bœuf, which we looked upon as a regular feast. Paul, the cook, was guilty of all sorts of base acts to get it; he promised Mr. M., the butcher, and Madame M. a permit for one of the forts to get a view of the Prussians.") These confidential communications between husband and wife, indicate the real state of matters better than any of the newspaper reports, which exaggerate on one side or the other. Famine has not yet actually made its appearance, but its forerunner, the high price rate, has. The Rothschilds and Pereires have still got their *dindon truffée.* The lowest classes are paid and fed by the government, but the whole middle class is starving, and has been so for a long time now. Such a state of matters cannot last long. Of course we assume that we shall conquer in the field of battle all the armies which continue to be raised against us.

Only the terrorism of the lawyer government makes it possible to provide such armies; they send them out to face the rough weather badly organized and without proper means of transport, without even ambulances or surgeons. These unfortunates, with all their bravery and all their patriotism, are quite unable to withstand our well-drilled troops. Their miseries in their bivouacs decimate them mercilessly, and the wounded lie in hundreds on the roads without any assistance until they are picked up by our ambulances — and the French fire even at these. The franctireurs are the terror of all the districts, bringing destruction wherever they go.

But enough of these sad things. God grant us an early and happy ending; and that such will come I do not doubt.

* * *

To his brother Fritz

Versailles,
12th December, 1870

. . . We have demanded an immediate exchange of prisoners through the American envoys in Paris, and we have indeed more of theirs in camp than is exactly pleasant; but the French have so few of ours that they can only be retaining them on account of our having made this request. The suggestion has remained unanswered. But, please God, the day is not far distant when all the prisoners shall be free. The French have now their executive power in three places — in Bordeaux, in Paris, and in front of Paris, for Trochou[8] has now formally separated himself from the town.

My compliments to General Hanenfeldt, Scheller, Glisczynski, and whoever else remembers me. It is already late, and I must close. Best love, and a merry Christmas.

To his brother Adolph

Versailles,
22nd December, 1870

. . . The French made another useless attempt yesterday, with a great waste of force, to break through our lines. Just as hens announce by cackling that they intend to lay their eggs, so do the Parisians announce their intention of making a move by a furious cannonade from all their forts. . . .

Versailles,
3rd February, 1871

You will already have learned from the newspapers that a three weeks' armistice has been arranged. We have occupied all the forts, and Paris herself is for us the huge prison in which we are guarding the captive armies. Not a single armed Frenchman can get out, and none of us go in. In the meanwhile we are dismantling the walls and guns of the forts, and should the armistice not result in peace we shall have it in our power to reduce the proudest city in the world to a heap of ruins, besides putting an end to the import of provisions which at present goes on.

Now that all the French armies have been defeated, and a third of the whole country is occupied by us, one might almost expect to find some sign of yielding. The French, however, are so overmastered by phrases that one cannot answer for anything. A dozen passionate orators can lead the entire *Assemblée Nationale* [the newly elected house of parliament][9] on to the most unlooked-for resolutions. A quite recent example is furnished by Gambetta's last decree, which chants, discordantly with his colleague Favre, the old barbarian song, "War to the Death." If all the vagabond members of the government were to join in this we should very soon have two ruling bodies, and by-and-by twenty, which means none at all. The country is, in fact, threatened with anarchy. We must, therefore, be fully prepared for the continuation of the combat; and the exasperation of our men, which already is great, will become terrible.

Versailles,
4th March

. . . the preliminaries of peace have been ratified, and that with such haste, too, that our troops were only twice twenty-four hours in Paris. Our mere *acte de présence* [appearance], however, is quite sufficient.

The definite treaty of peace will presumably not be made until about two months have elapsed, during which period we shall continue to occupy the whole district of France east of the Seine, and also all the forts of Paris similarly situated. We shall only be able for the present to disband the landwehr, and must continue to keep half a million of soldiers in the country. The emperor will remain fourteen days longer with the army in order to inspect the troops, but will have to be in Berlin in time for the opening of the first Reichstag. . . .

We have here just now the most delightful spring weather, just as it is at home in the beginning of May. The little shrubs are already beginning to get green, and I fancy in about a fortnight the cherry trees will be in bloom. And then how beautiful are the surroundings of this splendid capital, unhappily full of burnt-out houses and heaps of ruins and the tracts of destroyed woodlands. But already the people have commenced to rebuild, and there is such wealth in the country that they will be able to repair the destruction wrought by the war within a few years if only they obtain a strong government. But how in the future there will be any possibility of ruling—and especially in France where the fullest freedom of speech and of the press prevail—that I quite fail to see. The great danger in all countries lies at present in socialism. I consider it to be a very fortunate thing that we are now on the way to good relations with Austria. The French will, as they have done before, pant for revenge; but when they recover their strength again they will be more likely to turn against England than against the strong central power which is forming itself in Europe; the English will then reap the fruits of their short-sighted policy.

Berlin,
21st March

We have arrived here in good health and spirits; but the peace is not yet to be relied upon. Paris is at the present moment, as you may have observed from the newspapers, entirely in the hands of the insurgents. If the government cannot soon get the mastery over them, and if it turns out that the troops of the line are of the same mind with the mutineers, then France is doomed to the most complete anarchy, and the handle will then be missing which, up to the present, has enabled the situation to be grasped. So far as we are concerned the *Assemblée Nationale* is official France. It is the most freely elected assembly that has ever been brought together. The country people and the rated classes are sufficiently represented in it. If they submit to be governed by the Paris mob and the foreign agitators they will betray their own country, and only a new military dictatorship will be able to remake France.

Meanwhile six hundred thousand of our men remain in the country, and we have only sent the landwehr home. Yesterday it was just fifty-six years since Napoleon I. landed in France from Elba. As circumstances are it would have been very fitting if his nephew had also made his *acte de présence* there. However, he landed at Dover yesterday.

31st.—It is quite impossible to say with certainty when we shall be able to bring the troops home. The Guards and the Fifth Corps had already begun their return march when a general halt was ordered, and only the landwehr were allowed to go home. To us as well as to France it is a heavy burden that we have to remain there with over six hundred thousand men. With a government of such wretched weakness, however, one has to be prepared for everything; it has no credit, and no one is willing to lend it the money without which we shall not leave, so long as Paris does not submit. With a view to this we have agreed to eighty thousand men being left assembled near Versailles. That little prattler, Thiers,[10] however, still thinks that without the shedding of blood, and simply by proclamation and phrases he will be able to disperse those bands of robbers who have just declared the *Assemblée Nationale* to be deposed, and wish its members to be impeached, and who would very soon hunt them altogether out of Versailles. The man's vanity prevents his putting the power which he himself does not know how to use properly into the hands of an able general, a measure without which the troops cannot be relied upon. This is what happens when dilettantes get into power. So far as France is concerned, matters can only be brought to a settlement by a dictator, who cannot do otherwise than begin with a blood bath in Paris. We are here with one hundred and fifty siege guns ready to second him in this. If such a man cannot be found anarchy and civil war are unavoidable.

To his brother Fritz

Berlin,
13 June, 1871

. . . On Friday the festivities connected with the entry will take place. They are to last for five hours. If the weather is as it is now, it will be a pity. I am so sorry you will not be able to see the entry of the troops. Colossal stands have been erected from the Linné Street, right on to the Brandenburg Gate, capable of holding a hundred thousand persons. At the Halle Gate and the Leipzig Gate they have put up gigantic statues of Germania and Alsacia, which will no doubt be rendered quite shapeless by the continuous rain, unless indeed they put a gigantic umbrella into their hands. The Belle-Allianceplatz is entirely covered with two huge stands which reach right up to the second floors of the houses; the Opernplatz, the university, and the Lustgarten in the same way. Innumerable masts for flags and banners line the *via triumphalis.* And in Unter den Linden from the gate to the palace there is formed an avenue of cannon and mitrailleuses axle to axle, over a thousand pieces, but scarcely a fourth part of those we have captured. . . .

To his sister-in-law Jeanette

Berlin,
28th June, 1871

. . . If only she [his wife had died in 1868] had lived through this thanksgiving time, how her patriotic heart would have rejoiced; but it is better as it is. She knows now, in all certainty, what moves the minds of those who were nearest to her. Only for us who remain will life grow ever poorer. . . .

NOTES

1. A reference to Napoleon III's disastrous attempt in 1840 while an exile to "invade" France at Boulogne with a small force from England. He was arrested, tried and imprisoned, but escaped to England again, remaining there until the revolution of 1848.

2. Henri Rochefort, Republican aristocrat and journalist, enemy of Napoleon III, editor of *La Lanterne,* and later Communard.

3. Republican deputy, opponent of Napoleon III, now Foreign Minister

in the provisional government of the Republic proclaimed in Paris, September 4, 1870; negotiated with Bismarck for armistice terms.

4. Léon Gambetta, Republican deputy, enemy of the Napoleonic regime, now Minister of the Interior and principal exponent of rallying armies in the provinces to continue the war against the Germans.

5. Isaac [Adolphe] Crémieux, Minister of Justice in the provisional government.

6. Marshal François Achille Bazaine, bottled up in Metz with a large army, finally surrendered October 27th, and was later tried and condemned to death for dereliction of duty; his sentence was reduced to 20 years, and he escaped to Italy in 1874; he removed to Spain and died there.

7. The reference is to the relationship of the south German states with the North German Confederation created by Bismarck in 1867; the war and Bismarck's prestige resolved the problem when King William I was prevailed upon to accept the title of German Emperor, and in the formal ceremony in the Hall of Mirrors at Versailles, January 18, 1871, all were joined together as the German Empire.

8. General Louis Jules Trochu, President of the provisional government, Minister of War and Military Governor of Paris; the government had split, Gambetta and others leaving the besieged capital to rally the provinces, making their way from Tours to Bordeaux.

9. Elected February 8, 1871, the Assembly met at Bordeaux to consider the German peace terms, accepted them, and moved to Versailles; outraged by the armistice and by the conservative attitudes of the Assembly, Paris erupted in rebellion against this "assembly of country bumpkins," established the Commune, and was ultimately put down in a week of fire and violence by troops loyal to the new government and the Assembly, May 21–28, 1871.

10. Adolphe Thiers, former Minister under Louis Philippe, opponent of Napoleon III, now Chief of the Executive, and the bitter enemy of the Paris Commune.

12

Imperialism "Is the Law of the Universe, and We Cannot Alter It"

WHILE WAR in Europe tended to die away after 1871, the siren call of imperialism was answered by all. A host of defenders of the imperial idea rose on all sides. One of the literate defenders of national mission was the journalist Harold Frazer Wyatt (d. 1925), a strong supporter of navalism and compulsory military service. His unqualified certainty, which by comparison indicates how remote the era of European and white dominion has now become, is seen in the following essay.

The Ethics of Empire

THAT CONVERSION of the armed States of Europe into world Powers which has been the chief feature of the political history of the world during the last twenty years has, in fact, had the effect of bringing to the front, as matters of immediate and momentous import, certain ethical considerations of which the interest must previously have been academic only.

These questions may be briefly described as those which refer to (1) the morality of the acquisition of empire, (2) the morality of the retention of empire, (3) the morality of competing with other nations for extension of dominion, or for the gain of points of vantage, even at the risk of war. Twenty years ago such questions as these would have attracted the attention of very few. To-day it is not too much to say that the fate of the British Empire and of the British people—intending by that phrase the men and women of British

From THE NINETEENTH CENTURY (1897), vol. 41, pp. 516–530.

blood and speech who inhabit it—depends upon the right determination of this subject of inquiry.

Although the questions named are not usually formulated, they yet meet us at every turn. In the press, on the platform, in periodical literature, and in casual conversation, they are everywhere to be found. And this clashing of diverse ideas, this ambiguity of moral belief, are reflected indirectly, but not the less surely, in the conduct of public affairs. When Mr. Gladstone accomplished the famous surrender that followed Majuba Hill,[1] the acquiescence of England was largely obtained on the ground that it was immoral to coerce a people—namely, the Boer farmers—who were rightly 'struggling to be free.' When Gordon died at Khartoum in 1885,[2] when the troops of England were withdrawn from the Sudan, when by that withdrawal a whole population were handed over to fire and the sword, the same argument was used, the same moral compulsion was applied. To coerce the strong, to save at the point of the bayonet, to incur the sin of 'blood-guiltiness'—these were acts from from which the sensitive conscience of a large part of the United Kingdom shrank with horror. Nor are there wanting now similar instances to which the same train of thought applies. . . .

When the peace which followed after Waterloo closed at last our age-long rivalry with France, Britain was left in a position of actual power and of potential greatness such as no other country known to us in the recorded history of mankind has ever reached. The sea was hers. Because her navy had proved stronger in the game of war than the navies of her opponents, therefore her merchant fleet had waxed while theirs had waned, and the ports and coasts of all the uncivilized portions of the earth lay open to her, and there was none to say her nay. What she willed, that she could do. . . .

It is not quite a barren endeavour to recall those gigantic opportunities which Britain has had and lost. Half a century ago, there can be little doubt that it was open to her, without fear of European rivalry, to conquer and annex the whole of Southern China, and thus to create an Anglo-Chinese Empire, to rival that great dominion which we actually possess in Hindustan. Nor was there at that time —namely, in the early forties—any European Power which would have been likely seriously to challenge our right to proceed as we would in the Far East. Again, in Africa, the whole continent was, practically speaking, open to our approach, save only its Northern shores and those territories on the Eastern and Western coast which lay in the hand of Portugal. Nor can it be doubted that in the Pacific we might have annexed any islands or groups of islands which we chose. I recall these points not at present as an argument to prove that we should have used the opportunities which we did not use, but merely in order to show (1) that, though the extension of our empire since Waterloo undoubtedly has been great, this actual extension is insignificant beside the expansion which was possible; and (2) to point the contrast now existing between past and present opportunity. Assuredly the temptation of a too facile extension of dominion is not now presented to us. The teeming millions of China, groping in the darkness of a semi-barbarism and a spiritual torpor which have endured for thousands of years, are not now likely to be awakened to a new and more vigorous life through impulse communicated by men of British blood. The Russian, not the Briton, has his grasp upon China, and unless the force of England, exerted whether in diplomacy or in war, be sufficient to loosen that grip, the vast potential wealth which the undeveloped resources of the Celestial Empire offer to mankind are likely to enrich, not the British, but the Russian people.

In Africa, again, we have now mighty rivals. . . .

Thus, then, in regard to the more recent acts by which our empire has been increased, the choice has not lain between the extension of our dominion and the maintenance of the *status quo,* but between such an extension and the abandonment of the regions concerned to a foreign rival. As in South Africa, as in East Africa, as in Siam, as in Burmah, this has been the alternative presented to our Government. But if the competition of rival nations be so great and so keen, all the more necessary is it that our action should be unfettered by the haunting presence of unnecessary moral doubt. It does not appear that the action of France, or of Russia, or of Germany has been restrained by any such considerations as those to which I refer. . . . The British Empire, past, present, and prospective, is commonly assailed by the same speakers with arguments derived from a violent selfishness and also from as violent an altruism. With the argument from selfishness I have nothing to do in this article. It runs something like this: 'What use is the British Empire to me? What does it matter to me what's being done out in Australia, or amongst the blacks anywhere. All I want is victuals. What's the British Empire? Damn the British Empire!' The argument from altruism, on the other hand, may be paraphrased thus: 'The British

Empire is simply the result of a long course of fraud and robbery. Just as a man picks pockets or robs on the highway, so have the people of Britain during generations past been filching or violently robbing the lands of other nations. The making of the empire has been, as it were, one gigantic theft.' This is the argument with which I now propose to deal.

In the first place, it proceeds upon the assumption that every nation has a vested right to the territory which it inhabits, similar to the right that an individual has to his watch or to the clothes which he wears, and for which he is presumed to have paid. Who gave to a nation this right, or by what means was it acquired? The history of the great nations of Europe shows that, as a matter of fact, they acquired the territories which they now own by one means only—namely, force. . . .

If we now turn our regard to the history of uncivilised peoples, we shall find that that appearance of right, so called, which long ownership appears to confer is utterly wanting. The title-deed, instead of being concealed under the dust of ages, is in full view. The edge of the naked steel still glitters. . . . Like waves of the sea, so successive waves of invasion have passed over and submerged the territories held by weaker clans.

* * *

. . . In Bancroft's *History* of the latter it is stated that towards the close of the seventeenth century the total number of the various tribes of Indians who roamed the vast regions lying between Hudson's Bay on the one side and the Mississippi valley on the other did not exceed one hundred and eighty thousand. Is it to be seriously contended that the ethical sentiment inherent in man, the conscience of mankind, should have for ever restrained both our ancestors and all other civilised people from establishing themselves on the other side of the Atlantic? Greater cruelty, greater barbarity than was exercised by the North American tribes towards one another could not easily be conceived. Wandering over enormous realms, of which the potential wealth was unknown to them, and would have been, if known, useless, these tribes scalped and slaughtered according to the natural promptings of their tiger-like hearts. Was it then the intention of the Universe that these fair regions should be for ever possessed by a few scattered savages? Has civilised mankind sinned in finding, in that vast expanse of fertile soil, new outlets for millions of its members whose whole lives must otherwise, if they had been born at all, have been 'cribbed, cabined, and confined'?

* * *

But, turning from that part of the British Empire of which, when we first came to possess it, the population was scanty in the extreme, to that other portion of it which, when conquest gave it to us, was already thronged with many millions of inhabitants, we have now to ask whether here at least the objection taken on the ground of robbery may not be valid. Suppose, then, the argument urged to have been accepted by the nations of Europe, and to have held good thenceforth for all time upon this planet. Then would that welter of chaos and bloodshed which existed in Hindustan when the arms of France and England contended there for mastery have continued so far as human eye can see into the centuries to come? War, slaughter, the countless barbarities, the unspeakable infamies which prevail under Oriental rule, would have remained unchecked by the strong hand of England; there would have been no gleam of a brighter day. And not merely would those miseries have continued which have actually been arrested, but for that still greater mass of human suffering, for which as yet not even English rule has provided a remedy, there would have been no hope of a brighter morrow. The condition of women in India, as in most if not all Oriental countries, is one of infinite misery. There, one-half of the population suffer disabilities and restraints amounting to slavery at the hands of the stronger being, man. Child marriages, with all the subsequent horrors which early widowhood there entails, have not yet been put a stop to. But the touch of our civilisation upon the mind of India has not been wholly without effect. Here and there are symptoms that the chains of a convention which has endured for unnumbered ages may be broken at last. Surely, if we believe that the order and sequence of human things tend ever upwards, we must see that it is necessary that the higher civilisation should have power to dominate the lower.

* * *

. . . Nations which use and do not abuse their opportunities grow strong and expand; those which neglect them wither, and, in the long run, become subject peoples. This is the law of the universe, and we cannot alter it.

* * *

. . . If a tree, or a blade of grass, were to arrive suddenly at a conviction that competition was immoral, and were therefore to cease to contend with its compeers for the nutriment of Mother Earth, that tree, or that blade of grass, would perish. In a strictly analogous manner, if the English people under the British flag become so altruistic as to withdraw from the ceaseless competition for national existence and the means of national growth in which for centuries past they have been engaged, the result must be that sooner or later, and probably sooner than later, they must wither away and cease to operate as a moving factor in the affairs of men.

Would that mighty disappearance tend to the advantage of mankind as a whole? Has the British people, in common with the children of its race in the United States, no appointed work and function in the life of the world? To that question history supplies an emphatic answer. Freedom, justice, the spirit of humanity, representative institutions — all these have had their origin amongst ourselves. From us the Western nations of Europe have derived whatever is best amongst them. As the English Revolution of the seventeenth century is admitted to have been the parent of the French Revolution in the eighteenth, so has the English Parliament been the great pattern which Continental peoples have striven to copy. Amongst us, as the anti-Turkish agitation, however otherwise futile, sufficiently proves, sympathy with the distressed is more poignant and more powerful than it is elsewhere. In his poem upon Nelson, Mr. Swinburne has given noble expression to this thought: —

> As earth hath but one England, crown and head
> Of all her glories, till the sun be dead,
> Supreme in war and peace, supreme in song,
> Supreme in freedom, since her rede was read,
> Since first the soul that gave her strength grew strong,
> To help the evil, and to right the wrong.

And not by example alone has the British people helped mankind, but by the might of its sea power and by the sinews of its wealth. Those very European nations which now revile and deride us owe their freedom from the yoke of Napoleon to the blood and the treasure which our great grandfathers unstintedly poured out, in the days when a bastard and spurious altruism did not obtain. And if the work accomplished by Britain in bygone time has been vast and important, not less certain is it that labour as mighty and as noble awaits her in the future, if only she look not back from the plough. In India, and in Africa, the life-history of innumerable millions of as yet unborn human creatures will depend upon whether the task of shaping their destiny shall be carried forward by us, whom the course of our history has fitted for that great duty, or shall pass to other and to harsher hands.

Of that which comes to pass when the obligations of empire have been evaded and national duty has been shunned the British people have unfortunately in their own recent record a terrible and vivid instance in the horrors occasioned by that withdrawal from the Soudan which has been already alluded to. As the direct result of that abandonment a multitude of human beings perished, whose exact number will never be known, but which certainly exceeds by ten times the whole number of the vicitims of the Armenian atrocities, . . .

At whose door then lies the responsibility for this mass of human pain, to which not Bulgaria and not Armenia offers a parallel?[3] To answer that, let us consider what were the causes which led Britain to draw back from her task in the Soudan, to leave Gordon unavenged, to leave her work undone. The causes were two. They were, first, the cry in England of the humanitarians whose tender hearts could not bear the thought of striking down what they represented as the nascent freedom of a people, and, secondly, the fact that we were at that time so deeply involved in foreign complications that our Government feared to risk an English army in Africa. The existence of the first of these two causes becomes clear to any one who either remembers or takes now the trouble to re-read the feelings expressed in the press and in Parliament at that date. The humanitarians, as usual, were too high-minded to verify their facts. Their protest was one which proceeded from a radical misconception and a complete ignorance of the actual phenomena. They supposed the rising in the Soudan to represent an heroic attempt to throw off foreign — that is to say, Egyptian — dominion. We now know the reverse of this to have been the case. The Mahdi's movement has been in the main an attempt made by slave-owning Arabs, acting with certain tribes, and using Mahomedan fanaticism as their instrument, to subjugate other tribes and to possess their goods. In this regard the humanitarians stand before the bar of history condemned by the logic of actuality.

The second of the two causes which I have named was stated by Mr. Chamberlain,[4] in a speech made in the House of Commons in the early part of last year, as his reason for having acceded to the policy of withdrawal. . . : our military resources were so limited that the locking up even of this small body of men meant that the power of England to send the necessary reinforcements to India, should war with Russia break out, was crippled.

Why was the British army so small that we were compelled to abandon several millions of human beings to misery and death? Is not the cause in a very great measure, indeed, to be found in the ceaseless cry raised by these same humanitarians and other good people of a like kidney against any increase in the national armaments? Men of the very same stamp with those who have been recently shrieking aloud that our Government should fight the world rather than allow Armenians to be massacred, or Greeks to lose their chance of annexing Crete,[5] have been the most persistent opponents of such an increase in the fleet and army of Britain as should enable her to fulfil the mission which the processes of her past have laid upon her. Between their cry against the use of armaments on the one hand, and the result of their long-sustained agitation against the maintenance of these armaments on the other, the action of Britain was paralysed, and the face of the vast region which we call the Soudan was blasted with slaughter and desolation. If we measure policy, as in this world we must measure it, not by motive but by event, it is terribly true to say that the policy at once dictated and caused by the protestmongers in 1885 has been more fatal to human life than the policy of their favourite *bête noire,* Abdul Aziz[6] himself. Abdul has killed his thousands, but the humanitarians their tens of thousands. It is they, then, who are mainly responsible, in the twofold manner already shown, for that great act of abandonment which subsequent history has declared to have been at once base and a blunder. Now, twelve years afterwards, we are tardily endeavouring to repair that fearful mistake. But no valour and no enterprise can restore the dead to life.

The head of Gordon fixed on that tree in Omdurman, whence the sightless eyes might be thought still to look in death for the help, not for himself but for his people, which in life they had sought for long, and in vain; the plains strewn with the bones of those who have died of privation and despair, or who have been struck down by their brutal captors; the memory of women who have been outraged, of children left to perish, all bear testimony never to be forgotten, while English records last, to that which follows when the weapons of England are allowed to rust, and when sentiment, in place of reason, is permitted to sway the counsels of the empire. In the Soudan, at least, the work of the sentimentalist has been brought almost to a finish. From vast tracts of country the population is gone. Wild beasts prowl in the desolated villages, and the hyena might laugh, as it clashes its jaws on the fleshless skulls of the dead, at the rich products of the new humanity.

. . . If the humanitarians do indeed wish the great nation, into which they have been born, to be the friend of the friendless and the helper of the distressed; if they really cherish the noble ambition of succouring, not the Armenians or the Cretans only, but all races or peoples that are weak and oppressed; if they desire the sword of Britain to be keen to smite the oppressor, and the arm of Britain to be strong to save, then in the name of common-sense let them see to it that the sole means of achieving these ends, the navy and the army, shall be rendered adequate to the task which they have to perform. Yet so strange a thing sometimes is human intelligence, that the very persons who are foremost in expressing what passes for generous sympathy with the victims of tyranny are usually those who are opposed most bitterly to any increase in the national armaments.

They would have Britain help—yes; but there shall be no antecedent expenditure to enable her to help effectually. They would have her risk war with the world for the sake of the suffering—yes; but they would not vote for one extra battleship to put her in a position to war successfully. Between the thought of the righteousness of risking a conflict and the thought of what would happen if the conflict actually began, there seems to be, for these persons, a mental gulf as untraversable as that which separated Dives from Lazarus.

Probably, however, the root cause of this astonishing discontinuity is to be found in the prevalence of the same profound fallacy which has been referred to earlier in this article. For if you press a sentimentalist, he will tell you at last that it is the duty of a nation, as of an individual, to 'follow the right' (by which he means, to obey any generous impulse), without conuting the cost. Evidently here arises again the old false analogy between the State and a single citizen of the State with which we have dealt before.

As a nation is imagined by the humanitarians to own its territory in the same manner in which a man owns an umbrella, so is it also imagined by them to be free, as an individual is sometimes free, to sacrifice itself for the sake of others. . . .

That the case is the reverse of this we all know. The responsibilities of the State are as much more tremendous than those of the individual as the aggregate of its interests exceeds his. Lord Salisbury[7] has recently said with much emphasis that the Government are in the position of trustees towards the nation. The simile might be extended, for it is equally true to say that the whole nation is in the position of a trustee towards posterity. This one living generation of British men and British women, who now walk this world's stage, does not constitute the whole British people. Far back into the past, and, surely, far forward into the future, the chain, of which we are but one link, extends. Inheritors of a mighty trust, we are bound by the whole course of our history, up to now, to pass it on, inviolate, to those who shall follow. For ages past, the labour of dead generations has been building up the house of the British nation. For centuries, our national character has been taking form under the impulse of some of the greatest spirits whom earth has known. In Asia and in Africa great native populations have passed under our hand. To us—to us, and not to others, a certain definite duty has been assigned. To carry light and civilisation into the dark places of the world; to touch the mind of Asia and of Africa with the ethical ideas of Europe; to give to thronging millions, who would otherwise never know peace or security, these first conditions of human advance: constructive endeavour such as this forms part of the function which it is ours to discharge. Once more—to fill the wide waste places of Australia and Canada with the children of Britain; to people with our race the lofty plateau through which the Zambesi rolls down towards the sea, and whence of old the sailors of Tyre brought the gold of Ophir to the temple of Solomon; to draw from the soil, or from beneath the soil, the wealth hoarded for uncounted ages for the service of man; and, lastly, to let the sound of the English tongue and the pure life of English homes give to the future of those immense regions its hue and shape: this, again, is a portion of the task which our past has devolved upon us.

Have we the moral right, supposing us to have the moral feebleness, to cast from us, as a thing of no account, this vast world-work which previous centuries have entrusted to our care? From the moment when Drake, three hundred years ago, lying on his face on the edge of the wild rock that forms the southernmost extremity of the American continent, looked out upon that Pacific Ocean whose waters he was first 'to plough with an English keel,' even up to the present day, the duty of Britain has been in process of birth and in process of growth. Has not a nation, like an individual—for here at length the analogy holds—a certain appointed task which, beyond all other nations, it is fitted to perform? Wilfully to neglect this ordained labour is, so to speak, the one unforgiveable sin, because it is to defeat the purpose of the Universe as shown in the aptitudes which have been produced by the previous course of things. To sustain worthily the burden of empire is the task manifestly appointed to Britain, and therefore to fulfil that task is her duty, as it should also be her delight. But if that duty should be opposed, if her path should be traversed by some rival State, what then would be the necessity laid upon the British Government and people? Evidently, if the considerations already advanced are valid, it then becomes straitly incumbent upon them to resist the assailant with the entire force which they can exert.

Viewed from this standpoint, it will be seen that the adequate maintenance of the national armaments is not merely a vital need, prompted by the strongest conceivable motives of self-interest, but also, in very truth, a high and sacred obligation of morality. Not to heed that obligation means that we are ready lightly to lay aside the work which constitutes the chief justification for our existence as a people among mankind. It means that we are contemners of the past, that we are faithless to charge, that we are as fraudulent life-tenants with regard to our heirs. First of all duties, because the primary condition of the fulfilment of all duties, is the obligation of self-defence.

Well is it indeed for us, in the presence of persons who cut their emotion loose from their reason, and let it run amuck in the world like a mad Malay, that in the fulness of time the old idea of devotion to the nation, and of debt owed to the nation, has at last begun to revive. As a little leaven leaveneth the whole lump, so has the Imperial idea, held ten years ago but by a few, spread until it has become a vital force. In the possessions of the British people beyond the seas, as in these islands, there are men who are working in utter earnest to recall to their countrymen those thoughts and those high impulses which gave them strength in days gone by. As the years roll on, a wider patriotism and a deeper resolve are becoming perceptible. There is growing into existence a sentiment of national being which overleaps the ocean, so that, to those whom it possesses, it matters not whether they were born in Cape Town or in London, in Melbourne or in Montreal. Equally are they members of one mighty community, and equally are they heirs to that mastery of the seas which must ultimately carry with it the hegemony of mankind.

NOTES

1. Prime Minister Gladstone concluded a peace treaty at Pretoria, April 5, 1881, recognizing the independence of Transvaal under British suzerainty, after the Boer revolt of December 1880 and the defeat of a small British force at Majuba Hill, February 27, 1881.

2. Following British occupation of Egypt, Gladstone sent General Charles Gordon to assure the Egyptian government's agreement upon evacuation of the Sudan and to try to reach a settlement with the Sudanese rebel leader, the Mahdi Mohammed Ahmed; reinforcements for Gordon were despatched too late, and he was massacred with his force by the Mahdi's forces at Khartoum, January 26, 1885.

3. Turkey crushed insurrection in Bulgaria, 1876, and in Armenia, 1894, with considerable savagery, provoking public outcry in western Europe.

4. Joseph Chamberlain, Secretary of State for Colonies in Lord Salisbury's ministry.

5. A Cretan revolt, fomented by Greece, in 1896, resulted in a Greco-Turkish war, 1897, from which the Greeks and Cretans were rescued only by European intervention and a settlement imposed by the great Powers securing a measure of Cretan autonomy under Ottoman sovereignty. Not until 1913 was Greece permitted to annex the island.

6. Sultan of Turkey, who repressed Christian uprisings in the empire until deposed by mob action in Constantinople, 1876.

7. Three times Prime Minister, and an outstanding Conservative Foreign Secretary who helped retain Britain's prestige in the Bismarckian era and after.

13

"Some Favored a United States Protectorate, Some Annexation, Some Free Cuba"

THE United States was tempted in the same way as England. Renewed revolt in Cuba after February 1895, luridly reported in the press, cast Spain in the worst light. The sinking of the Maine, *and the revelation of the Spanish Ambassador's low opinion of President McKinley, brought bellicose opinion to flashpoint. Senator Redfield Proctor (1831–1908), a Republican businessman, former Governor of Vermont and Secretary of War, told the Senate what he had observed on the island. Calm and yet strongly suggestive, his report was effective in rallying conservative opinion to the cause of compelling McKinley to request a state of war with Spain.*

Redfield Proctor's Speech to the Senate: March 17, 1898

MR. PRESIDENT, more importance seems to be attached by others to my recent visit to Cuba than I have given it, and it has been suggested that I make a public statement of what I saw and how the situation impressed me. This I do on account of the public interest in all that concerns Cuba, and to correct some inaccuracies that have, not unnaturally, appeared in reported interviews with me.

My trip was entirely unofficial and of my own motion, not suggested by anyone. The only mention I made of it to the President was to say to him that I contemplated such a trip and to ask him if there was any objection to it; to which he replied that he could see none.

From THE CONGRESSIONAL RECORD *(Washington), Senate, March 17, 1898 (55th Congress, 2nd Session), vol. 31, pt. 3, pp. 2916–2919.*

No one but myself, therefore, is responsible for anything in this statement. Judge Day gave me a brief note of introduction to General Lee,[1] and I had letters of introduction from business friends at the North to bankers and other business men at Habana, and they in turn gave me letters to their correspondents in other cities. These letters to business men were very useful, as one of the principal purposes of my visit was to ascertain the views of practical men of affairs upon the situation.

* * *

The Maine

It has been stated that I said there was no doubt the *Maine* was blown up from the outside. This is a mistake. I may have said that such was the general impression among Americans in Habana. In fact, I have no opinion about it myself, and carefully avoided forming one. I gave no attention to these outside surmises. I met the members of the court on their boat, but would as soon approach our Supreme Court in regard to a pending cause as that board. They are as competent and trustworthy within the lines of their duty as any court in the land, and their report, when made, will carry conviction to all the people that the exact truth has been stated just as far as it is possible to ascertain it. Until then surmise and conjecture are idle and unprofitable. Let us calmly wait for the report.

Sections visited

There are six provinces in Cuba, each, with the exception of Matanzas, extending the whole width of the island, and having about an equal sea front on the north and south borders. Matanzas touches the Caribbean Sea only at its southwest corner being separated from it elsewhere by a narrow peninsula of Santa Clara Province. The provinces are named, beginning at the west, Pinar del Rio, Habana, Matanzas, Santa Clara, Puerto Principe, and Santiago de Cuba. My observations were confined to the four western provinces, which constitute about one-half of the island. The two eastern ones are practically in the hands of the insurgents, except the few fortified towns. These two large provinces are spoken of to-day as "Cuba Libre."

Habana, the great city and capital of the island, is, in the eyes of the Spaniards and many Cubans, all Cuba, as much as Paris is France.

But having visited it in more peaceful times and seen its sights, the tomb of Columbus, the forts—Cabana and Morro Castle, etc.—I did not care to repeat this, preferring trips in the country. Everything seems to go on much as usual in Habana. Quiet prevails, and except for the frequent squads of soldiers marching to guard and police duty and their abounding presence in all public places, one sees few signs of war.

Outside Habana all is changed. It is not peace nor is it war. It is desolation and distress, misery and starvation. Every town and village is surrounded by a "trocha" (trench), a sort of rifle pit, but constructed on a plan new to me, the dirt being thrown up on the inside and a barbed-wire fence on the outer side of the trench. These trochas have at every corner and at frequent intervals along the sides what are there called forts, but which are really small blockhouses, many of them more like large sentry boxes, loopholed for musketry, and with a guard of from two to ten soldiers in each.

The purpose of these trochas is to keep the reconcentrados in as well as to keep the insurgents out. From all the surrounding country the people have been driven in to these fortified towns and held there to subsist as they can. They are virtually prison yards, and not unlike one in general appearance, except that the walls are not so high and strong; but they suffice, where every point is in range of a soldier's rifle, to keep in the poor reconcentrado women and children.

Every railroad station is within one of these trochas and has an armed guard. Every train has an armored freight car, loopholed for musketry and filled with soldiers, and with, as I observed usually, and was informed is always the case, a pilot engine a mile or so in advance. There are frequent blockhouses inclosed by a trocha and with a guard along the railroad track. With this exception there is no human life or habitation between these fortified towns and villages, and throughout the whole of the four western provinces, except to a very limited extent among the hills where the Spaniards have not been able to go and drive the people to the towns and burn their dwellings. I saw no house or hut in the 400 miles of railroad rides from Pinar del Rio Province in the west across the full width of Habana and Matanzas provinces, and to Sagua La Grande on the north shore, and to Cienfuegos on the south shore of Santa Clara, except within the Spanish trochas.

There are no domestic animals or crops on the rich fields and pastures except such as are under guard in the immediate vicinity of the towns. In other words, the Spaniards hold in these four western provinces just what their army sits on. Every man, woman, and child, and every domestic animal, wherever their columns have reached, is under guard and within their so-called fortifications. To describe one place is to describe all. To repeat, it is neither peace nor war. It is concentration and desolation. This is the "pacified" condition of the four western provinces.

West of Habana is mainly the rich tobacco country; east, so far as I went, a sugar region. Nearly all the sugar mills are destroyed between Habana and Sagua. Two or three were standing in the vicinity of Sagua, and in part running, surrounded, as are the villages, by trochas and "forts" or palisades of the royal palm, and fully guarded. Toward and near Cienfuegos there were more mills running, but all with the same protection. It is said that the owners of these mills near Cienfuegos have been able to obtain special favors of the Spanish Government in the way of a large force of soldiers, but that they also, as well as all the railroads, pay taxes to the Cubans for immunity. I had no means of verifying this. It is the common talk among those who have better means of knowledge.

The reconcentrados—the country people

All the country people in the four western provinces, about 400,000 in number, remaining outside the fortified towns when Weyler's[2] order was made were driven into these towns, and these are the reconcentrados. They were the peasantry, many of them farmers, some landowners, others renting lands and owning more or less stock, others working on estates and cultivating small patches; and even a small patch in that fruitful clime will support a family.

It is but fair to say that the normal condition of these people was very different from what prevails in this country. Their standard of comfort and prosperity was not high measured by ours. But according to their standards and requirements their conditions of life were satisfactory.

They lived mostly in cabins made of palms or in wooden houses. Some of them had houses of stone, the blackened walls of which are all that remain to show the country was ever inhabited.

The first clause of Weyler's order reads as follows:

I ORDER AND COMMAND.

First. All the inhabitants of the country or outside of the line of fortifications of the towns shall, within the period of eight days, concentrate themselves in the towns occupied by the troops.

Any individual who, after the expiration of this period, is found in the uninhabited parts will be considered a rebel and tried as such.

The other three sections forbid the transportation of provisions from one town to another without permission of the military authority, direct the owners of cattle to bring them into the towns, prescribe that the eight days shall be counted from the publication of the proclamation in the head town of the municipal district, and state that if news is furnished of the enemy which can be made use of, it will serve as a "recommendation."

Many, doubtless, did not learn of this order. Others failed to grasp its terrible meaning. Its execution was left largely to the guerrillas to drive in all that had not obeyed, and I was informed that in many cases the torch was applied to their homes with no notice, and the inmates fled with such clothing as they might have on, their stock and other belongings being appropriated by the guerrillas. When they reached the towns, they were allowed to build huts of palm leaves in the suburbs and vacant places within the trochas, and left to live, if they could.

Their huts are about 10 by 15 feet in size, and for want of space are usually crowded together very closely. They have no floor but the ground, no furniture, and, after a year's wear, but little clothing except such stray substitutes as they can extemporize; and with large families, or more than one, in this little space, the commonest sanitary provisions are impossible. Conditions are unmentionable in this respect. Torn from their homes, with foul earth, foul air, foul water, and foul food or none, what wonder that one-half have died and that one-quarter of the living are so diseased that they can not be saved? A form of dropsy is a common disorder resulting from these conditions. Little children are still walking about with arms and chest terribly emaciated, eyes swollen, and abdomen bloated to three times the natural size. The physicians say these cases are hopeless.

Deaths in the streets have not been uncommon. I was told by one of our consuls that they have been found dead about the markets in the morning, where they had crawled, hoping to get some stray bits of food from the early hucksters, and that there had been cases where they had dropped dead inside the market surrounded by food. Before Weyler's order, these people were independent and self-supporting. They are not beggars even now. There are plenty of professional beggars in every town among the regular residents, but these country people, the reconcentrados, have not learned the art. Rarely is a hand held out to you for alms when going among their huts, but the sight of them makes an appeal stronger than words.

The hospitals

Of these I need not speak. Others have described their condition far better than I can. It is not within the narrow limits of my vocabulary to portray it. I went to Cuba with a strong conviction that the picture had been overdrawn; that a few cases of starvation and suffering had inspired and stimulated the press correspondents, and that they had given free play to a strong, natural, and highly cultivated imagination.

Before starting I received through the mail a leaflet published by the Christian Herald, with cuts of some of the sick and starving reconcentrados, and took it with me, thinking these must be rare specimens, got up to make the worst possible showing. I saw plenty as bad and worse; many that should not be photographed and shown.

I could not believe that out of a population of 1,600,000, two hundred thousand had died within these Spanish forts, practically prison walls, within a few months past from actual starvation and diseases caused by insufficient and improper food. My inquiries were entirely outside of sensational sources. They were made of our medical officers, of our consuls, of city alcaldes (mayors), of relief committees, of leading merchants and bankers, physicians, and lawyers. Several of my informants were Spanish born, but every time the answer was that the case had not been overstated. What I saw I can not tell so that others can see it. It must be seen with one's own eyes to be realized.

The Los Pasos Hospital, in Habana, has been recently described by one of my colleagues, Senator GALLINGER, and I can not say that his picture was overdrawn, for even his fertile pen could not do that. But he visited it after Dr. Lesser, one of Miss Barton's very able and efficient assistants, had renovated it and put in cots. I saw it when 400 women and children were lying on the floors in an indescribable state of emaciation and disease, many with the scantiest covering of rags — and such rags! — sick children, naked as they came into the world; and the conditions in the other cities are even worse.

* * *

When will the need for this help end? Not until peace comes and the reconcentrados can go back to the country, rebuild their homes, reclaim their tillage plots, which quickly run up to brush in that wonderful soil and clime, and until they can be free from danger of molestation in so doing. Until then the American people must in the main care for them. It is true that the alcaldes, other local authorities, and the relief committees are now trying to do something, and desire, I believe, to do the best they can. But the problem is beyond their means and capacity, and the work is one to which they are not accustomed.

General Blanco's[3] order of November 13 last somewhat modifies the Weyler order, but is of little or no practical benefit. Its application is limited to farms "properly defended," and the owners are obliged to build "centers of defense." Its execution is completely in the discretion of the local military authorities, and they know the terrible military efficiency of Weyler's order in stripping the country of all possible shelter, food, or source of information for an insurgent, and will be slow to surrender this advantage. In fact, though the order was issued four months ago, I saw no beneficent results from it worth mentioning.

I do not impugn General Blanco's motives, and believe him to be an amiable gentleman, and that he would be glad to relieve the condition of the reconcentrados if he could do so without loss of any military advantage; but he knows that all Cubans are insurgents at heart, and none now under military control will be allowed to go out from under it.

I wish I might speak of the country — of its surpassing richness. I have never seen one to compare with it. On this point I agree with Columbus, that this is the "most rich and beautiful that ever human eye beheld," and believe everyone between his time and mine must be of the same opinion. It is indeed a land —

> Where every prospect pleases
> And only man is vile.

The Spaniard

I had little time to study the race question, and have read nothing on it, so can only give hasty impressions. It is said that there are nearly 200,000 Spaniards in Cuba out of a total population of 1,600,000. They live principally in the towns and cities. The small shopkeepers in the towns and their clerks are mostly Spaniards. Much of the larger business, too, and of the property in the cities, and in a less degree in the country, is in their hands. They have an eye to thrift, and as everything possible in the way of trade and legalized monopolies, in which the country abounds, is given to them by the Government, many of them acquire property. I did not learn that the Spanish residents of the island had contributed largely in blood or treasure to suppress the insurrection.

The Cuban

There are, or were before the war, about 1,000,000 Cubans on the island, 200,000 Spaniards (which means those born in Spain), and less than half a million of negroes and mixed bloods. The Cuban whites are of pure Spanish blood and, like the Spaniards, dark in complexion, but oftener light or blond, so far as I noticed. The percentage of colored to white has been steadily diminishing for more than fifty years, and is not now over 25 per cent of the total. In fact, the number of colored people has been actually diminishing for nearly that time. The Cuban farmer and laborer is by nature peaceable, kindly, gay, hospitable, light-hearted, and improvident.

There is a proverb among the Cubans that "Spanish bulls can not be bred in Cuba"—that is, Cubans, though they are of Spanish blood, are less excitable and of a quieter temperament. Many Cubans whom I met spoke in strong terms against the bull fights: that it was a brutal institution, introduced and mainly patronized by the Spaniards. One thing that was new to me was to learn the superiority of the well-to-do Cuban over the Spaniard in the matter of education. Among those in good circumstances there can be no doubt that the Cuban is far superior in this respect. And the reason of it is easy to see. They have been educated in England, France, or this country, while the Spaniard has such education as his own country furnishes.

* * *

The political situation

The dividing lines between parties are the straightest and clearest cut that have ever come to my knowledge. The division in our war was by no means so clearly defined. It is Cuban against Spaniard. It is practically the entire Cuban population on one side and the Spanish army and Spanish citizens on the other.

I do not count the autonomists in this division, as they are so far too inconsiderable in numbers to be worth counting. General Blanco filled the civil offices with men who had been autonomists and were still classed as such. But the march of events had satisfied most of them that the chance for autonomy came too late.

It falls as talk of compromise would have fallen the last year or two of our war. If it succeeds, it can only be by armed force, by the triumph of the Spanish army, and the success of Spanish arms would be easier by Weyler's policy and method, for in that the Spanish army and people believe.

There is no doubt that General Blanco is acting in entire good faith; that he desires to give the Cubans a fair measure of autonomy, as Campos[4] did at the close of the ten-year war. He has, of course, a few personal followers, but the army and the Spanish citizens do not want genuine autonomy, for that means government by the Cuban people. And it is not strange that the Cubans say it comes too late.

I have never had any communication, direct or indirect, with the Cuban Junta in this country or any of its members, nor did I have with any of the juntas which exist in every city and large town of Cuba. None of the calls I made were upon parties of whose sympathies I had the least knowledge, except that I knew some of them were classed as autonomists.

Most of my informants were business men, who had taken no sides and rarely expressed themselves. I had no means of guessing in advance what their answers would be, and was in most cases greatly surprised at their frankness.

I inquired in regard to autonomy of men of wealth and men as prominent in business as any in the cities of Habana, Matanzas, and Sagua, bankers, merchants, lawyers, and autonomist officials, some of them Spanish born but Cuban bred, one prominent Englishman, several of them known as autonomists, and several of them telling me that they were still believers in autonomy if practicable, but without exception they replied that it was "too late" for that.

Some favored a United States protectorate, some annexation, some free Cuba; not one has been counted favoring the insurrection at first. They were business men and wanted peace, but said it was too late for peace under Spanish sovereignty. They characterized Weyler's order in far stronger terms than I can. I could not but conclude that you do not have to scratch an autonomist very deep to find a Cuban. There is soon to be an election, but every polling place must be inside a fortified town. Such elections ought to be safe for the "ins".

I have endeavored to state in not intemperate mood what I saw and heard, and to make no argument thereon, but leave everyone to draw his own conclusions. To me the strongest appeal is not the barbarity practiced by Weyler nor the loss of the *Maine,* if our worst fears should prove true, terrible as are both of these incidents, but the spectacle of a million and a half of people, the entire native population of Cuba, struggling for freedom and deliverance from the worst misgovernment of which I ever had knowledge. But whether our action ought to be influenced by any one or all these things, and, if so, how far, is another question.

I am not in favor of annexation: not because I would apprehend any particular trouble from it, but because it is not wise policy to take in any people of foreign tongue and training, and without any strong guiding American element. The fear that if free the people of Cuba would be revolutionary is not so well founded as has been supposed, and the conditions for good self-goverment are far more favorable. The large number of educated and patriotic men, the great sacrifices they have endured, the peaceable temperament of the people, whites and blacks, the wonderful prosperity that would surely come with peace and good home rule, the large influx of American and English immigration and money, would all be strong factors for stable institutions.

But it is not my purpose at this time, nor do I consider it my province, to suggest any plan. I merely speak of the symptoms as I saw them, but do not undertake to prescribe. Such remedial steps as may be required may safely be left to an American President and the American people.

NOTES

1. U.S. Consul in Havana.

2. General Valeriano Weyler y Nicolau, Governor of Cuba, 1896–97, recalled by the liberal ministry in Spain in the autumn of 1897.

3. General Ramón Blanco y Erenas, Weyler's more liberal successor, who introduced "autonomy" to the island following Spanish military collapse, but with no great calming effect on the revolt.

4. General Arsenio Martínez de Campos, statesman, political counsellor to the Spanish royal family, "pacifier" of Cuba in 1878.

14

"Every One Must Put His Hand to the Work Which Falls to His Share"

INTERNATIONAL *conflict had its domestic counterpart. The quarrel between rich and poor became so sharp that under Leo XIII the Catholic Church felt moved to recall men to their obligations and duties. Born Gioacchino Pecci (1810–1903), of an impoverished aristocratic family, Leo served as Bishop of Perugia from 1846 until his elevation to the Holy See, February 20, 1878. Old and frail, he continued along a mildly reformist path for 25 years, as hostile to the Italian state as Pio Nono before him, but working otherwise for better Church-state relations in the Christian world. Austere, economical and literate, he died at 93 on July 20, 1903.*

De Rerum Novarum: May 15, 1891

To our Venerable Brethren, All Patriarchs, Primates, Archbishops, and Bishops of the Catholic World, in grace and communion with the Apostolic See, Pope Leo XIII. Venerable Brethren, Health and Apostolic Benediction

IT IS NOT surprising that the spirit of revolutionary change, which has long been predominant in the nations of the world, should have passed beyond politics and made its influence felt in the cognate field of practical economy. The elements of a conflict are unmistakable: the growth of industry, and the surprising discoveries of science; the changed relations of masters and workmen; the enormous fortunes of individuals, and the poverty of the masses; the

From ENCYCLICAL LETTER OF OUR HOLY FATHER BY DIVINE PROVIDENCE POPE LEO XIII ON THE CONDITION OF LABOR *(Boston, n.d.), pp. 1–16.*

increased self-reliance and the closer mutual combination of the working population; and, finally, a general moral deterioration. The momentous seriousness of the present state of things just now fills every mind with painful apprehension; wise men discuss it; practical men propose schemes; popular meetings, legislatures, and sovereign princes, all are occupied with it—and there is nothing which has a deeper hold on public attention.

Therefore, Venerable Brethren, as on former occasions, when it seemed opportune to refute false teaching, We have addressed you in the interests of the Church and of the common weal, and have issued Letters on Political Power, on Human Liberty, on the Christian Constitution of the State, and on similar subjects, so now We have thought it useful to speak on

The condition of labor

It is a matter on which We have touched once or twice already. But in this Letter the responsibility of the Apostolic office urges Us to treat the question expressly and at length, in order that there may be no mistake as to the principles which truth and justice dictate for its settlement. The discussion is not easy, nor is it free from danger. It is not easy to define the relative rights and the mutual duties of the wealthy and of the poor, of capital and of labor. And the danger lies in this, that crafty agitators constantly make use of these disputes to pervert men's judgments and to stir up the people to sedition.

But all agree, and there can be no question whatever, that some remedy must be found, and quickly found, for the misery and wretchedness which press so heavily at this moment on the large majority of the very poor. The ancient workmen's Guilds were destroyed in the last century, and no other organization took their place. Public institutions and the laws have repudiated the ancient religion. Hence by degrees it has come to pass that Working Men have been given over, isolated and defenceless, to the callousness of employers and the greed of unrestrained competition. The evil has been increased by rapacious Usury, which, although more than once condemned by the Church, is nevertheless, under a different form but with the same guilt, still practised by avaricious and grasping men. And to this must be added the custom of working by contract, and the concentration of so many branches of trade in the hands of a few individuals, so that a small number of very rich men have been able to lay upon the masses of the poor a yoke little better than slavery itself.

Socialists and private property

To remedy these evils the *Socialists,* working on the poor man's envy of the rich, endeavor to destroy private property, and maintain that individual possessions should become the common property of all, to be administered by the State or by municipal bodies. They hold that, by thus transferring property from private persons to the community, the present evil state of things will be set to rights, because each citizen will then have his equal share of whatever there is to enjoy. But their proposals are so clearly futile for all practical purposes, that if they were carried out the working man himself would be among the first to suffer. Moreover they are emphatically unjust, because they would rob the lawful possessor, bring the State into a sphere that is not its own, and cause complete confusion in the community.

. . . The *Socialists,* therefore, in endeavoring to transfer the possessions of individuals to the community, strike at the interests of every wage-earner, for they deprive him of the liberty of disposing of his wages, and thus of all hope and possibility of increasing his stock and of bettering his condition in life.

Man's natural right to private property

What is of still greater importance, however, is that the remedy they propose is manifestly against justice. For every man has by nature the right to possess property as his own. This is one of the chief points of distinction between man and the animal creation. For the brute has no power of self-direction, but is governed by two chief instincts, which keep his powers alert, move him to use his strength, and determine him to action without the power of choice. These instincts are self-preservation and the propagation of the species. Both can attain their purpose by means of things which are close at hand; beyond their surroundings the brute creation cannot go, for they are moved to action by sensibility alone, and by the things which sense perceives. But with man it is different indeed. He possesses, on the one hand, the full perfection of animal nature, and therefore he enjoys, at least as much as the rest of the animal race, the fruition of the things of the body. But animality, however perfect, is far from being the whole of humanity, and is indeed humanity's humble handmaid, made to serve and obey. It is the mind, or the reason, which is the chief thing in us who are human beings; it is this which makes a human being human, and distinguishes him essentially and completely from the brute. And on this account—viz., that man alone among animals possesses reason—it must be within his right to have things not merely for temporary and momentary use, as other living beings have them, but in stable and permanent possession; he must have not only things which perish in the using, but also those which, though used, remain for use in the future.

This becomes still more clearly evident if we consider man's nature a little more deeply. For man, comprehending by the power of his reason things innumerable, and joining the future with the present—being, moreover, the master of his own acts—governs himself by the foresight of his counsel, under the eternal law and the power of God Whose Providence governs all things. Wherefore it is in his power to exercise his choice not only on things which regard his present welfare, but also on those which will be for his advantage in time to come. Hence man not only can possess the fruits of the earth, but also the earth itself; for of the products of the earth he can make provision for the future. Man's needs do not die out, but recur; satisfied to-day, they demand new supplies to-morrow. Nature, therefore, owes to man a storehouse that shall never fail, the daily supply of his daily wants. And this he finds only in the inexhaustible fertility of the earth.

Nor must we, at this stage, have recourse to the State.

Man is older than the state;

And he holds the right of providing for the life of his body prior to the formation of any State. And to say that God has given the earth to the use and enjoyment of the universal human race is not to deny that there can be private property. For God has granted the earth to mankind in general; not in the sense that all without distinction can deal with it as they please, but rather that no part of it has been assigned to any one in particular, and that the limits of private possession have been left to be fixed by man's own industry and the laws of individual peoples. . . .

. . . For that which is required for the preservation of life, and for life's well-being, is produced in great abundance by the earth, but not until man has brought it into cultivation and lavished upon it his care and skill. Now, when man thus spends the industry of his mind and the strength of his body in procuring the fruits of nature, by that act he makes his own that portion of nature's field which he cultivates — that portion on which he leaves, as it were, the impress of his own personality; and it cannot but be just that he should possess that portion as his own, and should have a right to keep it without molestation. . . .

* * *

That right of property, therefore, which has been proved to belong naturally to individual persons, must also belong to a man in his capacity of head of a family; nay, such a person must possess this right so much the more clearly in proportion as his position multiplies his duties. For it is a most sacred law of nature that a father must provide food and all necessaries for those whom he has begotten; and, similarly, nature dictates that a man's children, who carry on, as it were, and continue his own personality, should be provided by him with all that is needful to enable them honorably to keep themselves from want and misery in the uncertainties of this mortal life. Now in no other way can a father effect this except by the ownership of profitable property, which he can transmit to his children by inheritance. A family, no less than a State, is, as We have said, a true society, governed by a power within itself, that is to say, by the father. Wherefore, provided the limits be not transgressed which are prescribed by the very purposes for which it exists, the Family has, at least, equal rights with the State in the choice and pursuit of those things which are needful to its preservation and its just liberty.

The state may not abolish nor absorb paternal rights

The idea, then, that the civil government should, at its own discretion, penetrate and pervade the family and the household, is a great and pernicious mistake. True, if a family finds itself in great difficulty, utterly friendless, and without prospect of help, it is right that extreme necessity be met by public aid; for each family is a part of the commonwealth. In like manner, if within the walls of the household there occur grave disturbance of mutual rights, the public power must interfere to force each party to give the other what is due; for this is not to rob citizens of their rights, but justly and properly to safeguard and strengthen them. But the rulers of the State must go no further: nature bids them stop here. . . .

. . . The Socialists, therefore, in setting aside the parent and introducing the providence of the State, act *against natural justice,* and threaten the very existence of family life.

* * *

Thus it is clear that the main tenet of *Socialism,* the community of goods, must be utterly rejected; for it would injure those whom it is intended to benefit, it would be contrary to the natural rights of mankind, and it would introduce confusion and disorder into the commonwealth.

* * *

Let it be laid down, in the first place, that humanity must remain as it is. It is impossible to reduce human society to a level. The *Socialists* may do their utmost, but all striving against nature is vain. There naturally exist among mankind innumerable differences of the most important kind; people differ in capability, in diligence, in health, and in strength; and unequal fortune is a necessary result of inequality in condition. Such inequality is far from being disadvantageous either to individuals or to the community; social and public life can only go on by the help of various kinds of capacity and the playing of many parts, and each man, as a rule, chooses the part which peculiarly suits his case. . . .

. . . To suffer and to endure, therefore, is the lot of humanity; let men try as they may, no strength and no artifice will ever succeed in banishing from human life the ills and troubles which beset it. If any there are who pretend differently — who hold out to a hard-pressed people freedom from pain and trouble, undisturbed repose, and constant enjoyment — they cheat the people and impose upon them, and their lying promises will only make the evil worse than before. There is nothing more useful than to look at the world as it really is—and at the same time to look elsewhere for a remedy to its troubles.

The Christian interdependence of capital and labor

The great mistake that is made in the matter now under consideration, is to possess oneself of the idea that class is naturally hostile to class; that rich and poor are intended by nature to live at war with one another. So irrational and so false is this view, that the exact contrary is the truth. . . . Mutual agreement results in pleasantness and good order; perpetual conflict necessarily produces confusion and outrage. Now, in preventing such strife as this, and in making it impossible, the efficacy of Christianity is marvelous and manifold.

. . . Thus Religion teaches the laboring man and the workman to carry out honestly and well all equitable agreements freely made; never to injure capital, nor to outrage the person of an employer; never to employ violence in representing his own cause, nor to engage in riot and disorder; and to have nothing to do with men of evil principles, who work upon the people with artful promises, and raise foolish hopes which usually end in disaster and in repentance when too late. Religion teaches the rich man and the employer that their workpeople are not their slaves; that they must respect in every man his dignity as a man and as a Christian; that labor is nothing to be ashamed of, if we listen to right reason and to Christian philosophy, but is an honorable employment, enabling a man to sustain his life in an upright and creditable way; and that it is shameful and inhuman to treat men like chattels to make money by, or to look upon them merely as so much muscle or physical power. . . . Doubtless before we can decide whether wages are adequate, many things have to be considered; but rich men and masters should remember this—that to exercise pressure for the sake of gain, upon the indigent and the destitute, and to make one's profit out of the need of another, is condemned by all laws, human and divine. . . .

* * *

Christianity teaches practically the right use of money

. . . Whoever has received from the Divine bounty a large share of blessings, whether they be external and corporal, or gifts of the mind, has received them for the purpose of using them for the perfecting of his own nature, and, at the same time, that he may employ them, as the minister of God's Providence, for the benefit of others. *He that hath a talent,* says St. Gregory the Great, *let him see that he hideth not; he that hath abundance, let him arouse himself to mercy and generosity; he that hath art and skill, let him do his best to share the use and the utility thereof with his neighbor.*

The dignity of labor

As for those who do not possess the gifts of fortune, they are taught by the Church that, in God's sight, poverty is no disgrace, and that there is nothing to be ashamed of in seeking one's bread by labor. . . .

* * *

Social evils to be remedied only by return to Christian life and institutions

. . . When a society is perishing, the true advice to give to those who would restore it is, to recall it to the principles from which it sprung; for the purpose and perfection of an association is to aim at and to attain that for which it was formed; and its operation should be put in motion and inspired by the end and object which originally gave it its being. . . .

The Church seeks the material welfare of the poor

Neither must it be supposed that the solicitude of the Church is so occupied with the spiritual concerns of its children as to neglect their interests temporal and earthly. Its desire is that the poor, for example, should rise above poverty and wretchedness, and should better their condition in life; and for this it strives. By the very fact that it calls men to virtue and forms them to its practice, it promotes this in no slight degree. Christian morality, when it is adequately and completely practised, conduces of itself to temporal prosperity, for it merits the blessing of that God who is the source of all blessings; it powerfully restrains the lust of possession and the lust of pleasure —twin plagues, which too often make a man without self-restraint miserable in the midst of abundance; it makes men supply by economy for the want of means, teaching them to be content with frugal living, and keeping them out of the reach of those vices which eat up not merely small incomes, but large fortunes, and dissipate many a goodly inheritance.

Moreover, the Church intervenes directly in the interest of the poor, by setting on foot and keeping up many things which it sees to be efficacious in the relief of poverty. . . .

. . . The Church has stirred up everywhere the heroism of charity, and has established Congregations of Religious and many other useful institutions for help and mercy, so that there might be hardly any kind of suffering which was not visited and relieved. At the present day there are many who, like the heathen of old, blame and condemn the Church for this beautiful charity. They would substitute in its place a system of State-organized relief. But no human methods will ever supply for the devotion and self-sacrifice of Christian charity. Charity, as a virtue, belongs to the Church; for it is no virtue unless it is drawn from the Sacred Heart of Jesus Christ; and he who turns his back on the Church cannot be near to Christ.

The state's share in the relief of poverty

. . . The first duty, therefore, of the rulers of the State should be to make sure that the laws and institutions, the general character and administration of the commonwealth, shall be such as to produce of themselves public well-being and private prosperity. . . . And the more that is done for the working population by the general laws of the country, the less need will there be to seek for particular means to relieve them. There is another and a deeper consideration which must not be lost sight of.

To the state the interests of all are equal

. . . No matter what changes may be made in forms of government, there will always be differences and inequalities of condition in the State; Society cannot exist or be conceived without them. Some there must be who dedicate themselves to the work of the commonwealth, who make the laws, who administer justice, whose advice and authority govern the nation in times of peace, and defend it in war. Such men clearly occupy the foremost place in the State, and should be held in the foremost estimation, for their work touches most nearly and effectively the general interest of the community. Those who labor at a trade or calling do not promote the general welfare in such a fashion as this; but they do in the most important way benefit the nation, though less directly. We have insisted that, since it is the end of Society to make men better, the chief good that Society can be possessed of is Virtue. Nevertheless, in all well-constituted States it is a by no means unimportant matter to provide those bodily and external commodities, *the use of which is necessary to virtuous action.*[1] . . .

It is only by the labor of the working man that states grow rich

Justice, therefore, demands that the interests of the poorer population be carefully watched over by the Administration, so that they who contribute so largely to the advantage of the community may themselves share in the benefits they create — that being housed, clothed, and enabled to support life, they may find their existence less hard and more endurable. It follows that whatever shall appear to be conducive to the well-being of those who work, should receive favorable consideration. Let it not be feared that solicitude of this kind will injure any interest; on the contrary, it will be to the advantage of all; for it cannot but be good for the commonwealth to secure from misery those on whom it so largely depends.

* * *

Special consideration due to the poor

Rights must be religiously respected wherever they are found; and it is the duty of the public authority to prevent and punish injury, and to protect each one in the possession of his own. Still, when there is question of protecting the rights of individuals, the poor and helpless have a claim to special consideration. The richer population have many ways of protecting themselves, and stand less in need of help from the State; those who are badly off have no resources of their own to fall back upon, and must chiefly rely upon the assistance of the State. . . .

The state should safeguard private property

It must be borne in mind that the chief thing to be secured is the safe-guarding, by legal enactment and policy, of private property. Most of all is it essential in these times of covetous greed, to keep the multitude within the line of duty; for if all may justly strive to better their condition, yet neither justice nor the common good allows anyone to seize that which belongs to another, or, under the pretext of futile and ridiculous equality, to lay hands on other people's fortunes. . . .

The state must protect the laborers' rights

When work-people have recourse to a strike, it is frequently because the hours of labor are too long, or the work too hard, or because they consider their wages insufficient. The grave inconvenience of this not uncommon occurrence should be obviated by public remedial measures; for such paralysis of labor not only affects the masters and their work-people, but is extremely injurious to trade, and to the general interests of the public; moreover, on such occasions, violence and disorder are generally not far off, and thus it frequently happens that the public peace is threatened. The laws should be beforehand, and prevent these troubles from arising; they should lend their influence and authority to the removal in good time of the causes which lead to conflicts between masters and those whom they employ.

* * *

Save the laborers from the cruelty of speculators in labor

If we turn now to things exterior and corporeal, the first concern of all is to save the poor workers from the cruelty of grasping speculators, who use human beings as mere instruments for making money. It is neither justice nor humanity so to grind men down with excessive labor as to stupefy their minds and wear out their bodies. Man's powers, like his general nature, are limited, and beyond these limits he cannot go. His strength is developed and increased by use and exercise, but only on condition of due intermission and proper rest. Daily labor, therefore, must be so regulated that it may not be protracted during longer hours than strength admits. How many and how long the intervals of rest should be, will depend upon the nature of the work, on circumstances of time and place, and on the health and strength of the workman. Those who labor in mines and quarries, and in work within the bowels of the earth, should have shorter hours in proportion as their labor is more severe and more trying to health. Then, again, the season of the year must be taken into account; for not unfrequently a kind of labor is easy at one time which at another is intolerable or very difficult. Finally, work which is suitable for a strong man cannot reasonably be required from a woman or a child.

* * *

Employers' moral obligation to pay fair wages

. . . Let it be granted, then, that, as a rule, workman and employer should make free agreements, and in particular should freely agree as to wages; nevertheless, there is a dictate of nature more imperious and more ancient than any bargain between man and man, that the remuneration must be enough to support the wage-earner in reasonable and frugal comfort. If through necessity or fear of a worse evil, the workman accepts harder conditions because an employer or a contractor will give him no better, he is the victim of force and injustice. In these and similar questions, however — such as, for example, the hours of labor in different trades, the sanitary precautions to be observed in factories and workshops, etc. — in order to supersede undue interference on the part of the State, especially as circumstances, times, and localities differ so widely, it is advisable that recourse be had to Societies or Boards such as We shall mention presently, or to some other method of safe-guarding the interests of wage-earners; the State to be asked for approval and protection.

The state should favor multiplication of property owners

If a workman's wages be sufficient to enable him to maintain himself, his wife, and his children in reasonable comfort, he will not find it difficult, if he is a sensible man, to study economy; and he will not fail, by cutting down expenses, to put by a little property: nature and reason would urge him to do this. . . .

. . . If working people can be encouraged to look forward to obtaining a share in the land, the result will be that the gulf between vast wealth and deep poverty will be bridged over, and the two orders will be brought nearer together. Another consequence will be the greater abundance of the fruits of the earth. Men always work harder and more readily when they work on that which is their own; nay, they learn to love the very soil which yields in response to the labor of their hands, not only food to eat, but an abundance of good things for themselves and those that are dear to them. It is evident how such a spirit of willing labor would add to the produce of the earth and to the wealth of the community. And a third advantage would arise from this: men would cling to the country in which they were born; for no one would exchange his country for a foreign land if his own afforded him the means of living a tolerable and happy life. These three important benefits, however, can only be expected on the condition that a man's means be not drained and exhausted by excessive taxation. The right to possess private property is from nature, not from man; and the State has only the right to regulate its use in the interests of the public good, but by no means to abolish it altogether. The State is, therefore, unjust and cruel if, in the name of taxation, it deprives the private owner of more than is just.

* * *

Found the organizations on religion

Speaking summarily, we may lay it down as a general and perpetual law, that Workmen's Associations should be so organized and governed as to furnish the best and most suitable means for attaining what is aimed at, that is to say, for helping each individual member to better his condition to the utmost, in body, mind, and property. It is clear that they must pay special and principal attention to piety and morality, and that their internal discipline must be directed precisely by these considerations; otherwse they entirely lose their special character, and come to be very little better than those societies which take no account of Religion at all. What advantage can it be to a Workman to obtain by means of a Society all that he requires, and to endanger his soul for want of spiritual food?

What doth it profit a man if he gain the whole world, and suffer the loss of his own soul?[2]

. . . The foundations of the organization being laid in Religion, We next go on to determine the relations of the members, one to another, in order that they may live together in concord, and go on prosperously and successfully. The offices and charges of the Society should be distributed for the good of the Society itself, and in such manner that difference in degree or position should not interfere with unanimity and good-will. Office-bearers should be appointed with prudence and discretion, and each one's charge should be carefully marked out; thus no member will suffer wrong. Let the common funds be administered with the strictest honesty, in such way that a member receive assistance in proportion to his necessities. The rights and duties of employers should be the subject of careful consideration as compared with the rights and duties of the employed. If it should happen that either a master or a workman deemed himself injured, nothing would be more desirable than that there should be a committee composed of honest and capable men of the Association itself, whose duty it should be, by the laws of the Association, to decide the dispute. Among the purposes of a Society should be to try to arrange for a continuous supply of work at all times and seasons; and to create a fund from which the members may be helped in their necessities, not only in cases of accident, but also in sickness, old age, and misfortune.

* * *

At this moment the condition of the working population is the question of the hour; and nothing can be of higher interest to all classes of the State than that it should be rightly and reasonably decided. . . .

. . . Every one must put his hand to the work which falls to his share, and that at once and immediately, lest the evil which is already so great may by delay become absolutely beyond remedy. Those who rule the State must use the law and the institutions of the country; masters and rich men must remember their duty; the poor, whose interests are at stake, must make every lawful and proper effort; and since Religion alone, as We said at the beginning, can destroy the evil at its root, all men must be persuaded that the primary thing needful is to return to real Christianity, in the absence of which all the plans and devices of the wisest will be of little avail.

* * *

Given at St. Peter's in Rome, the fifteenth day of May, 1891, the fourteenth year of Our Pontificate.

LEO XIII., POPE.

Original Notes

1. St. Thomas of Aquin. De Regimine Principum, I. cap. 15.
2. St. Matthew XVI. 26.

15

"We Shall Remember the Splendid Acts of Self-Sacrifice, We Shall Recall Our Noble Friends . . ."

CONCERNED with the masses, this century still cared for the individual. Alfred Dreyfus (1859–1935), son of an Alsatian Jewish manufacturer, an artillery officer arrested for intelligence with Germany, was publicly degraded and sent for life to Devil's Island off the French Guiana coast, where he arrived March 15, 1895. Despite army resistance, the case erupted into the cause célèbre of the age. Dreyfus was returned for retrial, again found guilty (with extenuating circumstances) and pardoned. In 1906 the judgment of 1894 was finally quashed. Reinstated, decorated, Dreyfus served in the First World War, and lived on until July 12, 1935. The Affair itself became part of the mythology of the Republic. The following letters between Dreyfus and his wife span the period from his first conviction to his return to France.

Letters of Captain Alfred Dreyfus and his wife Lucie

Dépôt de Saint-Martin-de-Ré,[1]
January 21, 1895

Ma bonne chérie:

YESTERDAY they gave me your sad letter, and then your telegram, to which I replied. How wretched we are! I think that no one in the world has ever suffered as we two. You know there are

From Donald C. McKay (ed.), THE DREYFUS CASE, BY THE MAN—ALFRED DREYFUS, AND HIS SON—PIERRE DREYFUS (New Haven, 1937), pp. 78–108. Translation by Donald C. McKay.

times when I am sorry that I promised you to live. After my conviction I had prepared everything for my death. I was ready to appear before God, my conscience clear and at peace. You could have vindicated my memory quite as well, and you would not have suffered as much at the thought of my own torment. What is really terrible about this situation is that I am completely in sympathy with the measures which have been taken. Beginning today, I am for everyone a convict, and one condemned for the most heinous crime a soldier can commit. I am for everyone an object of contempt. What can I say — that I am innocent! But then why am I condemned, they quite logically ask?

What is essential, my dear, and what must be the object of your every thought, is to discover the truth, by every means possible, by using our whole fortune. Money is nothing, honor is all.

If the Government would show a little pity for me . . . if it would a little lessen my spiritual suffering, I should ask only one thing — that I should be cast nameless on a desert island which I might not leave, where I should see no one, until that day when, thanks to the investigations which must follow, the Government should discover the truth and restore my honor.

Take every care of your health, my dear, you need all your strength. Think of the children before you think of me. They need you, and they have only you now. You must not give yourself up to your grief. You have a task too lofty and too noble still to fulfill. . . .

ALFRED

January 21, 1895

Mon bon chéri:

Your good telegram of yesterday brought me great happiness. I was terribly worried without news of you, and so far no letter has come. Happily I didn't read the newspapers yesterday morning, and they tried to hide from me the sordid scene at La Rochelle. Otherwise I should have been mad with anxiety. What a terrible thing an angry mob is, poor Fred; what a frightful time you had! In any event you were not struck, I hope. I wept with anger, but there is nothing surprising in the attitude of the crowd; it is the result of reading these nasty sheets which live only by slander and filth, and which print no end of fables and lies, always readily accepted by the mob. But take courage, for among thinking men a great change has taken place, a change which everyone recognizes. I receive great numbers of letters from people who are indignant, people who swear your innocence and who tell me that we must have confidence and courage, that the truth will come to light. Only this morning I received, among others, a letter from an English lady with a bouquet of violets, emblem of innocence. She asked me to give it to you when I saw you again: "Bravest of the brave," she said, "that is the name your husband deserves. You can be proud of him. My sympathies were with the French Army in '70. Today I am proud of that sympathy, because I can tell everyone of the admirable conduct of a French officer in these circumstances. No officer, no matter of what nation, could have borne himself more bravely. The thought of Captain Dreyfus will remain an example to preserve me from all meanness in this life." That was so touching and so profoundly true that tears came to my eyes. Yes, *mon mari adoré,* I am proud of you. I have always had a profound love for you. Now I admire you, and wish only to be with you and never again to leave you.

Your children are too young to know how fine you are, but as soon as they reach the age of understanding they will deeply respect their father. They will restore to you in their affection and devotion the happiness which has been taken from you by this odious condemnation.

Adieu, mon bon chéri, je t'embrasse comme je t'aime mille et mille fois.

LUCIE

Saint-Martin-de-Ré,
Thursday, January 31, 1895

Ma chère Lucie:

. . . I ask myself in truth how I go on living. Night and day my thoughts are my only companions. There is nothing for me to do but to weep over our misfortunes.

Last night, as I thought back over my life, how I had struggled and worked to gain an honorable position . . . then, when I compared all that to my present situation, sobs caught in my throat and I thought my heart would break. I was so ashamed of my weakness and so afraid that the guards would hear me that I had to stifle my sobs in my covers. Really, this is too cruel!

Ah! how deeply I feel today that it is sometimes more difficult to live than to die! To die means a moment of suffering but then oblivion for all one's afflictions. . . . But I have no right to die, we have no right to die. We shall have that right only when the truth has been discovered, and my honor has been restored. Until then we must live.

How are our poor dear children? When I think of them, I burst into tears. And you? I hope that your health is good. You must take care of yourself, my dear. First the children, and then the mission which is yours — these impose duties on you, and you cannot fail.

Je t'embrasse comme je t'aime.

ALFRED

Salvation Islands
Tuesday, March 12, 1895

Ma chère Lucie:

On Thursday, February 21, some hours after you left, I was taken to Rochefort and there embarked.

I shan't tell you of my voyage! I was transported as the vile wretch whom I represent would merit; that was only just. One can accord no pity to a traitor; he is the lowest of all scoundrels. So long as I represent this wretch, I can only approve these measures. My situation here is to be understood in the same light.

But your heart will tell you all that I have suffered, and that I suffer now. It is horrible. It is only my spirit which keeps me alive and which gives me hope that I shall soon see the triumphant day of vindication. It is that alone which gives me the strength to live. Without honor, a man is unworthy to live.

You who are truth itself, you swore to me on the day of my departure that you were sure of succeeding soon. I only kept alive during this terrible voyage, and I only live now, because of this promise of yours — and this you must remember.

I landed just a few minutes ago, and I secured permission to send you a cable. I am hastily writing these few words, which will go on the fifteenth by the English mail. It is a comfort to speak to you in this way — you whom I love so deeply. There are two mails a month for France — one by an English boat on the fifteenth, and one by a French boat on the third. There are likewise two mails a month coming to the Islands, one French and one English. Find out what the dates are and write me by both.

What I must say to you yet again is that, if you would have me live, bring about my vindication. Mere personal convictions, no matter what their character, help me not at all; they do not change my situation. What is essential is a judgment of rehabilitation.

When I agreed to live on after this tragic affair, I made for you the greatest sacrifice possible for a man of courage. I did it because of the conviction you have given me that truth inevitably comes to light. It is for you then, my dear, to do everything humanly possible in order to discover the truth.

Wife and mother, this is a task to move the hearts of wives and mothers, and induce them to yield the key to this terrible mystery. I must have my honor, if you wish me to live. That we must have for our dear children, too. Your sentiments are affecting your logic and that is never good. A judgment exists. Nothing will be altered in our tragic situation, until that judgment is reviewed. . . .

ALFRED

When you have good news for me, send a cablegram. Each day I await it like the coming of the Messiah.

Salvation Islands,
July 15, 1895

Ma chère Lucie:

I have written you so many and such long letters during these months when I have been without news of you, that I have said and repeated many times all my thoughts and all my sufferings. Let me return no more to the latter. As to my thoughts, they are clear and invariable — and you know them well.

I appeal to my strength to stifle the beating of my heart, to bridle my impatience to learn that my innocence has finally been recognized everywhere and by every one. Although my energy is entirely passive, yours should be wholly active and animated by the ardent inspiration of my own.

If it were a question merely of torment, that would be nothing. But the honor of a name is at stake, the honor of our children. I will not have it — and of this you are well aware — that our children should ever be obliged to lower their heads. The light must be fully shed upon this tragic affair. Hence, nothing should be allowed to weary or to discourage you. Every door will open and every heart will beat for a mother who seeks only the truth, so that her children may have life.

It is almost from the grave that I say these words to you — for my life is not unlike death, with this added affliction, that I have a soul. . . .

ALFRED

Sunday, July 21, 1895

Mon Fred chéri:

Today it is raining, and I can't take the children for their walk. And so I have spent the entire afternoon reading the letters you have written since our frightful disaster. I have been terribly shaken. I have relived, hour by hour, those painful crises through which we passed. But all of that is over now; let us speak no more of it. I am calm now and full of confidence. I feel that happiness is coming. I should like to tell you what a touching thing Pierrot said to me. He came into my room just as I had burst into tears, and said to me: "Mama, you are very unhappy. Tell me why, and I will comfort you." I replied only with difficulty: "When you are older, you will understand." The poor little fellow stayed by my door for an age, returning often to repeat: "Mama, tell me, you are grieving because Papa is gone; are you less unhappy than you were a little while ago?" The music of his childish voice went to the bottom of my heart. Ah, if you could only hear the little dear! It would be such happiness for you. A ray of joy would warm your poor heart. Our children are very promising. They are strong, lively, fine looking, mischievous, and generous—willful, but persevering. They have all the elements which, properly guided, go to the making of fine character. We shall do our best and work to that end together, shall we not, my dear?

Bonsoir, mon mari adoré, je t'embrasse bien fort.

LUCIE

December 15, 1896

Mon cher Alfred:

I hoped that I should still receive some letters from you this month. I should have been so happy to have had a good long talk with you. But I received nothing, and so I went back to your October letters, and read and reread them. To my great happiness, I found there again that splendid strength which I so admire. It is this strength that sustains you in the terrible struggle you have accepted with such noble courage, a struggle which will lead us on to our supreme object, your vindication. The sentiments which you express, I share. We have each a duty to accomplish, however difficult it may be. Your duty is to strengthen yourself physically, with all the will that you possess; to dominate your nerves, so that you may not be disheartened. Thus you will be able to witness, with us all, the glorious triumph of truth. My duty, too, is simple and clear: to achieve our just right — the full and complete truth!

For two years we have been working toward this end, and we are certain that we shall achieve it. But how many obstacles we have encountered, how many difficulties we have overcome! Each effort carries us one step farther forward, and today we are sure of success.

LUCIE

[For two months the letters of Mme. Dreyfus to her husband reached the latter only in the form of copies written by a member of the penal administration.]

January 7, 1898

Mon chéri:

Courage, courage, I can see approaching the end of our suffering, the moment when we shall finally be reunited, happy, cleansed of this frightful stain which has been cast upon our name. Your martyrdom will end and nothing will remain of these sad days of suffering but a painful memory, which will, alas, never be effaced, but whose sharpness will be lessened by the happiness we shall find in being together once more, surrounded by our poor children. My poor husband, how unhappy you have been. What can I do to make you forget your martyrdom? . . . I have so often said to you that it was your example which has been my strength in this period of struggle and distress, your example which sustained and prevented me from yielding to despair. In the face of your heroism and the greatness of spirit with which you endured this torture, I had no right to falter. You were so splendid, so noble, I had such admiration for your resolution and your courage, that I wished to show myself worthy of you. Proud to be your wife, I was determined to be equal to my task. It was thus that I avoided all weakness, all yielding. You sketched for me the way of my duty; the road was there, I had only to follow it. . . .

YOUR LUCIE

Salvation Islands,
January 25, 1898

Ma chère et bonne Lucie:

I shan't write you a long letter, for I suffer too much in thinking of you and the children. . . .

I have asked for my rehabilitation and the review of my case in letters to the President of the Republic, the Minister of War, and General de Boisdeffre. . . . I am awaiting their reply with feverish impatience and with what strength remains to me. . . .

ALFRED

Salvation Islands,
January 26, 1898

Ma chère Lucie:

In the last letters I wrote I told you what I had done, to whom I had confided our fate and that of our children, what appeals I had made. I need not tell you with what anxiety I await a reply and how long the minutes are. . . .

Here is the situation as I think I understand it, and I fancy that I am not far from the truth. I believe that General de Boisdeffre has never refused us justice. We have been deeply wounded, and we ask him for the truth. It has no more been in his power than in ours to reveal the truth. That will be done in a future which none can foresee. Men have probably been embittered, blunders have perhaps been committed—I know not—and all this has envenomed a situation already so painful. We must go back and raise ourselves above all this suffering so that we may envisage our situation objectively. As for myself, the greatest victim . . . for more than three years; I, who am almost dying, have just given you counsels of wisdom and of calmness. . . .

March 17, 1898

Mon bien cher Alfred:

I read and reread your good letters very often. In spite of their profound sadness and the impression of pain and anguish which they breathe, it seems that I hear you speaking to me. And that is so sweet that it encourages me and brings me much comfort.

You seem to think, my dear, that our efforts have not succeeded, and that for three years we have sought the truth in vain. Thus, in your letter of the ninth of January last, you said: "The truth which we have been awaiting for three years has not come to light; it will do so in a future of which we know nothing." Fortunately I can tell you that you are entirely mistaken. The truth has come to light, it continues to come to light, and, in the very near future, it will blaze forth in the eyes of all.

We have been slow, that is indeed true! Three years, for all of us who suffer, and above all for you, who endure a martyrdom without name: three horrible years, the equal of a century. The first two years were especially terrible; we found ourselves in the blackest night. But if you only knew how our burden has been lightened, what mountains we have uplifted, and how much shorter the road ahead is, than that which we have come!

When I think of the darkness in which we were plunged and of which you, *pauvre cher ami,* could know nothing, I feel profoundly relieved and deeply gratified by the tremendous progress we have made. . . . My feeling that we shall soon be happy is so deep that I want very much to bring this certainty to you.

I know so well that your innocence will be discovered and recognized, that I only wish I could share with you this confidence, this certainty. I implore you to have faith in me, to keep up your courage! I swear to you that your vindication is coming, that nothing can hinder the march of truth. The truth is too strong, too pure, too evident for any human will to prevent it from becoming manifest. . . .

Lucie

[The following letter was not transmitted, and the Colonial Ministry did not give it to Dreyfus until October, 1900. Moreover, it is known that an order of the Court of Cassation was required to force the Government to advise Dreyfus that his request for an appeal had been allowed.]

October 29, 1898

Mon bien cher Alfred:

Finally, after terrible anguish, disillusionment, and frantic hopes, I was informed of the decision of the Court of Cassation — a happy judgment indeed, initiating the procedure of review, first stage in your vindication. My request for an appeal has been allowed by the highest court, and an investigation ordered to prepare all aspects of the case which have not been thoroughly sounded.

This was our most cherished desire. We wanted a striking demonstration of the truth, and, although this method may take longer, we would rather endure this melancholy situation in order that we may finally reach a solution so clear and so evident that no one on this earth can protest further. We know that you share this view, and that, to regain your honor in all its purity, you stand ready to prolong your suffering yet a while.

At last you will be told, at last you will learn this joyous good news. What would I not give to witness your happiness; to see the first smile on your beloved face; gently — very gently, to prepare you for all these emotions; to tend you with my loving care! *Mon Dieu,* what happiness, what mad joy for you and for us all. My heart beats as though it would break at the very thought. What will it be like when the reality is ours? It is too beautiful; one can't imagine such happiness. And the children, what will they say when they see their dear papa! They know that I am happier; they see me less sad. They never cease talking of you and making all kinds of plans for your return. How much we shall have to say to each other! What inexhaustible subjects! Above all, how much to forget, how many crimes and acts of baseness we shall prefer not to mention. We shall remember the splendid acts of self-sacrifice, we shall recall our noble friends, and we shall lack both words and years in which to show them our respect and love.

I am hoping with all my heart that this letter will never reach you, that, when the mail arrives, you will have left that dismal island and be on your way to our beloved France. God grant that this torture continue no longer, and that we find happiness at last.

Je t'embrasse comme je t'aime de toutes les forces de mon coeur.

Lucie

CABLEGRAM

Cayenne, June 6, 1899

Mme. Dreyfus. Salvation Islands, June 5. Heart and soul with you, children, all. I leave Friday. Await with great joy happy moment of embracing you. Kisses to all. Alfred.

Thursday, June 22, 1899

Mon bon chéri:

I want you to have a word from me upon your arrival, so that you may know that I am there near you in the same town, my heart beating with joy and emotion at the thought that I am going to see and embrace you. I know that we shall be violently shaken. One wonders how human flesh can withstand such terrible shocks.

How can I tell you what I felt the day I received your wire, with news of your departure. I was so happy that I thought I was living in a dream. All was changed within me, and I began to live again after long years passed with a bleeding heart. And what a solace it must have been to you to leave that dismal island, and how good those first moments must have seemed when you felt almost free and were on the way to your own country.

How I should like to have taken this journey with you, a journey I have often followed in my thoughts! It was so sweet to think that each hour, each minute, brought you nearer to me, and that we should soon find ourselves in each other's arms after this terrible, endless separation. What happiness, *Mon Dieu!* But one more step to surmount, that of the Court-Martial, and then we shall be free of this horrible nightmare. This will mean yet another terrible ordeal, *mon pauvre ami,* but I have confidence. I know you will endure it bravely and with the serenity which comes from a pure conscience.

I shall leave our dear children on Saturday, the twenty-fourth, in the care of Marie. I have permission to see you, and I shall hasten to the prison as soon as the Governor will let me. . . .

Lucie

Rennes, Saturday, July 1, 1899

Mon bien cher Alfred:

It is four years now that I have fought and prayed and ardently hoped for this blessed day. I had prepared myself for this shock. I wanted to be strong and without weakness, but it needed super-human effort on the part of both of us to control ourselves and to hold our nerves in check, so that we might bravely endure this great ordeal.

How quickly that hour passed. It seemed to me a dream, a beautiful dream, filled with emotion and sweet torment. I wanted to tell you a thousand things, to speak to you of the children, of our families, of all those whom we both love, but I was afraid to overtax you by introducing such affecting subjects. *Pauvre ami,* you, who have not spoken for nearly five years; you, who have suffered every affliction—you are still brave and courageous. You are worthy of everyone's admiration. The many tributes which I receive for you from France and from all parts of the world will prove to you how you are loved and honored.

A few weeks now and we shall have our happiness. These will be days of work, for you have much to do to inform yourself of all that has happened, and to acquaint yourself with the characters of the men who have taken part in this terrible drama. Some of them are vile and base, and deserve only pity. Others are great souls, with a purity, an elevation of mind, and a devotion which make one forget much villainy.

6 a.m., Sunday

I wrote you yesterday. My heart was too full, and needed to pour out its burden. And where should I find sweeter sympathy than from you, *mon pauvre ami?* The joy of having you near me, in the same town, made me sleep more calmly. My heart pains less, and I rejoice at having seen you. I wait for this afternoon with a feverish impatience. . . .

Your devoted,
Lucie

NOTE

1. Located about fifteen miles from La Rochelle, on the Island of Ré; strongly fortified since the days of Vauban, and the concentration point for convicts bound for French Guiana.

16

Burckhardt Reflects that "the Great Harm Was Begun in the Last Century. . ."

LIKE JUSTICE, other values did not triumph as easily as material progress. Not everyone believed the century was on the right track. An underlying stoic pessimism showed through in the private opinions of Jakob Burckhardt (1818–97), professor of history at Basle, 1849–93, and author of the famous book on The Civilization of the Renaissance in Italy *(1860). From early days he had an aristocratic attitude, beholding the "disgusting optimism" of the bourgeois world with a distaste tempered by a quiet resignation. Knowing "what beggars we mortals are at the gates of happiness," he determined to "die at peace with the world." Before his retirement, he had refused many substantial offers, including succeeding the great Leopold von Ranke in Berlin. Stretching across half a century, the following letters illustrate a certain unity of mood from youth to old age.*

Letters

To Hermann Schauenburg

5 May 1846

I THINK I can detect a look of silent reproach in your eyes, because I am off so light-heartedly in search of southern debauchery, in the form of art and antiquity, while in Poland everything is going to pieces and the messengers of the Socialist Day of Judgment are at the gates. Good heavens, I can't after all alter things,

From Alexander Dru (ed.), THE LETTERS OF JAKOB BURCKHARDT (London, 1955), pp. 97, 107–108, 145–148, 150–151, 190–191, 206–208, 219–220, 232–233. Translation by Alexander Dru. Reprinted by permission of Routledge & Kegan Paul Ltd. and Pantheon Books.

and before universal barbarism breaks in (and for the moment I can foresee nothing else) I want to debauch myself with a real eyeful of aristocratic culture, so that, when the social revolution has exhausted itself for a moment, I shall be able to take an active part in the inevitable restoration — 'if the Lord wills, and we live,' of course. Just wait and you will see the sort of spirits that are going to rise out of the ground during the next twenty years! Those that now hop about in front of the curtain, the communist poets and painters and their like, are mere *Bajazzi,* just preparing the public. You none of you know as yet what the people are, and how easily they turn into a barbarian horde. You don't know what a tyranny is going to be exercised on the spirit on the pretext that culture is the secret ally of capital, that must be destroyed. Those who hope to direct the movement with the help of their philosophy, and keep it on the right lines, seem to me completely idiotic. They are the Feuillants of the coming movement, and like the French Revolution it will develop like a natural phenomenon, involving everything that is hellish in human nature. I do not want to experience those times, unless I am obliged to do so; for I want to help to save things, as far as my humble station allows. For you I have no fears; I know well enough on which side events will find you. We may all perish; but at least I want to discover the interest for which I am to perish, namely, the old culture of Europe. It seems to me as though, when the time comes, we should meet in the same holy company. Shake yourself free from your illusions, Hermann! Out of the storm a new existence will arise, formed, that is, upon old and new foundations; that is your place and not in the forefront of irresponsible action. Our destiny is to help build anew when the crisis is past.

Basle, (before 14) September 1849

. . . I hope for nothing from the future; possibly we shall be granted a few half-bearable decades, a sort of Roman Empire. For I am of the opinion that democrats and proletarians, even though they make most furious efforts, will have to yield to an increasingly violent despotism, for our charming century is made for anything rather than genuine democracy. A more detailed explanation of all this would only sound uncharitable. It is no longer possible to link up a real social organism with our ageing Europe; anything of the kind has been forfeit since 1789.

I am delighted to see that you have achieved a considerable degree of resignation! I have grown so prudent that I now know that the philistines are not the worst; misplaced genius, however, is the very devil. I may not be very much at home in the present world, but I shall nevertheless try to learn to meet it affectionately and gently. . . .

To Friedrich von Preen

Basle, New Year's Eve 1870

. . . What has not happened in the last three months! Who could have believed that the struggle would have lasted far into a horrible winter, and would still show no sign of ending on the last day of the year? I shall remember the end of this year my whole life long! And not as regards my own, private, fate. The two great intellectual peoples of the continent are in the process of completely sloughing their culture, and a quite enormous amount of all that delighted and interested a man before 1870 will hardly touch the man of 1871—but what a tremendous spectacle, if the new world is born in great suffering.

The change in the German spirit will be as great as in the French; at first the clergy of both confessions will look upon themselves as the heirs of the spiritual disintegration, but something quite different will soon make itself felt, to one side. The shares of the 'Philosopher' will rise sharply, whereas Hegel, after this year's jubilee publications, may very possibly make his definitive jubilee retirement.

The worst of all this is not the present war, but the era of wars upon which we have entered, and to this the new mentality will have to adapt itself. O, how much the cultured will have to throw overboard as a spiritual luxury that they have come to love! And how very different from us the coming generation will be. It may well be that, to the young, we shall appear very much as the French *émigrés,* intent on a life of pleasure, appeared to those to whom they fled.

Just think how much of all that has been written up to now is going to die out! What novels and dramas are people going to look at? Are the authors, loved by publisher and public alike, because they met and flattered the needs of the century, indeed, of the year and the month, going to survive? Anything that is to live on must contain a goodly portion of the eternal. And if anything lasting is to be created, it can only be through an overwhelmingly powerful effort of real poetry.

To me, as a teacher of history, a very curious phenomenon has become clear: the sudden devaluation of all mere 'events' in the past. From now on in my lectures, I shall only emphasize cultural history, and retain nothing but the quite indispensable external scaffolding. Just think of all the defunct battles in the note-books of all the VV.EE. ["Your Excellencies"] in their Professorial Chairs! Fortunately for me I never went in very much for that kind of thing. But I see I am again talking about myself, when the times may well laugh at all our personal hopes and activities.

We are hourly expecting a battle in the neighbourhood, somewhere between Besançon and Belfort, and hourly expecting a great decision, who knows where, in France. The position of Switzerland, however strong our determination to maintain a strict neutrality, will not remain what it was, even though peace were signed today. The rest must be left to God.

'Put your house in order,' etc., is the wisest thing we can all do, in central Europe. It is going to be different from what it has been.

And with all that I am dreaming of a little tour this summer in Southern Germany, in the course of which I might call on you in Bruchsal. How incurable our optimism. . . .

Basle, 2 July 1871

Now that the terrible days, under the impression of which your last letter was written, lie a month behind us, what you say gives me once again to think. Yes, petroleum in the cellars of the Louvre and the flames in the other palaces are an expression of what the Philosopher calls 'the will to live'; it is the last will and testament of mad fiends desiring to make a great impression on the world; from all that one has read since in intercepted papers, etc., the mainspring of it all was, at bottom, Herostratic.[1] And now they are building schools. Those who arranged those things could all read, write and even compose newspaper articles and other literature. And the ones in Germany who mean to do the same sort of thing are certainly no less 'educated.' But just look at England, bursting with wealth, and secretly kept in a state of siege by analogous elements! Up till now, for two hundred years, people in England have imagined that every problem could be solved through Freedom, and that one could let opposites correct one another in the free interplay of argument. But what now? The great harm was begun in the last century, mainly through Rousseau, with his doctrine of the goodness of human nature. Out of this plebs and educated alike distilled the doctrine of the golden age that was to come quite infallibly, provided people were left alone. The result, as every child knows, was the complete disintegration of the idea of authority in the heads of mortals, whereupon, of course, we periodically fall victim to sheer power. In the meanwhile, the idea of the natural goodness of man had turned, among the intelligent strata of Europe, into the idea of progress, i.e. undisturbed money-making and modern comforts, with philanthropy as a sop to conscience. But the day before yesterday the victorious Prussians found it necessary to declare a state of siege in Königshütte.

The only conceivable salvation would be for this insane optimism, in great and small, to disappear from people's brains. But then our present-day Christianity is not equal to the task; it has gone in for and got mixed up with optimism for the last two hundred years. A change will and must come, but after God knows how much suffering. In the meanwhile you are building schools—at least you can take the responsibility for that before God; while I instruct my pupils and audience. I make no great secret of my philosophy to my students; the clever ones understand me, and as at the same time I do everything in every way I can to honour the real happiness that study and knowledge give one—however little it may be in itself—I am able to give each one some degree of consolation.

To Arnold von Salis

Basle, 21 April 1872

. . . What you say about this being a transitional period is felt by all thinking people about everything. But there is one particular point I want to draw your attention to: the worries and troubles in store for all spiritual things within the next few years, resulting from the ever-increasing emphasis on material things, from the general change in mundane affairs that is bound to follow on the coming rise in the cost of living (one and a half times), and from the fact that we are at the beginning of a series of wars, etc. Things have reached the point at which first-class minds, which ten years ago devolved to scholarship, the Church or the Civil Service are moving over in appreciable numbers to the *business* party. And as to the extent to which the Universities are feeling the lack of *timber* when they have to stop a gap (that is to say of sufficiently respected young scholars who are neither deaf nor blind from special research), on that score I have heard quite incredible admissions from a well-informed source.

If I am not mistaken, I told you my fundamental beliefs during the last war: something great, new and liberating must come out of Germany, and what is more *in opposition* to power, wealth and business; it will have to have its martyrs; it must be something which of its very nature will swim above water and survive political, economic and other catastrophes. But what? There you outquestion me. It might even be that we too should fail to recognize it if it came into the world.

In the meanwhile let us attend assiduously, and where we are concerned, learn and learn till we bust.

To Max Alioth

London, 2 August 1879

. . . Where will our history of art lead us, if people go on collecting at the present rate, and nobody tries to take a really general view of it? If I had a year to spend here, I would turn up my sleeves, spit on my hands and do what I could, with the help of others, to formulate as clearly as possible the living law of *forms.* However, I can't change the course of my life for the sake of such splendours. And what good do these great aesthetic incitements do the Londoner, if the look of the town is to be ruined all the same by a colossal horror on purely utilitarian grounds, by comparison with which our new bridge is perfectly innocent![2] A disgusting, high, straight, cast-iron bridge has been built slap across the main vista of the town, a main-line railway laid across it, and a hideous great round-topped lady's trunk built above it (the main station at Charing Cross). As I strolled in the moonlight yesterday evening, on Waterloo Bridge, and saw how the wonderfully picturesque view of the Houses of Parliament, Westminster Abbey and Lambeth Palace was cut in half, I could have cried. The evening light and the full moon rising made it all the more painful. Further down too, towards London Bridge, there is a similar monstrosity in cast iron, also leading to a colossal terminus. O Lord! what is not going to be sacrificed to the *practical sense* of the nineteenth century! And what will London look like in a hundred years' time, or even in ten years, if more and more of these terrible decisions have to be taken on account of the growing population? I am daily astonished, in the meanwhile, that the crowds don't crush one another to pieces, and that the supply and maintenance is so orderly.

Tomorrow in, I hope, fine weather, to Hampton Court.

Queen Victoria gets off lightly; her face on stamps and coins remains the same as at the beginning of her reign, whereas in truth it must be looking a bit rough.

To Friedrich von Preen

Basle, 13 April 1882

. . . Stick to your frivolous happiness; I do the same with all my strength, and do not allow the prospect of what is to come (although it's pretty clear) get the better of me. Each and every cheerful mood is a genuine gain, and then you have your sons to translate the things of this world into youth and hopefulness. My circle of friends is limited to cheerful people, for there is nothing to be got from those who have gone sour. Nor do I think that anyone in my neighbourhood could complain that I had damped their spirits; and then, as old people are wont to do, I am really beginning to love solitude (linked to a bit of music).

Everybody has a right to think as they please about the situation, peace or war. There are still, of course, diplomatic secrets on the question, but they are no longer decisive; the danger is in the full light of day, for everyone to see. One principal difference between the present and the former years lies in the fact that the Governments of great countries, for example France, are no longer capable of secret negotiations, because the ministries change so often and no form of discretion can be assured. The same is true of Italy; who would dream of trusting or confiding anything to Signor Mancini[3] and his friends?

But the incredible insolence which is spreading everywhere in

Russia, far beyond the control of the Cabinet, is very significant. It is not the nihilists who are the most dangerous, but the impertinence of those in high places. I am not surprised that everything points to direct elections with you; parties all over the world are of the opinion that there is perhaps something to be won in that lucky dip, and that anyway there is nothing to be lost, so full steam ahead!—in a mood of despair.

It has long been clear to me that the world is moving towards the alternative between complete democracy and absolute, lawless despotism, and the latter would certainly not be run by the dynasties, who are too soft-hearted, but by supposedly republican Military Commands. Only people do not like to imagine a world whose rulers utterly ignore law, prosperity, enriching work, and industry, credit, etc., and who would rule with utter brutality. But those are the people into whose hands the world is being driven by the competition among all parties for the participation of the masses on any and every question. The *ultima ratio* [final argument] of many conservatives has been familiar here for a long time: 'It's bound to come,' as you put it, 'and it is useless to resist,' referring to complete democratization.

At the same time, the older stratum of workers is quite out of fashion, and people of assured position are more and more seldom found in office—that too is a phenomenon with which we are long familiar, and anyone who wants to see it on a really large scale need only to look at France and its present governing personnel.

Your position in local government, my dear Sir, gives you an insight into the real ethos of the times which is entirely wanting to many a 'man of the people,' and which he would in any case forbid himself. One of the principal phenomena which you emphasize reveals itself as clearly as can be in Switzerland: a flight from the risks of business into the arms of the salary-paying State is manifest in the fact that the moment farming is in a bad way the numbers who want to enter classes for teachers increases. But where on earth is it to end—the enormous luxury of learning side by side with that of teaching? Here in Basle we are now faced again with disbursements of two millions for new school buildings! It's a single chain of related facts: free instruction, compulsory instruction, a maximum of thirty per class, a minimum of so and so many cubic metres per child, too many subjects taught, teachers obliged to have a superficial knowledge of too many subjects, etc. And, naturally, as a result: everyone dissatisfied with everything (as with you), a scramble for higher positions, which are of course very limited in number. Not to mention the absolutely insane insistence upon scholarship that goes on in girls' schools. A town is at the present time a place to which parents without resources want to move simply because there their children are taught all manner of pretentious things. And like many other bankruptcies, the schools will one day go bankrupt, because the whole thing will become impossible; but it may well be accompanied by other disasters, which it is better not to think about. It may even be that the present educational system has reached its peak, and is approaching its decline.

Baden, 24 July 1889

. . . Bit by bit I am acquiring really mythical eyes, perhaps they are those of an old man once again approaching childhood? I have to laugh when I think that I used to polish off twenty battles and wars, so and so many changes of territory, and whole series of genealogica in a single lecture. Wolfgang will bear me out in this.

Old legends are not my sole concern; like you I recapitulate my own varied past from time to time, only perhaps I have more cause to wonder than you, having made so many foolish decisions and done so many foolish things; who could describe how blind one has been in decisive matters, and the importance one has attached to inessentials, and the degree of emotion! On the whole I really cannot complain, it might all have gone much less well. What we both have in common on our earthly pilgrimage, at least since a certain year, has been the need to be satisfied with the moment through one's work, and what is more a varied and stimulating work. The leaden roller that flattens out so many people has not passed over us.

How the younger generation will survive, and build its nest, is something which, seeing the complete inconstancy of things, one ought really not to worry about too much. The young folk in my family, at any rate, look out on the world just as cheekily as we did in our day, and one of my principles is to conceal my fears for the future entirely from them. The forty-year-olds are of course beginning to notice things for themselves. The picture I have formed of the *terribles simplificateurs* [terrifying simplifiers] who are going to descend upon poor old Europe is not an agreeable one; and here and there in imagination I can already see the fellows visibly before me, and will describe them to you over a glass of wine when we meet in September. Sometimes I meditate prophetically on how our learning and quisquilian researches will fare when these events are in their very early stages, and culture, in the interval, has only sunk a peg or two. Then, too, I picture to myself something of the lighter side of the great renovation: how the pale fear of death will come over all the careerists and climbers, because once again real naked power is on top and the general *consigne* [password] is: 'shut your mouth.' In the meanwhile, what is the most grateful task for the moment? Obviously: to amuse people as intensively as possible.

To a Theological Student

Basle, 26 May 1895

. . . I am now entering upon my seventy-eighth year and am not only old but thoroughly tired, and attend quite objectively at the campaign which my excellent and valued doctor (also a nephew) is fighting against my illness with the help of frequent examinations and three alternating medicines. However, I have my eyes and my ears, sleep tolerably and will not complain.

Be true to art 'in all its branches,' to music, to poetry and to painting, and persevere in believing that it is not for nothing that it is given to one to have one's life exalted by these glorious things. There are of course admirable people who do without all these things and they will be granted an *Ersatz* [compensation], but it is better to have them. And how much better placed the youth of the present day is than ours was, when there were no cheap editions of music, no cheap books, no photographs, and no trains either, to make travelling easy. But one of the blessings of youth is a marvellous memory for everything seen and heard, and for things too, that one has only enjoyed once.

The art of today has long ago vanished almost entirely from my horizon and I hardly know, or don't know at all, what the catchwords mean. In great old age one only wants peace, and that is best found when one no longer hears anything about the quarrels in art and in literature. That only goes for very old people, for in one's youth one must know about such things, and must be able to adopt a position, for one's contemporaries and friends do the same. . . .

NOTES

1. Herostratus, an Ephesian, set fire to the Temple of Artemis at Ephesus on the night Alexander the Great was born, 356 B.C. He confessed under torture that he had fired the temple to immortalize himself. His name was condemned to oblivion, but seemingly Burckhardt could count upon von Preen knowing the incident. 'The Philosopher' is, as elsewhere, Schopenhauer.

2. The new bridge in Basle that Burckhardt strongly disapproved of.

3. Pasquale Stanislao Mancini, liberal Neapolitan jurist, Italian Minister of Justice, and Foreign Minister 1881–85.

17

Zola on the Armed Peace: "It Is War Killing War. . . ."

ONE OF those looking unflinchingly at his times was the novelist Émile Zola (1840–1902). He was famous for his denunciatory open letter to President Faure on the Dreyfus Affair which appeared in the newspaper l'Aurore, *January 13, 1898, under the headline "J'Accuse! . . ." A successful and wealthy writer, Zola in this letter deliberately created a scandal to compel a review of the case. Though his novels were often considered scandalous too, his part in the defense of Dreyfus was the most celebrated episode of his life. He was found dead, mysteriously asphyxiated, in his Paris home, on September 29, 1902, and was given a state funeral. The following essay reflects both realism and a certain optimism as the century closed.*

On War

WE ARE, I hope, witnessing in our day a slow transformation of the object of war. In the beginning of humanity, in heroic times, war was essentially an aggressive measure: a people attacked its neighbors intending to rob them of their country and reduce them to slavery. To-day, if such be the intention, at least it is not avowed. There is no longer question of anything but war of defense: one's domestic peace and possessions are threatened, and one enters the field merely in self-defense. The most military nations of the day, those most thoroughly organized and best equipped for war, excuse themselves for being upon such a footing on the plea that it is solely for the eventual defense of their country. Not one of them would confess that it meditates an attack upon its neighbor and seeks the conquest of the world. It seems, therefore, that purpose of war is losing its virulence, since it no longer dares to be one of conquest and

From the NORTH AMERICAN REVIEW *(1900), vol. 70, pp. 449–463.*

seeks its justification in the single necessity of defending the frontiers.

All this leads me to estimate the actual state of Europe. Since 1870, all the large European countries have been converted into immense intrenched camps. This state of affairs is, I believe, due to our defeats; in fact, it is certain that the formidable war footing on which Europe now lives is the result of the situation created by Germany's victories and by her conquest of the two provinces which she took from us. As Germany wished to retain these two provinces she was obliged to keep herself strongly armed; and as we, on the other hand, were anxious to regain them, we had to put ourselves on an equal footing with Germany. It necessarily followed that Austria, Italy, and even Russia, were constrained to do likewise, and therefore, as I have said, all the great nations of Europe are to-day possessed of troops innumerable, and may indeed be compared to huge intrenched camps. Such a situation has naturally produced very serious consequences. First of all, there is obligatory military service—whole nations under arms and at an incalculable cost to their respective treasuries. Next comes the question of equipment, and a great expenditure is required for fortifications, arms, provisions and all war materials. Besides, modern improvements in the manufacture of arms have caused weapons made at an earlier date to be discarded as useless and replaced by new ones, thereby greatly increasing national expenses, and, since 1870, the war budgets of European nations have consumed millions.

This state of affairs has begotten a peculiar social and political condition which threatens precipitate ruin. Business is more or less paralyzed; the money of the different countries goes into the war budget, this budget grows larger from year to year, and it really seems that, if things so continue, these nations must inevitably become bankrupt. And underlying it all there is much anxiety; it may not be admitted, but I am convinced that in poor countries, such as Italy, which has really gone to extremes in the matter of armament, the people know full well that, in case of war, their exorbitant military expenses would exhaust the national fund.

In the Conference held at The Hague there was an indication of this fear. I do not care to analyze the reasons which prompted the Emperor of Russia to convoke this Conference, but, be they what they might, they were born of the situation, they were in the very air. All nations are preoccupied. It is a universally evident fact that the war budget of each people is gradually consuming its fortune and that such a condition of affairs cannot continue indefinitely, unless the nations come to grief. Consequently, to the question of army equipment may be referred the financial, political and social anxiety now prevailing throughout Europe.

As has been said, the Conference of The Hague has been prolific of no practical result; still, I consider it a highly important event, a very propitious occurrence, inasmuch as it brought up the question. It showed the uneasiness of nations, indicated that they fully realize that the social and economic crisis through which they are passing is the issue of the terrible war footing on which the people of Europe are obliged to live. The opinion is an intelligent one: the existing situation is indeed awful, and may, in the near future, lead to catastrophe. I therefore consider the Conference of The Hague important, since it called forth a momentous question which must sooner or later be solved. Besides, in the thousands of millions uselessly expended by those nations which, without profit, are exhausting their finances in maintaining standing armies; in the continual improvement of military equipment which is ever making the engines of war more and more deadly — in all this, I, the avowed enemy of war, can see its approaching end. And why? Because it is evident that such a condition of affairs cannot last. Nations cannot remain forever under arms, for if they did, national production and social life would, in the long run, be arrested, hemmed in and sacrificed. Moreover, arms are becoming daily more murderous. With long-distance guns, with shells which are ever more destructive, with other late inventions, machines and explosives which, at a distance of kilometres, can annihilate entire regiments, it is evident that the character of warfare is changing; it is no longer a test of physical courage, a hand-to-hand encounter with sword or bayonet, but a sort of science by the practice of which one can destroy the enemy without approaching him. The aspect of warfare is indeed becoming so terrifying that henceforth one nation, before declaring war upon another, will probably pause and think a second time. It is no longer a question of hirelings fighting a duel in a corner, with two nations for witnesses; no, it is the two nations themselves falling upon each other with intent so abominable that, to terminate the bloody quarrel, either assailant must be destroyed.

Under such conditions war becomes execrable, and humanity should be spared like attacks. It is understood that before plunging into such excesses every possible means is employed to bring about an understanding, the more so, since at present, granting that all

Europe is in arms, a war would not be confined to two nations, but would entangle all the neighboring countries till, at length, all Europe would find itself within the mesh, and a general massacre would ensue. This explains why, for the last thirty years, despite threats of war, despite the strong hatred existing between France and Germany, and all that we have been led to fear, there has been no war. And the further we go, the more impossible war seems to become, the more it appears to develop into a crime of high treason against humanity—an atrocity for which no nation would be responsible.

If present difficulties have reached such a pitch that we could not lay down our arms without first fighting it out; if, in the near future, we were to suffer from a sort of general conflagration, I think that war would be forever at an end: because, after the great massacre, the nations would be unfit to resume the struggle, and exhausted, filled with horror and pity, they would be convinced that henceforth peace should reign among them. Yes, the whole world would hold this last abomination in such remorseful abhorrence that warfare would surely die.

When I declared myself the adversary of war, it was not that the martial ideal is not grandly poetic. And that it is poetic may be learned by observing what is at present taking place in the Transvaal.[1] Since the war broke out, we have beheld all nations intensely interested; the newspapers are replete with telegraphic dispatches and all correspondence from that quarter is eagerly perused, even we, the enemies of war, reading it most attentively.

* * *

. . . I know what a hold warlike exploits take upon the imagination of different peoples, and in vain do we endeavor to advance in civilization, since we must inevitably drift back to our primitive instinct: to the admiration of valor, to the hero-worship of those who fight, who kill or are killed. Therein danger and bravery are both exalted. War brings all men's passions into play, and the champions who consent to die stir the innermost emotions of our souls. Peaceful philosophers, poets, confined within their sanctums, quiet men like myself, writers who believe in the superiority of the pen over the sword, who are convinced that civilization is the result not of battles, but of books—in a word, the passions of all studious men are irresistibly appealed to when they read the account of a battle. In vain do we aspire after universal peace, in vain do we seek to encourage fraternity among people, when there is in our very blood a sort of atavism which agitates and excites us as soon as a new war is announced; when we are seized with a species of delirium upon hearing that one nation attacks another, fights, exults and finally flaunts the flag of victory. We repudiate all this as a return of barbarism, thinking rather that humanity should advance toward a future city of peace and goodness; but I repeat that in our blood is that old warlike atavism which prompts us to applaud the conqueror even though he be in fault.

This fact is certainly ominous, and yet I believe that, sooner or later, warfare will have become a thing of the past. As I have stated, many reasons seem to indicate that it is being gradually eliminated from civilization; it will end by costing too high a price from being too murderous in its effects. Europe, not to mention a country which I know well, will be on the fair road to bankruptcy if she persist in keeping all nations on a war footing, if she continues the manufacture of guns that are becoming daily more costly and more destructive, and if she stock her arsenals with shells, which, when such missiles are required, must be discarded for those of later manufacture, the deadly secrets of which are as yet unknown to neighboring nations.

The chief reason for the eventual disappearance of war is that it will have become useless. When speaking thus, I have in mind the democratic movement, the great socialist movement which, within the last hundred years, has made such advancement. In my way of thinking, the real human struggle is no longer on the field of battle, but on that of labor; in industry, in agriculture, in fact in every human effort for production and prosperity. The mighty contest going on to-day is that between capital and remunerative labor. I am convinced that now, in our day, there is in progress as important and decisive a social transformation as took place in olden times, when slavery was abolished and paid labor introduced. It required a great change to bring about such an issue, a change which caused the overthrow of the Roman Empire. The idea of having no slaves for manual and agricultural labor, industrial and domestic work; the thought of abolishing slavery and replacing it by something else, could not be entertained, and called forth the most vehement protestations even from the intellectual and liberal-minded. It was deemed impossible to live without slaves, and the hue and cry arose: "By what can you replace them? How live without them?" And when slavery was superseded by paid labor, a new state of things was created, even empires being carried away. And therein Christianity played a great part. It declared all men equal, helped to destroy slavery and created, to a certain extent, the modern laborer, thereby immensely benefiting humanity.

Well, to-day the situation is pretty much the same. They say: "How can a nation exist without paid workmen? How can work be accomplished unless the workmen be remunerated? And by what can you replace workmen?" There have been precursors, apostles, like Saint Simon, Auguste Comte, Proudhon and above all, Fourier, who have sketched or outlined a future society in which the question of wages and salaries was not considered even by workmen themselves; in which there was co-operation, community of interests and responsibilities; in fact, an entirely new state of affairs which was destined to replace actual pay. And it is evident that we are tending toward just such a state. The contention that we witness is really between capital and labor, and will eventually lead us to that other state which, as yet, is not clearly defined, but which will surely exact a total reorganization of labor and bring about a new distribution of riches. Yes, I maintain that this state of future society is the object for which we are now struggling, the new ideal toward which we are advancing, in direct opposition to the ideal of war which has so long stirred the passions of nations.

It is certain that in this future society war will be unheard of because the reorganization of labor will everywhere beget greater solidarity, bind the different nations closer together, either by arbitration or some other means of which we have, as yet, formed no conception. War cannot be a factor in this future state which the struggles of a closing century will link to the century about to dawn. It will be doomed to disappear, for it will be incompatible with the new condition of things.

Is it a dream to believe that we are witnessing war's last agony? Do not a thousand symptoms indicate the fact? May not the furore caused by the question of military equipment and so forth, be regarded as the last fitful glow in the dying embers of war? Would it not be impossible for the men of to-day to engage in combat similar to that into which their ancestors ruthlessly plunged, combat which could bring about no good but would do much harm?

* * *

Ours is indeed a warlike past. Our history is replete with accounts of our secular combats with England, combats the memory of which is still with us; because, into the hatred which we are accredited with having for England, there evidently enters the recollection of our long struggle, all the rancor that could have been harbored against a neighbor with whom we fought for centuries. There were also our conflicts with Austria, Italy, Germany and Spain; in fact we were never known to remain quiet. France, the most turbulent nation of Europe, was constantly rekindling the flame of war. Our neighbors always considered us, and I think they hold the same opinion still, a people who could not remain quietly at home, but were ever looking after others and ready to interfere in their behalf; who, when we had no war question of our own to settle, felt that we must deliver Greece or Poland, and went meddling in foreign affairs, showing a truly chivalrous, but very restless, spirit, and remaining a constant menace to the peace of Europe.

This reputation of ours was well confirmed during the Napoleonic campaigns. These abounded in historic exploits to which I shall not now revert, but there was at length a supreme outburst of warlike sentiment in France; certain events helped it out, and, at a given moment, France was seen setting out to war against the combined nations of Europe, threatening and fighting them and acquiring vast lands. But it must be confessed that Napoleon failed to realize France's old dream—European domination. Moreover, the prodigious adventure was also the most cruel lesson that France could receive, as in the wake of Napoleon's dazzling warlike achievements came, first of all, defeat, then social discontent and exhausted finances, and, lastly, the degeneration of our country. This lesson teaches us that such conquests are always followed by dire results, as, for instance, interior difficulties arising from the foothold gained by political rings and parties, and the prolonged crisis which still holds us in the balance, rendering us unable to find our equilibrium. The perusal of Napoleonic history would tempt none but a madman to wish for a renewal of military feats which, glorious as they were, were followed by a dismal confusion from which our country still suffers.

This is why I cannot admit that France would ever so jeopardize her future as to try to make it a repetition of her warlike past . . . In 1789 her cry for deliverance re-echoed through all nations, and at that time she may be said to have instilled into the world the idea of liberty: her part to-day would be to inflame it with a spirit of justice.

I would have her take the lead in this great socialist movement, in the re-organization of labor, which, in my opinion, will be the great feature of the coming century. I would see her at the head of the nations which will beget that future society in which, thanks to the organization of labor, there will be an even distribution of riches. I would that France might be the handmaid of this future society, of this expected evolution which will transform the world by bringing into it a new civilization.

. . . Thought is supreme; it breaks swords and stops the cannon's roar. The world was never positively conquered except by thought. What remains of great ancient nations, of Syria, Egypt, Greece and Rome, is not warlike achievements, but books and monuments; in fact, whatever is the fruit of labor and of peace.

We may speak of Alexander and Cæsar, but their splendid conquests belong only to a dead past, even their empires have crumbled away, nothing being left of them but ruins, grains of sand which are carried off by the wind; whereas, the works of Homer and Virgil and all the monuments of legislation and civilization still live and form a part of our wealth. And we are the children of these ancestors of human thought. The exploits of war count only insofar as they procure for legislators, poets and artists that peace which they most need in order to be able to produce these monuments of the wisdom and beauty of man.

I know that, for belief in peace and future disarmament, the time is scarcely auspicious, as we are now beholding an alarming recrudescence of militarism. Nations which until now seem to have held aloof from the contagion, to have escaped this madness so prevalent in Europe, now appear to be attacked. Thus, since the Spanish War, the United States seem to have become a victim of the war fever. I am not quite competent to judge the situation in the United States, as I am not sufficiently well informed on the subject, and I speak merely from what I have seen in the newspapers and in some documents that were given me. However, I can see in that great nation a dangerous inclination toward war; I can detect the generation of vague ideas of future conquest. Until the present time, that country wisely occupied itself with its domestic affairs and let Europe severely alone, but now it is donning plumes and epaulettes and will probably be dreaming of possible campaigns and be carried away with the idea of military glory — notions so perilous as to have been responsible for the downfall of nations.

And England, since the resistance offered her in the Transvaal, that small Republic which she expected to subdue almost without an effort, even England has yielded to that most disturbing emotion, the growing desire of fostering the military spirit. To be sure, this state of mind is nothing new to the English. There is in England much of what we call *imperialism;* that is to say, a sort of national impulse which may lead her to extremes, a desire to extend her colonies, to make herself mistress of the most important posts in the world, or to acquire what the word imperialism denotes, dominion over the world.

Such is England's dream, and her symptoms in this regard are indeed alarming. Therefore, is Rudyard Kipling the most popular English novelist: it is no longer Dickens, the charming narrator, that the nation reads; no, Kipling is the author now winning loudest applause, Kipling, who is almost a soldier, a bugle sounding the charge. He fans all England's warlike passions, chooses his types from the new generation, and these types are those of men ready for war, putting in war their only hope, developing themselves morally and physically for war — in fact, having nought else in view but fighting and conquests. Until now, England has escaped the military spirit, in the sense that she has not had conscription. She has had no experience of that blood-tax, for she always had, and still has, paid troops. But the possibility of establishing military conscription in England, as it now exists in France and Germany, has already been discussed in the Houses of Lords and Commons. And this fact is singularly significant. After the battle of Waterloo and the defeat of Napoleon, England was wise enough not to be intoxicated with the glory of victory, and was satisfied with an army of hired soldiers; but to-day she is prone to introduce the system of military conscription. It can be clearly foreseen that if England should continue to meet with reverses in the Transvaal or, if victorious, should later be forced to defend herself or to attack stronger nations, she would hurriedly adopt conscription and exact military service from her subjects. This contingency is a serious one and shows that England is about to enter upon a new phase of her history. She has always been looked upon as being in retirement in her island, well protected by her coast defenses, proud and happy of her free institutions, sparing her subjects military conscription, living for commerce and for the development of the arts, when lo! she succumbs to the war passion which has reached her from the Continent, and becomes the latest victim of a folly which threatens the destruction of Europe in a frightful, general massacre.

It must be admitted that symptoms such as these are indeed terrifying. If the United States, on the one hand, and England on the other, were to arm all their male citizens, would not the situation become only the more alarming? On the other side of the seas would be found great fortified camps such as we have in Europe; there would be one in England and another in America, and both nations could truly be said to be under arms. Well may one tremble when peace is thus threatened. How, in face of it all, can we believe that war will soon have become a thing of the past?

Nevertheless, in conclusion, I shall repeat that I consider these terrifying symptoms the result of that ever-increasing uneasiness which is pushing to extremes the dread of war, is goading nations on to self-destruction, forcing them to make extravagant preparations for war in the hope that they will never again have to fight. The present crisis will, I feel, be the last, and is undoubtedly war's death-cry. It is war killing war; war making further war impossible; war forced to disappear because it is anti-social, because it ruins nations and impedes the progress of humanity toward the City of Peace and Justice, because it is a factor which, on account of its utter uselessness, must henceforth be banished from history.

NOTE

1. In the Boer War, 1899–1902, Great Britain successfully fought the Republics of Orange Free State and Transvaal to bring them under her sovereignty.

18

The Progressive Assault upon "an Excessively Individualized Democracy"

WHETHER THE *threat from armaments was growing or diminishing, some critics believed that great concentration of wealth threatened democracy. American Progressives such as Herbert Croly (1869–1930), journalist, editor, founder of* The New Republic *in 1914, argued that government must regulate economic life and curb the power of big business. In a widely read tract for the times,* The Promise of American Life, *Croly appealed to the middle class for an end to "chaotic individualism."*

How the Promise of American Life Has Been Realized

ALL THE conditions of American life have tended to encourage an easy, generous, and irresponsible optimism. As compared to Europeans, Americans have been very much favored by circumstances. Had it not been for the Atlantic Ocean and the virgin wilderness, the United States would never have been the Land of Promise. The European Powers have been obliged from the very conditions of their existence to be more circumspect and less confident of the future. They are always by way of fighting for their national security and integrity. With possible or actual enemies on their several frontiers, and with their land fully occupied by their own population, they need above all to be strong, to be cautious, to be united, and to be opportune in their policy and behavior. . . . We were for the most

From Herbert Croly, THE PROMISE OF AMERICAN LIFE *(New York, 1909), pp. 7–10, 17–18, 20–25, 452–454. Reprinted by permission of The Macmillan Company.*

part freed from alien interference, and could, so far as we dared, experiment with political and social ideals. The land was unoccupied, and its settlement offered an unprecedented area and abundance of economic opportunity. After the Revolution the whole political and social organization was renewed, and made both more serviceable and more flexible. Under such happy circumstances the New World was assuredly destined to become to its inhabitants a Land of Promise,—a land in which men were offered a fairer chance and a better future than the best which the Old World could afford.

No more explicit expression has ever been given to the way in which the Land of Promise was first conceived by its children than in the "Letters of an American Farmer." This book was written by a French immigrant, Hector St. John de Crèvecœur before the Revolution, and is informed by an intense consciousness of the difference between conditions in the Old and in the New World. "What, then, is an American, this new man?" asks the Pennsylvanian farmer. "He is either a European or the descendant of a European; hence the strange mixture of blood, which you will find in no other country. . . .

"He becomes an American by being received in the broad lap of our great *Alma Mater.* Here individuals of all nations are melted into a new race of men, whose labors and prosperity will one day cause great changes in the world. Here the rewards of his industry follow with equal steps the progress of his labor; this labor is founded on the basis of *self-interest;* can it want a stronger allurement? Wives and children, who before in vain demanded a morsel of bread, now fat and frolicsome, gladly help their father to clear those fields, whence exuberant crops are to arise to feed them all; without any part being claimed by a despotic prince, a rich abbot, or a mighty lord. . . . The American is a new man, who acts upon new principles; he must therefore entertain new ideas and form new opinions. From involuntary idleness, servile dependence, penury, and useless labor, he has passed to toils of a very different nature rewarded by ample subsistence. This is an American."

Although the foregoing is one of the first, it is also one of the most explicit descriptions of the fundamental American; and it deserves to be analyzed with some care. According to this French convert the American is a man, or the descendent of a man, who has emigrated from Europe chiefly because he expects to be better able in the New

World to enjoy the fruits of his own labor. The conception implies, consequently, an Old World, in which the ordinary man cannot become independent and prosperous, and, on the other hand, a New World in which economic opportunities are much more abundant and accessible. America has been peopled by Europeans primarily because they expected in that country to make more money more easily. To the European immigrant — that is, to the aliens who have been converted into Americans by the advantages of American life — the Promise of America has consisted largely in the opportunity which it offered of economic independence and prosperity. Whatever else the better future, of which Europeans anticipate the enjoyment in America, may contain, these converts will consider themselves cheated unless they are in a measure relieved of the curse of poverty.

This conception of American life and its Promise is as much alive to-day as it was in 1780. Its expression has no doubt been modified during four generations of democratic political independence, but the modification has consisted of an expansion and a development rather than of a transposition. The native American, like the alien immigrant, conceives the better future which awaits himself and other men in America as fundamentally a future in which economic prosperity will be still more abundant and still more accessible than it has yet been either here or abroad. No alteration or attenuation of this demand has been permitted. With all their professions of Christianity their national idea remains thoroughly worldly. They do not want either for themselves or for their descendants an indefinite future of poverty and deprivation in this world, redeemed by beatitude in the next. The Promise, which bulks so large in their patriotic outlook, is a promise of comfort and prosperity for an ever increasing majority of good Americans. At a later stage of their social development they may come to believe that they have ordered a larger supply of prosperity than the economic factory is capable of producing. Those who are already rich and comfortable, and who are keenly alive to the difficulty of distributing these benefits over a larger social area, may come to tolerate the idea that poverty and want are an essential part of the social order. But as yet this traditional European opinion has found few echoes in America, even among the comfortable and the rich. The general belief still is that Americans are not destined to renounce, but to enjoy.

* * *

The moral and social aspiration proper to American life is, of course, the aspiration vaguely described by the word democratic; and the actual achievement of the American nation points towards an adequate and fruitful definition of the democratic ideal. Americans are usually satisfied by a most inadequate verbal description of democracy, but their national achievement implies one which is much more comprehensive and formative. In order to be true to their past, the increasing comfort and economic independence of an ever increasing proportion of the population must be secured, and it must be secured by a combination of individual effort and proper political organization. Above all, however, this economic and political system must be made to secure results of moral and social value. It is the seeking of such results which converts democracy from a political system into a constructive social ideal; and the more the ideal significance of the American national Promise is asserted and emphasized, the greater will become the importance of securing these moral and social benefits.

The fault in the vision of our national future possessed by the ordinary American does not consist in the expectation of some continuity of achievement. It consists rather in the expectation that the familiar benefits will continue to accumulate automatically. In his mind the ideal Promise is identified with the processes and conditions which hitherto have very much simplified its fulfillment, and he fails sufficiently to realize that the conditions and processes are one thing and the ideal Promise quite another. Moreover, these underlying social and economic conditions are themselves changing, in such wise that hereafter the ideal Promise, instead of being automatically fulfilled, may well be automatically stifled. For two generations and more the American people were, from the economic point of view, most happily situated. They were able, in a sense, to slide down hill into the valley of fulfillment. Economic conditions were such that, given a fair start, they could scarcely avoid reaching a desirable goal. But such is no longer the case. Economic conditions have been profoundly modified, and American political and social problems have been modified with them. The Promise of American life must depend less than it did upon the virgin wilderness and the Atlantic Ocean, for the virgin wilderness has disappeared, and the Atlantic Ocean has become merely a big channel. The same results can no longer be achieved by the same easy methods. Ugly obstacles have jumped into view, and ugly obstacles are peculiarly dangerous to a person who is sliding down hill. The man who is clambering up hill is in a much better position to evade or overcome them. Americans will possess a safer as well as a worthier vision of their national Promise as soon as they give it a house on a hill-top rather than in a valley.

* * *

The conscious recognition of grave national abuses casts a deep shadow across the traditional American patriotic vision. The sincere and candid reformer can no longer consider the national Promise as destined to automatic fulfillment. The reformers themselves are, no doubt, far from believing that whatever peril there is cannot be successfully averted. They make a point of being as patriotically prophetic as the most "old-fashioned Democrat." They proclaim even more loudly their conviction of an indubitable and a beneficent national future. But they do not and cannot believe that this future will take care of itself. As reformers they are bound to assert that the national body requires for the time being a good deal of medical attendance, and many of them anticipate that even after the doctors have discontinued their daily visits the patient will still need the supervision of a sanitary specialist. He must be persuaded to behave so that he will not easily fall ill again, and so that his health will be permanently improved. Consequently, just in so far as reformers are reformers they are obliged to abandon the traditional American patriotic fatalism. The national Promise has been transformed into a closer equivalent of a national purpose, the fulfillment of which is a matter of conscious work.

The transformation of the old sense of a glorious national destiny into the sense of a serious national purpose will inevitably tend to make the popular realization of the Promise of American life both more explicit and more serious. . . .

The extent and the character of this revision may be inferred from a brief consideration of the effect upon the substance of our national Promise of an alteration in its proposed method of fulfillment. The substance of our national Promise has consisted, as we have seen, of an improving popular economic condition, guaranteed by democratic political institutions, and resulting in moral and social amelioration. These manifold benefits were to be obtained merely by liberating the enlightened self-interest of the American people. The beneficent result followed inevitably from the action of wholly selfish motives — provided, of course, the democratic political system of equal rights was maintained in its integrity. The fulfillment of the American Promise was considered inevitable because it was based upon a combination of self-interest and the natural goodness of human nature. On the other hand, if the fulfillment of our national Promise can no longer be considered inevitable, if it must be considered as equivalent to a conscious national purpose instead of an inexorable national destiny, the implication necessarily is that the trust exposed in individual self-interest has been in some measure betrayed. No preëstablished harmony can then exist between the free and abundant satisfaction of private needs and the accomplishment of a morally and socially desirable result. The Promise of American life is to be fulfilled—not merely by a maximum amount of economic freedom, but by a certain measure of discipline; not merely by the abundant satisfaction of individual desires, but by a large measure of individual subordination and self-denial. And this necessity of subordinating the satisfaction of individual desires to the fulfillment of a national purpose is attached particularly to the absorbing occupation of the American people,—the occupation, viz.: of accumulating wealth. The automatic fulfillment of the American national Promise is to be abandoned, if at all, precisely because the traditional American confidence in individual freedom has resulted in a morally and socially undesirable distribution of wealth.

In making the concluding statement of the last paragraph I am venturing, of course, upon very debatable ground. Neither can I attempt in this immediate connection to offer any justification for the statement which might or should be sufficient to satisfy a stubborn skeptic. I must be content for the present with the bare assertion that the prevailing abuses and sins, which have made reform necessary, are all of them associated with the prodigious concentration of wealth, and of the power exercised by wealth, in the hands of a few men. I am far from believing that this concentration of economic power is wholly an undesirable thing, and I am also far from believing that the men in whose hands this power is concentrated deserve, on the whole, any exceptional moral reprobation for the manner in which it has been used. In certain respects they have served their country well, and in almost every respect their moral or immoral standards are those of the great majority of their fellow-countrymen. But it is none the less true that the political corruption, the unwise economic organization, and the legal support afforded to certain economic privileges are all under existing conditions due to the malevolent social influence of individual and incorporated American wealth; and it is equally true that these abuses, and the excessive "money power" with which they are associated, have originated in the peculiar freedom which the American tradition and organization have granted to the individual. Up to a certain point that freedom has been and still is beneficial. Beyond that point it is not merely harmful; it is by way of being fatal. Efficient regulation there must be; and it must be regulation which will strike, not at the symptoms of the evil, but at its roots. The existing concentration of wealth and financial power in the hands of a few irresponsible men is the inevitable outcome of the chaotic individualism of our political and economic organization, while at the same time it is inimical to democracy, because it tends to erect political abuses and social inequalities into a system. The inference which follows may be disagreeable, but it is not to be escaped. In becoming responsible for the subordination of the individual to the demand of a dominant and constructive national purpose, the American state will in effect be making itself responsible for a morally and socially desirable distribution of wealth.

The consequences, then, of converting our American national destiny into a national purpose are beginning to be revolutionary. When the Promise of American life is conceived as a national ideal, whose fulfillment is a matter of artful and laborious work, the effect thereof is substantially to identify the national purpose with the social problem. What the American people of the present and the future have really been promised by our patriotic prophecies is an attempt to solve that problem. They have been promised on American soil comfort, prosperity, and the opportunity for self-improvement; and the lesson of the existing crisis is that such a Promise can never be redeemed by an indiscriminate individual scramble for wealth. The individual competition, even when it starts under fair conditions and rules, results, not only, as it should, in the triumph of the strongest, but in the attempt to perpetuate the victory; and it is this attempt which must be recognized and forestalled in the interest of the American national purpose. The way to realize a purpose is, not to leave it to chance, but to keep it loyally in mind, and adopt means proper to the importance and the difficulty of the task. No voluntary association of individuals, resourceful and disinterested though they be, is competent to assume the responsibility. The problem belongs to the American national democracy, and its solution must be attempted chiefly by means of official national action.

Neither can its attempted solution be escaped. When they are confronted by the individual sacrifices which the fulfillment of their national Promise demands, American political leaders will find many excuses for ignoring the responsibility thereby implied; but the difficulty of such an attempted evasion will consist in the reënforcement of the historical tradition by a logical and a practical necessity. The American problem is the social problem partly because the social problem is the democratic problem. American political and social leaders will find that in a democracy the problem cannot be evaded. The American people have no irremediable political grievances. No good American denies the desirability of popular sovereignty and of a government which should somehow represent the popular will. While our national institutions may not be a perfect embodiment of these doctrines, a decisive and a resolute popular majority has the power to alter American institutions and give them a more immediately representative character. Existing political evils and abuses are serious enough; but inasmuch as they have come into being, not against the will, but with the connivance of the American people, the latter are responsible for their persistence. In the long run, consequently, the ordinary American will have nothing irremediable to complain about except economic and social inequalities. In Europe such will not be the case. The several European peoples have, and will continue to have, political grievances, because such grievances are the inevitable consequence of their national history and their international situation; and as long as these grievances remain, the more difficult social problem will be subordinated to an agitation for political emancipation. But the American people, having achieved democratic institutions, have nothing to do but to turn them to good account. In so far as the social problem is a real problem and the economic grievance a real grievance, they are bound under the American political system to come eventually to the surface and to demand express and intelligent consideration. A democratic ideal makes the social problem inevitable and its attempted solution indispensable.

I am fully aware, as already intimated, that the forgoing interpretation of the Promise of American life will seem fantastic and obnoxious to the great majority of Americans, and I am far from claiming that any reasons as yet alleged afford a sufficient justification for such a radical transformation of the traditional national policy and democratic creed. All that can be claimed is that if a democratic ideal makes an express consideration of the social problem inevitable, it is of the first importance for Americans to realize this truth and to understand the reasons for it. Furthermore, the assumption is worth making, in case the traditional American system is breaking down, because a more highly socialized democracy is the only practical substitute on the part of convinced democrats for an excessively individualized democracy.

* * *

Democracy . . . may prove to be the most important moral and social enterprise as yet undertaken by mankind; but it is still a very young enterprise, whose meaning and promise is by no means clearly understood. It is continually meeting unforeseen emergencies and gathering an increasing experience. The fundamental duty of a critic in a democracy is to see that the results of these experiences are not misinterpreted and that the best interpretation is embodied in popular doctrinal form. The critic consequently is not so much the guide as the lantern which illuminates the path. He may not pretend to know the only way or all the ways; but he should know as much as can be known about the traveled road.

Men endowed with high moral gifts and capable of exceptional moral achievements have also their special part to play in the building of an enduring democratic structure. In the account which has been given of the means and conditions of democratic fulfillment, the importance of this part has been under-estimated; but the under-estimate has been deliberate. It is very easy and in a sense perfectly true to declare that democracy needs for its fulfillment a peculiarly high standard of moral behavior; and it is even more true to declare that a democratic scheme of moral values reaches its consummate expression in the religion of human brotherhood. Such a religion can be realized only through the loving-kindness which individuals feel toward their fellow-men and particularly toward their fellow-countrymen; and it is through such feelings that the network of mutual loyalties and responsibilities woven in a democratic nation becomes radiant and expansive. Whenever an individual democrat, like Abraham Lincoln, emerges, who succeeds in offering an example of specific efficiency united with supreme kindliness of feeling, he qualifies as a national hero of consummate value. But — at present — a profound sense of human brotherhood is no substitute for specific efficiency. The men most possessed by intense brotherly feelings usually fall into an error, as Tolstoy has done, as to the way in which those feelings can be realized. Consummate faith itself is no substitute for good work. Back of any work of moral conversion must come a long and slow process of social reorganization and individual emancipation; and not until the reorganization has been partly accomplished, and the individual released, disciplined and purified, will the soil be prepared for the crowning work of some democratic Saint Francis.

Hence, in the foregoing account of a possible democratic fulfillment, attention has been concentrated on that indispensable phase of the work which can be attained by conscious means. Until this work is measurably accomplished no evangelist can do more than convert a few men for a few years. But it has been admitted throughout that the task of individual and social regeneration must remain incomplete and impoverished, until the conviction and the feeling of human brotherhood enters into possession of the human spirit. The laborious work of individual and social fulfillment may eventually be transfigured by an outburst of enthusiasm — one which is not the expression of a mood, but which is substantially the finer flower of an achieved experience and a living tradition. If such a moment ever arrives, it will be partly the creation of some democratic evangelist — some imitator of Jesus will reveal to men the path whereby they may enter into spiritual possession of their own individual and social achievements, and immeasurably increase them by virtue of personal regeneration.

Be it understood, however, that no prophecy of any such consummate moment has been made. Something of the kind may happen, in case the American or any other democracy seeks patiently and intelligently to make good a complete and a coherent democratic ideal. For better or worse, democracy cannot be disentangled from an aspiration toward human perfectibility, and hence from the adoption of measures looking in the direction of realizing such an aspiration. It may be that the attempt will not be seriously made, or that, if it is, nothing will come of it. Mr. George Santayana concludes a chapter on "Democracy" in his "Reason in Society" with the following words: "For such excellence to grow general mankind must be notably transformed. If a noble and civilized democracy is to subsist, the common citizen must be something of a saint and something of a hero. We see, therefore, how justly flattering and profound, and at the same time how ominous, was Montesquieu's saying that the principle of democracy is virtue." The principle of democracy *is* virtue, and when we consider the condition of contemporary democracies, the saying may seem to be more ominous than flattering. But if a few hundred years from now it seems less ominous, the threat will be removed in only one way. The common citizen can become something of a saint and something of a hero, not by growing to heroic proportions in his own person, but by the sincere and enthusiastic imitation of heroes and saints, and whether or not he will ever come to such imitation will depend upon the ability of his exceptional fellow-countrymen to offer him acceptable examples of heroism and saintliness.

19

The House of Lords Debates Whether to "Perish in the Dark"

HEADLONG though its progress might seem, democracy still had its old enemies. A famous last stand occurred in England in 1909 when the House of Lords rejected the budget, breaking its 250-year-old custom of accepting financial legislation sent on by the Commons. Other issues envenomed the dispute. Herbert Asquith's Liberal government obtained passage of a Parliament Bill through the Commons, May 1910, canceling the Lords' veto on money bills and limiting it on others. Despite losses in two elections, it persuaded King George V to agree, if necessary, to create sufficient peers to secure passage in the Lords. On the stifling hot night of August 10, 1911, the upper house voted and acquiesced.

The Parliamentary Debate of August 10, 1911

The Marquess of Lansdowne[1]

YOUR anxiety on this Bench is that before the debate proceeds further, and in order that those who take part in the debate may know what they are talking about, the noble Viscount should tell us whether our interpretation of the undertaking given to His Majesty's Ministers by His Majesty was a correct or an incorrect interpretation. We placed upon it this interpretation, that His Majesty had promised the creation of a number of Peers sufficient to ensure the passing of the Parliament Bill in its House of Commons form. We understood that no number had been specified, and we understood further that when the pledge was implemented it would be implemented in such a way that the number of Peers

From THE PARLIAMENTARY DEBATES (OFFICIAL REPORT) (London, 1911), 5th Series, vol. ix, House of Lords, cols. 997–1074.

created would be amply sufficient to overcome any possible combination of Parties in this House.

* * *

Viscount Morley[2]

. . . I will, since the noble Marquess desires it, give a plain answer to his question. . . .

If the Bill should be defeated to-night His Majesty would assent to a creation of Peers sufficient in number to guard against any possible combination of the different Parties in opposition by which the Parliament Bill might again be exposed a second time to defeat. . . . That, I think, is pretty conclusive. However intense may be your disapprobation of that proceeding, in voting against my Motion by-and-by you are making that proceeding which you disapprove of with such intensity and such sincerity inevitable; and let every noble Lord who goes into the Lobby to-night against my Motion reflect before he goes there what it is that he is doing. . . .

* * *

The Earl of Rosebery[3]

My Lords, I certainly did not come here to-night with any intention of speaking, and I shall not trouble your Lordships for more than a minute. But the speech of my noble friend opposite, important and weighty as it is, and wholly convincing, as I think it is, on the point at issue in the Division to-night, does raise one or two more issues than perhaps he contemplated. The misfortune of this debate is that it is almost impossible to keep the name of the Sovereign out.

Deep as the waters may be in which we find ourselves to-night, and on my part I think they are as deep as the Pacific Ocean, we cannot overlook that grave consideration—going to a young and inexperienced King four or five months on the Throne to ask him for a third Dissolution, a second within the year, and accompanying that demand, as I understand the case—and this part of the case is wrapt in some obscurity—with a request for a contingent guarantee, before they had read their Bill perhaps, even once in the House of Commons, that should that Bill not meet with acceptance in the House of Lords, there should be an immense creation of Peers. Deep as our waters may be, I venture to say that we cannot exaggerate the enormous gravity of the position brought about by the Government at that time. That was the true Constitutional crisis. I think myself it would have been open to the Sovereign to say that before he acceded to so enormous a demand he should be allowed to take counsel with ex-Ministers and not be left entirely in the hands of His Majesty's Government, an *ex parte* body pleading their own cause with one who was hitherto unversed in such affairs. But that is all history. It does give an unpleasant savour to the whole of this transaction. No words that I can use, and I do not mean to use any such words, would exaggerate the effect that such a transaction would produce on any impartial and thinking man in this country.

Now I come to a far more important point, the announcement that the noble Viscount has categorically made this evening. I confess I am not very well qualified to advise your Lordships as to rejecting a measure supported by two General Elections. I am not a good adviser, because ever since I have been in this House, some 43 years, I have always been under the impression, though I was as jealous of the honour of this House as any member of it, that it was not a political instrument that was capable of achieving the purposes which its leaders thought it capable of producing. I never thought it was an instrument that could be used for rejecting what might even appear to be the will of the people without causing an exasperation and a reaction pre-eminently dangerous to the fortunes of this House. For taking that line on more than one occasion I have been reproached with cowardice in this House, and if I continued to sit here I might again make myself liable to that charge; but it is my conviction that an unreformed, hereditary House of Lords is wholly unfitted to resist great popular movements, and that is why all the time I have been in this House I have endeavoured to further the cause for reform. I do not think that this House is a body that could resist a cause or a measure supported by two General Elections.

* * *

Viscount Milner[4]

. . . If the Government are going to act upon the powers with which they are armed to the full extent by creating an artificial majority in this House—if that is what they contemplate it adds enormously to the outrageousness of their proceedings; but it does not, to my mind, affect the course which noble Lords who regard this measure in the manner in which I do ought to take. We should indeed have been shortsighted if we had ever entered upon this campaign not foreseeing the possibility of such a declaration as has been made by the noble Viscount to-night. My feeling remains what it has always been — that if we regard this measure as bad, if we regard the methods by which it has been forced upon this House as abominable, then it would be better that it should be passed, if it must be passed, by the votes of men who believe in it, rather than that it should owe its presence on the Statute Book to the acquiescence, or still worse to the votes, of those who think it a thoroughly bad Bill. I believe it would be better for the country, for the wholesomeness of our political life, and for the honour and character of all those concerned in this transaction. . . . A great deal has been said about the abuse, as we think it to be, of the Royal Prerogative. The defence offered by Ministers is that it was inevitable, that they were driven to it, that there was no other way out. It was only inevitable because they have pressed forward this measure in a spirit of pure partisanship and without the slightest vestige of a constructive idea. . . . Their policy is simply to reduce the proceedings of this House to such a farce that it no longer matters whether opportunities are equal or not. . . . No political controversy of great magnitude in this country has ever been dealt with by the Government of the day with a more complete and total absence of the spirit of give and take. The Government say to us, in effect, "We have a majority in the House of Commons. This is the measure which is approved by that majority. You are free to alter it when you in your turn command a majority." . . .

It is not heroics, and it is not a desire to strike an attitude, but it is merely common sense to refuse to yield to such an unscrupulous abuse of power. . . .

* * *

. . . If we give way to-day we shall be exposed to the same threats again and again in the future. The Government may have — I have no doubt they have — the power of creating such a number of Peers as would entirely destroy the independence of this House. But it is also evident to any man who hears their speeches or reads their Press that a check given them to-night would put them in a position of the greatest embarrassment. Taking the view that I do, I hold that it is the duty of those who wish to defeat the policy of the Government to take every opportunity that they lawfully and honourably can to assist in increasing their embarrassment; not for the mere pleasure of embarrassing them — for that would, indeed, be a contemptible motive which I do not think would actuate any noble Lords in this House — but for a far better reason — in order to make them pay the penalty of their unscrupulous action.

There is one appeal which must commend itself to every loyal subject, the appeal that we should not compel His Majesty to take a step which we are glad and grateful to know is distasteful to him. But I cannot see how the keeping of a promise already given could injuriously affect the august position of His Majesty. In this instance, so far as His Majesty is concerned, the mischief has already been done by the unfair pressure which has been put upon him by his Ministers to give that promise. And as for the future, it seems to me that the fulfilment of that promise on the present occasion would be more likely than anything else to prevent the Royal Prerogative being made use of hereafter as the normal means of bringing pressure to bear on this House. If we are going to make it easy and comfortable for the advisers of the Crown thus to abuse the Royal Prerogative, it is not likely that they will not have recourse to it again. On the other hand, I am firmly convinced that once you swamp this House by a large creation of Peers in order to enable the Government to ride down their opponents, the storm of odium that will be aroused will prevent any Ministry in the future from abusing the Royal Prerogative in a similar manner and will thus preserve the King from being involved over and over again in our political controversies.

It has been stated that this is a mere question of tactics and procedure, but in my opinion it is in the highest degree a matter of principle. I consider, after what has happened, that this House is as good as wiped out as a real power in British politics, and that we shall have to look in other directions for checks and safeguards against the tyranny of the single-Chamber government with which we are threatened. The wire-pullers have got the people of England by the throat, and the struggle which lies before us in the future is a struggle to free the nation, and especially that part of the nation which is not too deeply devoted to either Party, from the tyranny of the House of Commons and the wire-pullers. In that struggle the incident of to-night is the beginning, as probably it may be regarded as the end of the importance of the historic House of Lords. . .

* * *

The Earl of Camperdown[5]

. . . I regard this Bill as an act of violence, as violent an act as if you marched soldiers up to this House and removed the Mace. It is a revolution, nothing else; and I must say I should have respected noble Lords opposite much more if they had not tried to minimise the effect of their measure so much, but had courageously stated what actually is the effect of their Bill and had stuck to that and said it was quite right. There is one other thing—that is, the bad effect which I am afraid has been created by this Bill and which I greatly fear will endure. This Bill has imported a feeling of bitterness into our politics far exceeding anything that has ever existed before. I admit that I feel indignation at this measure and the manner in which it has been brought forward, and when I say that I am in favour of supporting it on the present occasion I announce to your Lordships that I am doing it certainly not from any love of the Bill. I hate and detest the Bill, and I do not believe that there is any one in the House who entertains towards it feelings of a less friendly sort than I do. . . .

* * *

The Duke of Northumberland[6]

. . . From the very first I have held the opinion that we ought never to have yielded one iota to the proposal of this Bill, and that we ought to have rejected the Bill on the very first day we properly could have done so without giving the Government the smallest rope of any sort or kind. . . . I do not think we can understand the real character of the struggle in which we are engaged unless we take the history of it and look at it as a whole.

* * *

If we are to go into the history of this measure, it must be remembered that we are constantly told—we were told the other night from the Woolsack—that the origin of this Bill was our rejection of the Budget. I think the noble and learned Earl's words were that the rejection of the Budget made this Bill inevitable. But our memories are not quite so short as that. Do we not know that when Sir Henry Campbell-Bannerman[7] came into office the very first thing he did was to declare war against the House of Lords? I will admit that the rejection of the Finance Bill gave a very great excuse to the Government to attack the House of Lords. In December last the Government announced that they were going to appeal to the country, and they put this question in the forefront of the battle. . . .

We have heard a great deal about the verdict of the people at the last election. We have been told *ad nauseam* — we were told from the Episcopal Bench last night — that nobody can doubt that the last election was in favour of this Bill. I do not believe one word of it, and I cannot conceive how any one with experience of electioneering can honestly say such a thing. The whole country had been well bribed by the reckless finance of the Chancellor of the Exchequer[8] and the liberality of other people, and it was asked whether it liked the present Government. It liked them very much, naturally — not enough to give them an increased majority, for in fact they lost a few seats, but still I admit it liked them very much. But as to this Bill, they neither knew nor cared anything about it. The Reform Bill of 1832 has been quoted over and over again. I wonder whether the people who quote it have ever read the history of that Bill. There was some interest aroused in the country then, and a very unpleasant interest it was, too. The country was very nearly on the verge of revolution then; but when you compare the present state of things with the condition of things in 1832 and tell me that the people are anxious to change the Constitution of the country and to abolish the House of Lords, my answer is that they know nothing whatever about the question and do not care two brass farthings about it.

* * *

What is our record with regard to this Bill when we go before the country? We all admit that we have got a trust, a responsibility, in this House, and yet at no one stage of this Bill have we made any effective opposition at all, and we are not prepared even now to stand against it. I cannot conceive a more pitiable ending to the House of Lords. I have protested from the first against the Bill, and I protest to the end. There is the cry that we are going to restore the Constitution of this country at the first chance we get. That is a very good argument for those who stand to their guns, but not for those who are doubling to the rear as fast as they can go. That is the position we are placed in by noble Lords who make this cry. I have been asking myself, Why is it that we are to yield upon the present occasion, as is recommended to us by so many of our noble friends? First of all, they say it is a dreadfully unconstitutional thing that 300 or 400 or 500 Peers should be made. Of course it is. But when once you tell an unscrupulous Party, conscious that they will stick at nothing, that you will yield to threats of this kind, you may be perfectly certain that the liberties of this House have gone, and I do not care for my own part whether the Peers are made in 1911 or 1912 or 1913. One of two things is evident, either that you must be the slave of the House of Commons or you will have sooner or later this very creation of Peers which you are now seeking to avoid.

. . . It is far better, I am convinced, that the country should realise what it is that is being done. If there are introduced 200, or 300, or 400, or 500 Peers I do not think there will be any very immediate effect, but I am perfectly certain that the country would not stand it long. Something would have to be done, and as what I desire above all things is a strong Second Chamber I look forward with satisfaction to anything which will force upon the attention of the country and His Majesty's Government the absolute necessity for the reform of this House. I am not in the least frightened of the creation of these Peers. I cannot say that I welcome them or that I would have any respect for them, but I do not see that they can do us any harm, and I think they will indirectly do a great deal of good. . . .

The Earl of Meath[9]

Lord Rosebery told us that by yielding in 1832 we obtained a further existence of eighty years. I wish to goodness we had never had those eighty years. If only in 1832 a fight had been made we should have been a real live Assembly at this moment. The noble Lord said that after to-day we shall exist only for a few years in a miserable condition. I do not say those were his words, but that was the pith of his meaning. I ask your Lordships, Is it worth while, for the sake of a few years existence, to go on without any power or real authority whatever—a sort of painted fortress, with a perfectly useless *simulacrum* of power, which will only deceive the people? Is it not better and much nobler to say to the Government at once, "Force us. We are not going to yield until you fire. Do your worst."

* * *

Earl Curzon of Kedleston[10]

. . . I pay my noble friends the compliment of saying that the whole of their action during the past fortnight, their speeches, their letters, their resolutions have not been without effect in convincing the country of the existence of a revolution. I pay them that compliment. But if they think that the country is likely to be brought more face to face with revolution because 400 or 500 gentlemen are going to troop into this House and sit on the Benches opposite I respectfully differ from them. I would ask noble Lords for a moment to contemplate the positive consequences of the action which they propose to take. If you succeed to-night in defeating the Government and compelling the creation of a large number of Peers, is it not clear that you will be making an enormous and gratuitous addition to the power for mischief of the Party opposite? A noble Lord last night used this metaphor, that noble Lords on this side of the House who were taking such a line of action were committing suicide on the doorstep of their opponents. I think my noble friends to whom I am appealing would be doing much worse than that. They would be presenting a regiment, an army, to the enemy in the campaign upon which we are about to enter.

* * *

One last point. We are all Members of the House of Lords. We have reached it by different avenues, some of us by descent, some of us by election, some of us by service; but I believe there is no man who sits in this House, not even the latest recruit to it, who does not when he comes within these walls acquire some measure of inspiration, some idea that this House is the centre of a great history and of noble traditions—the idea that he is part of an Assembly that has wrought and is capable of doing in the future great and splendid service to this country. I have those feelings. I cannot contemplate with satisfaction anything which must effect the pollution—perhaps that is too strong a word—the degradation of this House, and I ask your Lordships to pause before you not only acquiesce in, but precipitate or facilitate, a course of procedure with regard to this House which cannot but have the effect of covering it with ridicule and of destroying its power for good in the future.

. . . What I mean is that it is in the power of 80 or 90 or 100 members of your Lordship's House to-night by the vote which you are going to give to dictate an action to the whole of the House. All I want is that your Lordships should clearly realise the responsibility you are assuming in this matter, because it may be that by a small majority, a majority of two or three or four of that small minority, you may impose upon the Government a course of action which may have a profound effect on the whole future of this country. I do not suppose a more momentous Division will ever have taken place in the House of Lords. It is possible that as a result of this Division 400 Peers may be created. If that is done, the Constitution is gone as we have known it. We start afresh to build up a new Constitution. God knows how we shall do it. We may do it with success or with failure. Let us realise what is before us—

The Marquess of Bristol[11]

It is because 400 Peers are going to run away to-night.

Earl Curzon of Kedleston

I would sooner run away with the Duke of Wellington than stand with the noble Lord.

The Marquess of Bristol

I would rather fight with Nelson at Copenhagen than run away with the noble Earl.

The Earl of Rosebery

. . . I cannot conceive a more painful position than being obliged to vote apparently for a Bill which is abhorrent to me as it practically abolishes the only Second Chamber which exists without substituting anything in its place. Happily that is not exactly the position I occupy to-night, because the strict question is whether we shall insist upon an Amendment with which I personally do not agree. Therefore I have not the least hesitation in saying, profoundly painful as it is, that I shall think it my duty to follow the Government into the Division Lobby.

The Earl of Selborne[12]

My Lords, I am not going to stand between you and the Division. I am only going to ask you to weigh the value of the advice you have just got from the noble Earl on the Cross Benches when I have read to you his words uttered in this House on May 29 last. The noble Earl said—

"I can see no use in prolonging the existence of this House as a useless sham to delude the people of this country into the belief that they still have a Second Chamber with control over

> the First. Far better let the naked truth appear. Far better let it be seen by the country that this House is a mere phantasy from which all substance has been stripped, than allow it to remain in the paralysed condition in which noble Lords opposite, and noble Lords opposite alone, wish to preserve it for their own purposes."

When Lord Rosebery said those words I believed him. Those views which he expressed are my views now. My noble friend Lord Midleton has found out to-night for the first time that there are great safeguards in this Bill. In my conscience and my heart I believe there are none. I believe that a Single Chamber — naked, as Lord Rosebery would say — would be safer for this country than a Constitution with a House of Lords emasculated according to this Bill. Therefore the Government's creation of Peers has no terrors for me.

But the choice before us to-night is this. The House of Lords as we have known it, as we have worked in it, is going to pass away. We ourselves, as effective legislators, are doomed to destruction. The question is — Shall we perish in the dark by our own hand, or in the light, killed by our enemies? . . .

* * *

Their Lordships divided: Contents, 131; Not-contents, 114.

NOTES

1. Sometime Governor General of Canada, Viceroy of India, Secretary of State for War, and for Foreign Affairs, leader of the Conservatives in the Lords, he sought the Bill's amendment, and abstained in the voting.
2. Liberal journalist and reformer, born John Morley and created Viscount in 1908, he piloted the bill through the Lords for the government.
3. Author, sometime Foreign Secretary, Gladstonian Liberal who left the party in 1905. An advocate of reform of the Lords since 1894, he was opposed to the bill but voted for it as a lesser evil.
4. German-born journalist and lawyer, created Viscount in 1902, defender of the imperial idea, he strongly opposed the bill.
5. Landowner, sometime Lord in Waiting and Lord of the Admiralty, he fiercely opposed the bill, but sacrificed himself and voted for it.
6. A diehard enemy of the bill.
7. Liberal Prime Minister, 1905–08.

8. David Lloyd George, champion of social and fiscal reform, general in the "war" on poverty, destined to lead the country to the victory of 1918.

9. Sometime diplomat, philanthropist, originator of "Empire Day," and diehard opponent of the Bill.

10. George Nathaniel Curzon, champion of empire, sometime Viceroy of India, created Earl in 1911, later Marquis, agreed that the Lords must submit.

11. Landowner, and Rear-Admiral in the Royal Navy, diehard opponent of the bill.

12. Sometime First Lord of the Admiralty and High Commissioner for South Africa, leading opponent of the bill.

20

"The Dark Shadow Moves over the Map of the Continent"

The last terrible lesson of the age was that popular institutions were not enough. Of those Americans who watched the onset in Europe, none was more committed than Walter Hines Page (1855–1918). A North Carolinian by birth, schoolteacher turned editor, he left the South in 1887 for the literary world of New York and Boston. As an early supporter of Woodrow Wilson, he was rewarded with appointment as Ambassador to the Court of Saint James in 1913, a post for which his Anglophile propensities rather than diplomatic training recommended him. His enthusiasm for the Allied cause outran the President's, but he remained on, despite ill health, until the autumn of 1918 when the final victory was within sight. Returning home, he died on December 21, 1918. The following letters to Wilson cover the days immediately prior to and the months immediately following the general outbreak of war. They reflect simplified contemporary views of the war, sanguine hopes and the dawning realization that neither Europe nor America would ever be the same again.

Letters of Walter H. Page to President Woodrow Wilson

American Embassy, London, July 29, 1914

Dear Mr. President:

YESTERDAY before the news came that war had begun between Austria and Serbia, yielding to the impulse that every American feels, I went to see Sir Edward Grey[1] and told him that I had come on my own initiative informally to ask him if he saw any way in

From Burton J. Hendrick, THE LIFE AND LETTERS OF WALTER HINES PAGE *(Garden City, 1922–25), vol. iii, pp. 125–130, 135–137, 141–147. Reprinted by permission of Dr. Ives Hendrick.*

which the good offices of our government could be used and that, if he did or should see any way, I prayed that he would inform me. He thanked me with feeling and said that he knew that the good influence of the United States could be counted on for peace, and he promised to inform me if he should see anything that we could do. I reminded him again that I had no instructions, but I reminded him also of your wish (of which I felt sure) and of the feeling of the whole American people. Then this morning came Mr. Bryan's[2] telegram of inquiry whether I saw a way for us to help. I immediately sent that to Sir Edward with a reminder of our conversation. There the matter for the moment rests. I do not yet see any way in which we could help, for England seems to me to be doing everything that can be done — England, with more direct influence on the Continental Powers than we could have. There has been running through my mind vaguely all day the query whether perhaps we might not in some way add our voice to England's — the wisdom or the uselessness of which you will have seen and decided before you receive this — in case the danger of a general war continue.

I think that every Ambassador here saw Sir Edward yesterday, and I purposely waited till late in the afternoon when they — all the rest — had gone. I think I shall never forget yesterday. There sat this always solitary man — he and I, of course, in the room alone, each, I am sure, giving the other his full confidence. He looked ten years older than he looked a month ago. He told me a day or two after the murder of the heir to the Austrian throne that he feared just what has happened and worse than has yet happened. He is, I imagine, the foremost Foreign Secretary in Europe. He has held this office eight years. He knows his European politics as perhaps no other man knows it. He is a forward-looking, liberal-minded man — a sort of sad and wise idealist, restrained and precise in speech and sparing in his use of words, a genuine clear-thinking man whose high hopes for mankind suffer sad rebuffs but are never quenched — a grave philosopher who feels the prodigious responsibility he carries. He had received Germany's refusal of his proposition of an ambassadorial conference. He was grieved, but I think not surprised. He still had hope that Russia and Austria would get together directly. "If Germany would give the word," said he, "war would be averted." Throughout his frank talk I felt the possibility of a sort of crack of doom for Continental Europe. This is the man who if the Liberals lose and win again in ten years, or if they hold on for a few years more, will be Prime Minister. Even the Conservative papers to-day, in spite of the intense party feeling, praise him and call on the whole nation to stand behind him.

A few hours later I went to dinner at Lord Glenconner's whose family are all especial friends of Sir Edward; and he was there. I do not often meet him dining out. He spends his evenings in the House and later at home with his dispatches and reports, and he frequently does several hours' work in bed in the morning. At dinner he was the same sad figure, saying little, absorbed, waking up once in a while with a smile and then slipping back into silence. After dinner there was music and he sat in a corner of the room—alone. He folded his arms and mechanically kept time with his foot, of course not hearing the music or anything else. The hostess sought him and marched him across the room, and he affected a certain gaiety which fooled nobody, not even himself. Lady Glenconner told me that he spent Sunday at her country house. In the afternoon he and she took a long walk and he told the whole European political story to her two or three times. After they came back to the house, he went off on a still longer walk alone.

All this is intensely interesting to me. Here is a great and sincere man working with a great government as his tool, working to save Europe from itself and (most likely) failing. Monarchy and privilege and pride will have it out before they die—at what cost! If they do have a general war they will so set back the march of progress in Europe as to set the day forward for American leadership. Men here see that clearly. Even in this kingdom every ship is ready, every crew on duty, and every officer of the Admiralty office in London sleeps with a telephone by his bed which he expects to ring, and the telegraph men are at their instruments every minute. But of all men here the most impressive is the brooding, saddened, solitary Foreign Secretary, at whom men turn back and gaze as he drives along the street and for whose success every wise man in all Europe prays to-night. And he will tell me with a melancholy smile the next time I see him of his unfortunate fate that he cannot go fishing.

It's the Slav and the German. Each wants his day, and neither has got beyond the stage of tooth and claw. While I was talking to Sir Edward, Mrs. Page was talking to Prince X, who wishes to fight, who talks like a mediæval man, and so loves the blood of his enemies that, if he can first kill enough of them, he is willing to be whipped.

He went home last night. Meantime, the price of bread has risen even in England.

Again and ever I thank Heaven for the Atlantic Ocean.

Very heartily yours,

Walter H. Page

London, Sunday night, August 2, 1914

Dear Mr. President:

It seems useless and almost silly to write by mail about this quickly changing drama, for whatever one might write will become obsolete before you get it. Yet the impulse to put down what one hears and fears is irresistible. I detect even in English opinion an acquiescence, almost a satisfaction, that war between England and Germany is certain. They feel that it must come some time — why not now and have it over? It is better to have it when Germany will have other enemies than England in the field than at some time when England might alone have to fight Germany — better, too, when the responsibility for starting it lies at Germany's door.

In one way at least race-hatred is at the bottom of it — the Slav against the Teuton. The time to have that fight out seems favourable to Russia; the old Austrian Emperor is in his last years, the Slav states of his empire are restive, not to say rebellious, England may be drawn in now to help weaken Germany, Russia feels the need of a patriotic race cry at this stage of her growth and the need of a war to cause forgetfulness of the Russian-Japanese disaster. I am told, too, that the Tsar — as, of course, most of his subjects — is really superstitious and that miracle-working priests — a sort of modern soothsayers — have a great influence over him; and of course the military party know how to use such machinery. We have to stop and think of such absurd things as this to realize the deplorable mediævalism of a large part of Europe and to understand why the criminal folly and the economic suicide of war do not have more effect on them. Russians, Germans, and even Frenchmen are, moreover, yet in that stage of evolution where the "glory" of war makes a strong appeal to them.

Already the foregoing is out of date. While I was writing, the news came of Germany's declaration of war against Russia and of her marching into Luxemburg, which of course means that France and England must become involved: I can see no escape from that. The general conflagration has begun.

My thoughts run quickly as to what *we* may do. On my own initiative I asked Sir Edward Grey nearly a week ago if he could use the good offices of the United States for peace. Sir Edward is very appreciative of our mood and willingness. But they don't want peace on the Continent — the ruling military classes do not. But they will want it presently, and then our opportunity will come — *your* opportunity to play an important and historic part. Ours is the only great government in the world that is not in some way entangled. (How wise our no-alliance policy is!) Of course I'll keep in daily touch with Sir Edward and with everybody who can and will keep me informed.

The imagination simply balks at what may happen — at what *is* happening. The Embassy is already besieged by people who wish to go to the United States and can't, who have travellers' checks for which they cannot get money, and who have other unexpected troubles. I hear of even worse confusion in Paris.

This island is even now practically cut off from the Continent. Three days ago we talked with Paris by telephone. Now it is impossible to get a private telegram through with any certainty, and telephone communication is wholly cut off.

Our shipping and foreign commerce will gain immensely; our chance to help settle the quarrel will surely come — there was nothing that we could have done to prevent it; and our intimate and frank and confidential relations with this country are such that we will, I am sure, be called on as soon as they are willing to call on anybody to point the way back to reason.

Events here alone seem to me likely to make your Administration historic. Let's watch closely for chances to serve.

Yours—dazed——

Walter H. Page

American Embassy, London, August 23, 1914

Dear Mr. President:

It has been impossible to write lately, except by telegraph. I have been kept at work from the time I waked till twelve or one or two o'clock every night this fortnight, every minute of the time. . . .

The thing of great and lasting importance of course is that the diplomatic work proper be done without error and without fumbling. When this involves direct dealing with four governments every day — well, I keep a straight path, a head not bothered with details, I get advice, and — follow my own judgment. The saving fact is (and the importance of this cannot be exaggerated) that I have dealt so candidly and frankly with Sir Edward Grey and so completely given him my confidence that his candour and confidence in me are now my shield and buckler. I could suggest no change in this relation. I have had conferences with him nearly every day these three weeks. I think he has told me every fact at every stage in this troublesome journey so far. I have seen this singularly self-contained, unemotional man weep in talking with me; I have seen him broken with care and lack of sleep — weighed down with an indescribable burden; and I have seen him roused with indignation, with a confident and invincible air. He could not be more frank or more friendly if I had known him always. That such a man should be in his post now is the first of our pieces of good fortune here. . . .

The dark shadow moves over the map of the continent bringing political, economic, and spiritual ruin; and again, I think, England will save Europe from itself. Turning from the awful spectacle on land and sea, it is inspiring to watch this nation — sad, dead-in-earnest, resolute, united — not a dissenting voice — silent. It will spend all its treasure and give all its men, if need be. I have never seen such grim resolution. They trust us to play our part of neutrality with scrupulous exactness and they know we will do it. It will be a hard fight, an experience of unimagined horrors. I am glad the chance comes to me to show our attitude — it calls for steadiness, clearness, frankness. These are not flashy qualities, being the brood rather of wisdom and common sense.

Yours most heartily,
Walter H. Page

American Embassy, London, September 22, 1914

Dear Mr. President:

The more fully the whole recent diplomatic story of the war and of the events that preceded it comes out, the clearer it becomes here that the German military party had deliberately planned the practical conquest of the world; that it had won the German people (or a large part of them) to believe in this as a necessity; and that the military firmly believed that they could do it; and that, believing in this programme as a necessity, they came to believe that any method whereby they could do this justified itself. The military party gave the whole people an extraordinary case of big-head. I find the evidence of these extraordinary facts incontrovertible. The English themselves go further than this in their conclusions—under the effects of war. But there is no need to go further to see that the English are not going to discuss peace except in Berlin. In other words, they will reject any terms that Germany will offer except on the basis of defeat. They are going to rid themselves and the rest of Europe of the menace that they have lived under for thirty years—a hostile military autocracy.

These are not a warlike people. They didn't wish to fight. In fact, the public took the war, after it had been declared, with indifference. It was thought for several weeks that the Government would have to conscript men to get enough. They were very slow in waking up. But now they can't find officers or quarters for the volunteer recruits, and you can't find an Englishman of any class who holds any opinion but that the war must go on until the Germans are completely disabled from continuing their military caste. All the resources of the Empire and all the men that they can get will be spent if they are needed to prevent another "assault on the continuity of civilization." For these reasons Mr. Straus's[3] peace activity was looked on here as a part of the German campaign to affect public opinion in the United States and as nothing else — as a move in the game of publicity to seem to put the responsibility for continuing the war on England, in spite of the fact that Germany had made no definite proposal whatever.

All the military men I see talk of a long war — from one to three years; and they think that it will be ended, when it ends, quite as much by starving the Germans as by fighting them. And England is preparing for an indefinite struggle, many talking even of three years. And one gets glimpses now and then of the quality that has made English history — that quality at work in these people. By sheer good luck I happen to have become pretty well acquainted with both Sir John French[4] and Sir John Jellicoe.[5] They are able and forcible men: I think anybody who knows them would say that. But six months ago nobody thought of them or spoke of them as great historic characters — as great heroes. But now the universal expectation is that they will play the parts of Wellington and Nelson; and if French saves his army and is in at the end, and if Jellicoe gets a chance at the German fleet, all this will come true. It'll be they who saved Europe and kept England free; they will be made peers; they will receive great residences and large grants and their families will become great families in the realm; and, more than that, the poets and the orators and the biographers will make them known, in heroic size, wherever English is read.

And you may be dead sure the story will be told well and, therefore, it will become history, and sung well, and therefore it will become literature. And the story will be the story of English freedom again saved and again broadened, of the Empire become bigger and very much more firmly knit — of India become really loyal and far better treated, of Ireland stripped of its grievance, of new African colonies to exploit and (more important yet) the common man of England claiming and getting more privileges and more power and a wider opportunity. These things are almost visible now. And, for us, in addition to an increase in our trade and financial power, we shall have the Monroe Doctrine still safe, as we should not have if Germany won.

All these things, in addition to the daily roll of the dead and the constant march of recruits and all such visible reminders of war, prevent us here from forgetting it for one moment — prevent us from ever changing the subject. It bears down on one very hard. There comes a kind of weariness that drives one to long sleep, which is the only way to get away from it. London seems muffled — a queer sort of silence; and dark — all the bright lights are out at night; and resolute — there are not even the common routine gaieties: if anybody has a few friends in to dinner, it is never spoken of.

The diplomatic work betwixt Great Britain and our country is, as you know, not difficult: they play the game squarely; they are wholly courteous and sincere and even more than ever they value our friendship and sympathy. But I see Sir Edward Grey four or five times a week; he gives his confidence; and we have only to keep strictly neutral. That is not hard to do here. Nor does the work of the German and Austrian Embassies cause difficulty; it is, on all sides, only the large volume of work, not its difficulty. We are beginning to see what the normal conditions of work will be so long as the war lasts and for a period after. . . .

. . . Lord Kitchener[6] told Colonel Squier, our Military Attaché, to-day, that the war would really begin next spring. He was not speaking in jest — there's no jest in Kitchener. Since England has only a small army they sent that over of course to help France. France will give the Germans the best tug they can this autumn and wear them down somewhat, and Russia will finish Austria. Meantime England will drill a million, perhaps a million and a half men, and have them as a fresh army in the spring. I shouldn't wonder if Kitchener himself will take command; and these are the fellows who will take Berlin; and Kitchener, if he go, will dictate the terms of peace; it'll be an English (not a French or a Russian) victory! These English are the only people in Europe who have the habit of success and who know the art of managing great things. Look also at their diplomacy. Sir Edward Grey was broken-hearted when he could no longer keep peace. But when war came Russia and France were already engaged before England went in; and yet it is primarily a war between England and Germany. Of the German allies, one did not come in and the other is already beaten. Of the English allies—so far they are doing practically all the fighting and England will come in at the end as victor! In other words, Grey and Kitchener are more than a match for the whole continent of statesmen and soldiers.

Now since it is essential to modern progress that this brutal, big-headed, stupid military caste in Germany be rooted up—nobody can live in security till it is—and since the English have the one great fleet and will have a great army, and since it has Grey and Kitchener and French and Jellicoe and English character and endurance behind them—peace-talk now is old women's prattle or else it is insincere and is "springes to catch woodcock"—a part of the German tactics.

It staggers one's reasoning powers to think back over the last thirty years, and it balks the imagination to try to think forward. The Germans, when as a boy I went to Berlin, were a philosophical, studious, mystical, musical folk with a simplicity of mind and with no ambition to conquer the earth—to win a place in the sun. Their great war machine and their "cult of valour" were just beginning. Their writers who have completely changed their thought and aims—or expressed this change of thought and aims—were just beginning to write. It is a frightful thing to think how a war party may change a whole nation in three decades. In the meantime England is the same as in other great crises, the leader, making other nations do much of her work, forgetting for the time her domestic differences, leaping from the lap of luxury into the battle trenches, tough and silent and grim. The duchesses (who, you will recall, spoiled Lowell[7]) are now working in hospitals; the great houses are taking in Belgian refugees—entertaining and caring for that whole buffer nation; the noble ladies come to see me to ask if I can get word of their dead or wounded sons or brothers or husbands, and they come dry-eyed and self-possessed with a bearing that Spartan women would have envied. This is the price they pay for Empire. England not only will gain territory and power and trade and even greater dominion at sea, she will also toughen her breed and make literature of the experience. The Germans deserve the fate that awaits them for their sheer stupidity in not understanding this.

The liberalization of Europe will follow. But, her strong enemy overcome, Great Britain will not so greatly need our friendship; and, when clashes of interest come, we shall need firmness. She doesn't become arrogant with success; she simply becomes more positive and more energetic. There never came so good a time to put our foreign service, at home and abroad, on a firm, liberal, and uniformly efficient basis — from the Department of State to the humblest consul. We have some wonderfully good men — wonderfully, as this stress is showing. But we have also in places the feeblest sort of touch. All news of both sorts comes to London. This war is showing how we are a part of the great world whether we wish to be or not. Could the next Congress not be induced to have a study made of the foreign service of other great states compared with ours?

Yours very heartily,

Walter H. Page

P. S. The reports of peace meetings in the United States as they have appeared in the London papers the last day or two produce the impression here of mutton-headed victims of German special pleaders.

This thought grows on me the more I ponder this world-changing series of events — that, when the war is ended, nothing will be precisely as it was before, not even England. England will not only be more powerful, but she will be under very definite bonds to — Russia and Japan. Russia and Japan, therefore, will be different. We shall need a new sort of diplomatic force in most parts of the world; we shall need somehow to wake up the American public to realize that our isolation is gone and that our perfunctory diplomatic work, which has done well enough in many places in the past, will not do anywhere in the future; and a stronger navy? There simply is no end to the changes that are coming.

W.H.P.